101 RECIPES YOU CAN'T LIVE WITHOUT

101 RECIPES YOU CAN'T LIVE WITHOUT

The Prevention® Cookbook

Lori Powell

RODALE.

© 2012 by Rodale Inc.

Rodale books may be purchased for business or promotional use or for special sales. For information, please write to:
Special Markets Department, Rodale Inc., 733 Third Avenue, New York, NY 10017.

Prevention® is a registered trademark of Rodale Inc.

Printed in the United States of America

Rodale Inc. makes every effort to use acid-free ∞, recycled paper ♻.

Book design by Kara Plikaitis

Photographs by Mitch Mandel/Rodale Images

Food styling by Mariana Velasquez; prop styling by Amy Wilson

Library of Congress Cataloging-in-Publication Data

Powell, Lori.
    101 recipes you can't live without : the Prevention cookbook / Lori Powell.
        p.   cm.
    Includes index.
    ISBN 978-1-60961-942-8 hardcover
    1. Cooking.   2. Health.   3. Functional foods.   I. Prevention (Emmaus, Pa.)
II. Title.   III. Title: One hundred one recipes you can't live without.
IV. Title: One hundred and one recipes you can't live without.
TX714.P686   2012
641.5—dc23   2012020529
Distributed to the trade by Macmillan

2   4   6   8   10   9   7   5   3   1   hardcover

RODALE.

We inspire and enable people to improve their lives and the world around them.
rodalebooks.com

*For everyone who wants to eat foods that
nourish the body and delight the taste buds*

CONTENTS

FOREWORD

Prevention is rooted in the idea that what you eat is a cornerstone of good health. Ever since 1950, when J. I. Rodale published the very first issue of *Prevention*, the magazine was ahead of its time in exploring and espousing the idea that eating the right food was key to living a long and healthy life . . . and that eating the wrong food would lead to weight gain and illness.

The idea was pioneering and powerful at the same time, and a natural progression of thought for a man who moved himself and his wife, Anna, from New York City to Pennsylvania, bought a 63-acre farm, and launched *Organic Farming and Gardening* magazine. In *Prevention*'s first decade of publication, the magazine took a stand against hot dogs and buns as one of the most unhealthy American staples around, strenuously objected to chemical additives in foods, and encouraged people to take natural supplements and herbs.

Fast forward more than 60 years, and such ideas are now well accepted and applauded. It's gratifying and inspiring to everyone at *Prevention* today to know how progressive our founder was—and the Rodale family continues to be—and to see how many people around the world are both advocating for healthier food and eating them in their daily lives.

That's the spirit in which this cookbook was born—to make it easy for you and your family to prepare good-for-you meals that will help you live longer and more healthfully. Along with nutritious ingredients, a hearty helping of passion went into every dish. Healthy food is the most delicious food possible, we strongly believe—and the scrumptious recipes on these pages prove that.

So, without waiting a moment longer, we encourage you to dig in!

Diane Salvatore
Editor in Chief
Prevention
Prevention.com

PREFACE

The world is chock-full of cookbooks of every variety—vegetarian, meat-based, Italian, Asian, gluten-free, heart-healthy, quick & easy, slow-cooking, chocolate only—and the list goes on. With all these options to choose from, do you really need one more? The answer is *yes,* because the cookbook you are holding in your hands is unlike any other. Sure, it's jam-packed with delicious recipes. Flip to any photo here and just observe the pleasure that floods your brain as you imagine the tastes and aromas of each dish. But this book goes one step further.

We've been bold enough to call it *101 Recipes You Can't Live Without,* and here's why. We began by selecting a baker's dozen of crucial nutrients, from magnesium to vitamin D, that you *literally* can't live without. Magnesium, for example, helps regulate your heart rhythm, keeps your digestive tract humming, brings on more blissful sleep, helps you sidestep diabetes, derails major headaches, and much more. But how many people consider magnesium when designing recipes? We did. We found the foods that offer the most, then put them together into recipes that are not only good for you, but packed with flavor, too. And we did the same for all of our essential 13 nutrients.

Better yet, when you get your essential 13 from food rather than supplements, they come packaged with hundreds of *other* nutrients—including still more vitamins, minerals, fiber, antioxidants, and compounds that stimulate your body's detoxification enzymes. In other words, you're getting benefits that stretch way beyond the protection of even our powerhouse 13. And forget any preconceived notions you may have about "healthy" foods not tasting good—or yummy dishes necessarily being sinful. These recipes would stand on their own, even if they weren't designed to maximize health. Independent taste-testing confirmed it. Now that's a book you can't live without!

Lori Powell
Food Director
Prevention

Anne Underwood
Nutrition Director
Prevention

Read enough nutrition news and you're guaranteed to come across plenty of controversy. Is high-fructose corn syrup really worse than sugar? Would we all be better off on a gluten-free diet? Are eggs safe for people worried about their cholesterol level? It's easy to find expert opinions on either side of issues like these, but there is one thing the majority of nutrition pros agree on: It's healthier to get your nutrients from food than from supplements.

EAT YOUR WAY TO A HEALTHIER BODY

1

WHILE THERE'S NO HARM
IN TAKING A MULTIVITAMIN, there's no evidence that it does you much good either. In a study of more than 180,000 men and women, University of Hawaii researchers found that multivitamin users did not live longer or have lower rates of cancer or heart disease than people who didn't take a pill.

What's not in doubt is the healing power of nutrients in food. Still, you often hear that you should take a multivitamin as a "backup." With the recipes in this book, you won't need one. These delicious dishes show you how to get everything you need for a healthy body from your plate.

IN CHAPTER 2, you'll read about the Essential 13—the nutrients that research has shown have the strongest disease-fighting potential against both chronic illnesses, such as heart disease and diabetes, and everyday concerns. For instance, calcium helps lower blood pressure and fight belly fat. When you eat a diet rich in vitamin C, you're reducing the kind of inflammation that can cause heart disease and preventing wrinkles. Fiber protects against diabetes and keeps you fuller longer, so it makes losing weight easier. And that's just a few examples.

But how do you make sure you're getting enough of the calcium, vitamin C, fiber, and other nutrients you need? That's where the recipes come in. Working in the leading sources of the Essential 13 is a snap. In fact, every one of the 101 easy-to-prepare dishes in this book supplies a hefty dose of one or more of the 13 key nutrients—at least one-quarter of your daily needs for nutrients where a recommended intake has been established. You can rest easy knowing that every bite you put into your mouth—from hearty breakfasts to mouthwatering desserts—is maximizing your health and satisfying your appetite. Case in point: Just one serving of Roast Pork Tenderloin with Edamame Succotash (page 173) gives you:

- 123 percent of your daily vitamin C
- 78 percent of your daily folate
- 36 percent of your daily potassium
- 28 percent of your daily fiber
- 27 percent of your daily magnesium

And the week's worth of menus on pages 232 to 234 shows you just how easy it is to mix and match these recipes to meet your nutritional needs.

FOOD VERSUS PILLS

It's the intricate blend of nutrients in foods that makes them superior to supplements. Of course, when you sit down to a meal that contains several different foods, you're getting a variety of nutrients. But even a single food can supply a multitude of benefits that would be hard to get in a pill. Take broccoli, for instance. It's a rich source of vitamin C, vitamin K, carotenoids, and folate, and it also supplies small amounts of fiber, potassium, iron, and vitamin E. It even contains a powerful cancer-fighting compound called sulforaphane. The natural combination of nutrients in foods works synergistically—that is, they complement each other, helping with digestion and absorption, and giving your body the greatest possible health advantage.

"The whole is truly greater than the sum of its parts," says Barbara Shukitt-Hale, PhD, a USDA researcher at the Human Nutrition Research Center on Aging at Tufts University in Boston. "We're seeing that if you start to take food apart, the individual components aren't as effective as the whole food. For instance, in the lab we might discover that component A has one function, component B does something else, and component C does yet another thing. But when all three work together, you get a greater health gain than you would from any one component working in isolation."

Single nutrients alone are not just less beneficial, they may actually be harmful, especially at high doses. In some studies where researchers have tried to separate specific nutrients from foods, the results were disturbing. After research showed that a diet rich in the antioxidant beta-carotene—the yellow-orange pigment found in foods like carrots, winter squash, and cantaloupe—might reduce the risk of cancer, scientists at the Fred Hutchinson Cancer Research Center in Seattle tested the effects of beta-carotene in supplement form. It turned out that people taking the pills had a 28 percent increased risk of lung cancer and 26 percent increased risk of cardiovascular disease. To make matters worse, the isolated form of beta-carotene used in supplements significantly lowers the concentration of lycopene—another powerful antioxidant—in the blood. At the National Cancer Institute, studies of yet another protective antioxidant led to similar conclusions: High doses of vitamin E supplements not only increased the risk of prostate cancer, but also upped the chance of death from any cause.

And, surprisingly, in the same way that some people think that opting for the large order of fries is no problem as long as they wash it down with a diet soda, taking a multi can give you a false sense of security and lead you to engage in unhealthy habits. The (faulty) logic is that the multi "covers" you, so you can skip a workout or not worry about getting enough fruits and vegetables in your diet. A recent study in the journal *Addiction* demonstrated that smokers who took vitamins actually smoked more and felt less vulnerable to disease.

TURN YOUR HEALTH AROUND IN 13 STEPS

If you want to feel better, lose weight, and stay healthy for years to come, you can't rely on pills. You need to know how to eat smarter. We based our recipes on 13 tried-and-true principles of healthy eating. There are no crazy gimmicks, like skipping fruit in the morning, or senseless restrictions like banning carbs after 3 p.m. The principles below break down healthy eating into simple, manageable steps, but the heart of this book comes down to just one thing: choosing nutrient-rich whole foods as often as possible. Since you're bound to encounter obstacles along the way (hello, late nights at the office), we've also put together tips and fixes for the most common eat-right roadblocks. After that comes the best part: 101 crave-worthy recipes that you can enjoy and share with family and friends for life.

1. **GO BACK TO BASICS.** Ending your dependence on processed foods, even "healthy" ones like granola bars, makes room in your diet for the superfoods your body needs. That's why we based our recipes on foods in their natural form—fresh produce, whole grains, grass-fed beef, and wild-caught seafood. To limit exposure to pesticides, choose organic produce when possible, especially when you'll be eating the skin. So make organic grapes and tomatoes a higher priority than organic bananas and avocados.

2. **EAT THE RAINBOW.** Filling at least half of your plate with a variety of colorful vegetables and fruits is an easy way to make sure you're getting more of the nutrients you need. There's nothing wrong with gorgeous green broccoli, kale, and spinach, but don't forget to go for orange hues (butternut squash, carrots), blues and purples (cabbage, beets, berries), and reds (tomatoes, bell peppers) in order to cover all your nutritional bases. Fruits and veggies are the best sources of many of the Essential 13.

     And as you'll see, most of the recipes featuring produce call for more than one kind, guaranteeing that every bite packs a spectrum of nutrients.

3. **REDEFINE "HEALTHY."** Food that tastes bland, leaves you unsatisfied, or makes it impossible to go to (or host) a dinner party with friends isn't what this approach is about. The key to sticking to this new way of eating is knowing that food can be healthy, delicious, and fun all at once. In that spirit, we've created these recipes with the goal that you'll share them at parties, picnics, and gatherings of all kinds.

4. **MAKE EVERY BITE COUNT.** Dessert should taste indulgent. But if one luscious serving of cheesecake (like the Cardamom Yogurt Cheesecake with Caramelized Plums on

page 226) also provides a major calcium boost, that's even better. With a little forethought, you can turn just about every meal and snack into an opportunity to maximize your daily nutrients. The star nutrients are called out in every recipe, so you know just how much good stuff you're getting in a single serving.

5. **PUMP UP THE VOLUME.** Studies have proven time and again that fueling up on nutritious foods makes it easier to control your weight. Our dishes won't leave you feeling deprived because the high water content of grains, beans, and just about every vegetable and fruit you can think of translates to filling portion sizes and low calorie counts. A study in the *Journal of the American Dietetic Association* spells it out: Reducing your calorie intake without decreasing the actual volume of food you eat is a savvy way to drop pounds without feeling hungry. Next time you consider blowing 540 calories on a fast-food burger, just picture what you could be eating instead: a hearty Tuscan Kale Salad with Almonds and Parmesan (page 210), a 5-ounce roasted chicken breast, and a Dark Chocolate Walnut Brownie (page 222), all for just 511 calories. No contest.

6. **SIP SMARTER.** According to a study in the *American Journal of Clinical Nutrition*, Americans consume 21 percent of their daily calories in liquid form. That's 420, or about a meal's worth, if you eat 2,000 calories per day. To add more bad news, most caloric beverages are low in nutrients and aren't as satisfying as something you can chew. So what should you drink? Coffee or tea with a splash of milk is fine, and seltzer mixed with fresh fruit juice is flavorful yet very low in calories. Low-fat milk is a good source of protein, calcium, vitamin D, and potassium. Alcohol isn't off-limits, but stick to a 5-ounce glass of wine (about 120 calories) or a 12-ounce light beer (about 100 calories). Of course, the ultimate beverage is water—for zero calories, it keeps you hydrated so you have more energy and experience fewer cravings.

7. **BE SELECTIVE ABOUT FAT.** It's not all created equal, and the best types ward off disease. Monounsaturated fats like olive and canola oil, and polyunsaturated fats like safflower oil can help improve cholesterol levels, control blood sugar, and prevent type 2 diabetes. Omega-3 fatty acids—found in salmon, walnuts, flaxseeds, and canola oil—may decrease the risk of coronary artery disease. Omega-3s have been shown to offer so many health advantages that we named them one of our Essential 13.

    In addition to the health benefits these fats supply on their own, researchers have proven that fat is essential to the absorption of other nutrients. A study at Iowa State University found significantly lower levels of beta-carotene and lycopene in the blood of men and women after eating a salad with carrots, tomatoes, and fat-free dressing than after eating the same salad with full-fat dressing. This means there's no reason to cut out healthy fats as long as you keep portions in check (1 tablespoon is an ideal serving, so measure it).

8. **PLAN NOW TO SUCCEED LATER.** Jot down your menu for the week. Get the grocery shopping done. And if you really want to ace this step, wash your produce as soon as you bring it home from the market. This way, you'll have nothing left to do in the middle of a busy week but open this book and get cooking. And you won't be caught off guard with nothing but an empty refrigerator and a drawer full of take-out menus. Ever wonder what the heck people are talking about when they say cooking is relaxing and meditative? With all of the mental effort finished ahead of time, you're about to find out.

9. **BYOL (BRING YOUR OWN LUNCH).** Speaking of planning ahead, brown bagging might just be one of the best eat right strategies there is. Again, it comes down to the numbers. A Sierra Turkey on Focaccia with Asiago Cheese from Panera Bread sets you back 920 calories and 49 grams of fat, while homemade Mediterranean Edamame Patties in Whole Wheat Pita with Tahini Sauce (page 86) provides more than 25 percent of your daily dose of fiber, folate, magnesium, iron, and vitamin C for just 366 calories and 12 grams of fat. The lesson here is that bakery bread, fatty spreads, and supersize portions of meat and cheese can turn restaurant sandwiches into calorie bombs that are less nutritious than the lunch you make yourself with natural, high-quality ingredients. Just turn to Chapter 4 for plenty of midday meal inspiration.

10. **MAXIMIZE FLAVOR.** If it doesn't taste good, you're not going to eat it, no matter how healthy it may be. Enjoying the food you cook and eat is an essential part of staying fit for life. In these recipes, you'll find fresh herbs, as well as dried; an array of spices; and low- or no-calorie add-ons like citrus juice and zest and flavorful vinegars. A handful of basil or dash of balsamic can punch up healthy foods and increase the nutrient value. Did you know that parsley provides potassium and vitamins A and C? Or that cinnamon contains antioxidants that may improve heart health? With so many flavorful ways to dress up your dishes, you can let your creativity soar and never get bored.

11. **SQUEEZE OUT SUGAR.** If weight control has been an uphill battle, start paying attention to sugar in your diet. The American Heart Association determined that Americans consume 355 calories worth of the sweet stuff each day on average, mostly from foods like soda and candy that contribute little or no nutritional value. Feeding those sugar cravings leads to weight gain, increasing your risk for type 2 diabetes and heart disease. Ready for some good news? These recipes make it a cinch to cut out added calories from sugar by helping you fill up on natural, unprocessed dishes (including desserts) that leave you satisfied and able to avoid the office vending machine for a 3 p.m. "energy" boost.

5 Snacks You Can't Live Without

The right in-between-meal nibbles can go a long way toward helping you meet your nutritional needs. Try these fast healthy options.

SMART SNACK: 1 slice low-fat Swiss cheese and an apple
NUTRITIONAL PAYOFF: 27 percent of your daily calcium, 16 percent of your daily fiber

SMART SNACK: 1 cup sliced strawberries and 1 cup low-fat plain Greek yogurt
NUTRITIONAL PAYOFF: 163 percent of your daily vitamin C, 25 percent of your daily calcium, 12 percent of your daily fiber

SMART SNACK: 1 medium pear and 1 tablespoon almond butter
NUTRITIONAL PAYOFF: 28 percent of your daily fiber

SMART SNACK: ½ cup salmon from a pouch mixed with 2 teaspoons mayo and ½ teaspoon Dijon mustard with ¼ whole wheat pita
NUTRITIONAL PAYOFF: 72 percent of your daily omega-3s

SMART SNACK: ½ cup black beans mixed with 1 tablespoon salsa on a 6-inch corn tortilla
NUTRITIONAL PAYOFF: 32 percent of your daily folate, 32 percent of your daily fiber

12. **SWITCH THINGS UP.** Sure, potatoes are a stellar source of potassium, but if you only rely on one particular food for your daily dose day in and day out, you might be cheating yourself nutritionally. That's why we highlighted multiple sources for each of the Essential 13 nutrients—and many of those foods supply a hefty chunk of more than one of them. Salmon, for instance, is rich in omega-3s and vitamin D. Beets contain not only more than 25 percent of your daily potassium needs in 2 cups, but also heart-healthy anthocyanins, 30 percent of your daily fiber, and a whopping 74 percent of your daily folate.

13. **SNACK SMARTER.** It's 2 hours until lunchtime and you're starving, despite the bowl of cereal you wolfed down on your way out the door this morning. What to do? Eating between meals isn't off-limits, as long as you choose wisely. A bag of trail mix from the vending machine, for example, could be the calorie equivalent of an entire meal (those little bags may contain anywhere from two to four servings). But the right snacks, like the ones in "5 Snacks You Can't Live Without" (*above*), give you the perfect opportunity to boost your nutrient intake for the day, while providing the energy you need to coast through a crazy morning. We know you can't always prepare a full recipe when you need a quick bite on the go. This book is meant to give you the tools you need to eat for optimal health (no pills required) and the flexibility you need to keep it up for life.

THE NO-EXCUSES GUIDE TO YOUR BIGGEST HEALTHY-EATING OBSTACLES

Even with a solid set of guidelines to follow, barriers to eating right abound (we're talking about you, coworker, who inaugurated "doughnut Wednesdays"). To combat these sneaky saboteurs, we came up with easy solutions and fast fixes for the things most likely to derail your best eating intentions.

EAT-RIGHT OBSTACLE: It's boring.

HEALTHY SOLUTION: Before you drizzle lemon juice and olive oil over yet another batch of steamed broccoli, remember that eating a variety of healthy foods is the easiest and tastiest way to maximize your nutrition—and this book gives you plenty of creative options. Plan to make at least one new recipe a week and purchase a new-to-you fruit or veggie every time you hit the produce section. Good-bye, boredom.

EAT-RIGHT OBSTACLE: It takes too much time.

HEALTHY SOLUTION: Do not, we repeat, do not make every meal from scratch. Cook a double batch of the Black Bean–Turkey Chili with Butternut Squash (page 162) on Sunday and eat it again on Wednesday. Transform tonight's Grilled Steak au Poivre (page 170) into tomorrow's steak sandwich. Come up with a personal fail-safe meal that you could cook in your sleep, and always keep the necessary ingredients on hand for those days when you really don't have time to shop for or cook one of the recipes in this book. For example, you can turn frozen shrimp, jarred marinara sauce, whole wheat spaghetti, and red-pepper flakes into Shrimp Fra Diavolo (that's Italian for "spicy shrimp pasta") in about 20 minutes. Remember, too, that although we've categorized dishes by meal type, there's nothing to say you can't have breakfast or lunch for dinner. Sweet Corn Frittata (page 69) makes a delicious dinner that's ready in 25 minutes. Or pair a Ham and White Cheddar Panini with Mango Chutney (page 91) with a green salad.

EAT-RIGHT OBSTACLE: Healthy foods are unfamiliar.

HEALTHY SOLUTION: Trust us, you're not the only one who doesn't know how to pronounce quinoa (it's "KEEN-wah," by the way). Think of it this way: Making these recipes is both helping your body nutritionally and sharpening your mind. Studies show that learning a new skill or veering from your normal routine builds new neural connections, keeping the brain active and stimulated. Navigating the bulk bins at your local health food store and experimenting in the kitchen certainly count!

EAT-RIGHT OBSTACLE: It's expensive.

HEALTHY SOLUTION: We're not going to pretend that organic apples cost less than your run-of-the-mill Granny Smiths, but we do have simple strategies to keep your wallet as healthy as your body. When it comes to produce, the stuff in season costs less. Skip blueberries in January (or try frozen), and get your anthocyanins from red cabbage instead. Buy grains, legumes, and nuts in bulk. They lack the fancy packaging that drives up the cost, and you can try a variety of new foods without committing to a large quantity. (Millet's not for everyone, right?) That said, eating natural, unprocessed foods can actually save you money. Premade meals and snacks are pricey, thanks to marketing, advertising, and manufacturing costs, and frequent dining out won't save you cash unless you stick exclusively to the dollar menu—not the healthiest or most flavorful strategy.

EAT-RIGHT OBSTACLE: My family and friends want what they want.

HEALTHY SOLUTION: This is one reason why we created nutrient-packed, lighter versions of favorite foods, such as Stuffed Shells with Peas and Mint (page 134), Swiss Chard, Eggplant, and Mushroom Lasagna (page 139), Baked Chicken Parmesan with Homemade Tomato Sauce (page 155), Dark Chocolate Pudding with Whipped Ricotta (page 217), and Dark Chocolate Walnut Brownies (page 222). Whether your crew is health-conscious or not, they'll love dishes like these because they don't sacrifice flavor for nutrition. If you're going out to dinner, check out the restaurant's menu online, zero in on the healthy options, and decide ahead of time what you'll order. Then have a healthy snack about an hour or so beforehand so you aren't ravenous when you arrive.

EAT-RIGHT OBSTACLE: Temptation. It's everywhere.

HEALTHY SOLUTION: No, you can't ban doughnuts and candy dishes from the office, drive 10 miles out of the way to avoid passing a single drive-thru, or skip your sister's birthday dinner because there will be cake. But, if you'd rather not succumb to treats at every turn, you need viable alternatives. It doesn't take much planning to make sure you always have yogurt in the office fridge and a banana or a bag of almonds in your car. As for that birthday cake, have a piece if it's homemade and absolutely amazing. If not, say you're stuffed and sip some tea instead. You'll rarely regret food you didn't eat.

Stocking a Healthy Kitchen

Choosing fresh, natural ingredients is paramount for eating right. But what happens next—you know, the actual cooking—can make or break your nutrition goals. To ensure success, we've compiled a list of the most important tools and pantry staples that will make prep time easier and even help you put together healthy meals on the fly.

PANTRY STAPLES

1. **OLIVE OIL** Great for both sautéing and making salad dressing.

2. **CANNED BEANS** Loaded with nutrients and filling fiber, they can stand in for meat in pastas, soups, grain dishes, and salads. Rinse before using to remove some of the sodium.

3. **CANNED NO-SALT-ADDED TOMATOES** The quickest route to homemade marinara sauce or a 30-minute weeknight pasta, they're also packed with lycopene, a powerful antioxidant.

4. **WHOLE WHEAT PASTA** Add a vegetable and a protein, and dinner is done.

5. **FROZEN STEAM-IN-THE-BAG VEGETABLES** As nutritious as fresh, but a hero on busy nights when all you have time for is hitting a few buttons on the microwave.

6. **FROZEN BERRIES** Full of vitamins and antioxidants, but oh-so-pricey for much of the year, fresh berries can be a luxury. Fortunately, the frozen ones are affordable anytime and perfect for smoothies or stirring into your morning yogurt or oatmeal.

7. **TOASTED NUTS** The recipe for success here is buy in bulk to save money. Toast a big batch. Store in the freezer. Every recipe calling for these nutritious nibbles just got a lot easier.

8. **FRESH SPICES** When it comes to getting the most flavor from ground spices like cumin, cinnamon, and chili powder, toss any that have been hanging around longer than a year. To avoid waste, buy in small quantities and use them often.

9. **WHOLE GRAINS** The ultimate stock-up staple. Pack your pantry with airtight containers or mason jars full of grains like quinoa, brown rice, barley, steel-cut oats, and bulgur and you'll always have a healthy side dish ready to go.

10. **LOW-SODIUM SOY SAUCE** Essential for many Asian recipes, it also adds flavor dimension to marinades, soups, cooked greens, and simple steamed vegetables. Just remember to use less salt (or skip it) since you'll get the seasoning from the soy.

TOOLS

1. **MICROPLANE GRATER** It's perfect for making citrus zest that's fine enough (not chewy) to add to quick breads, salad dressings, and soups.

2. **SALAD SPINNER** Washing and drying greens just went from arduous to easy.

3. **HANDHELD CITRUS JUICER** This is the fastest, easiest way to juice one or two lemons or limes for a quick burst of flavor.

4. **NONSTICK SKILLET** Many new models are free of Teflon (which may be toxic when heated to high temperatures) and make cooking with less oil a no-hassle job.

5. **PEPPER MILL** Adding freshly ground black pepper to your healthy dishes really does up the flavor compared to the preground stuff. You'll never go back.

6. **FRESH HERB KEEPER** These clever gadgets keep pricey herbs fresh longer. Add herbs to marinades, omelets, salads, sandwiches, soups, and steamed grains for low-calorie flavor and a nutrition boost.

7. **SMALL LEAKPROOF JARS** Shake up your own house-made vinaigrette in seconds. No whisking required.

8. **FISH SPATULA** Hate it when your perfectly cooked fish falls apart when you turn it? This tool is long enough to make flipping delicate fillets a cinch.

9. **CAST-IRON SKILLET** These inexpensive pans go from stove top to oven with no worries and only get better with years of use. Cast-iron is ideal for searing meat or browning vegetables, yet the surface acts like a nonstick pan, so you can cook with less oil.

10. **FOOD PROCESSOR** Decades ago, this appliance was celebrated for letting you make homemade mayonnaise with ease. Today, it's the perfect tool for healthy eats like pesto, hummus, pureed vegetable soups and sauces, and even yogurt cheesecake.

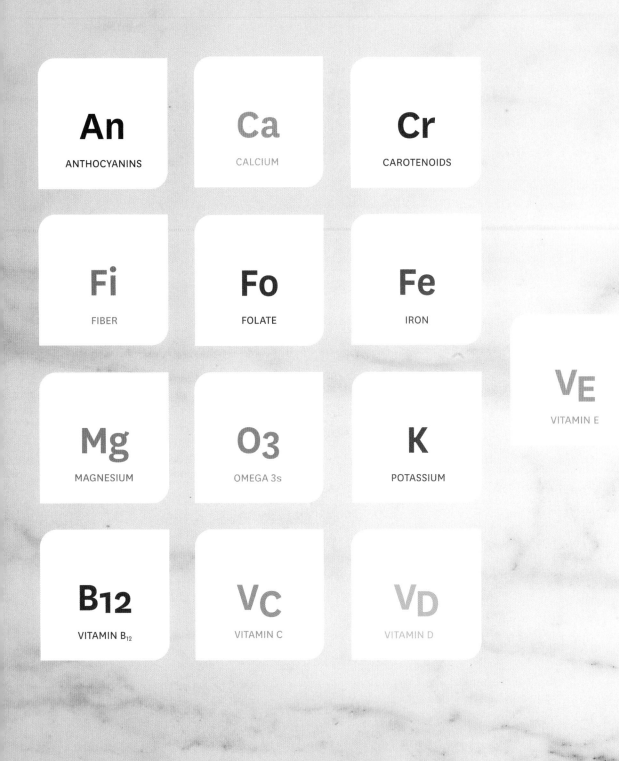

MEET THE ESSENTIAL 13

THERE ARE 16 MINERALS,

13 VITAMINS,

AND COUNTLESS OTHER COMPOUNDS in food that are required to keep our bodies functioning normally. Yet in this book, we've decided to focus on just 13 nutrients. Why? Because they actually do more than cover your basic needs—they maximize your health. Study after study shows that they help do everything from fight fatigue to control your weight to help prevent serious illnesses like heart disease and diabetes. Many of them are also nutrients that people have difficulty working into their diets.

Shrimp and Asparagus Stir-Fry with Rice Noodles (page 184) has carotenoids, folate, iron, and vitamin C.

IN THIS CHAPTER, we present the evidence for just how powerful these nutrients are and tell you how much you should aim to consume each day. We based our daily doses on the Daily Values (DV), the recommended intake set by the FDA for use on food labels. They're expressed as percentages. For instance, a glance at the calcium section on the label of a carton of fat-free milk shows you that 1 cup supplies 31 percent of the DV. What the label doesn't list (and this book does) is the total DV, in this case 1,000 milligrams. We chose the DVs instead of the other set of dietary recommendations, called the Dietary Reference Intakes, because they're familiar to most people and they're designed to meet the needs of all healthy people regardless of gender or age. Three of the nutrients we've included—anthocyanins, carotenoids, and omega-3 fatty acids—don't have DVs, but the research strongly suggests that they're protective and that we should all be eating more of them.

At the end of the chapter, we list the recipes that are high in each nutrient. To make the grade, one serving of the dish has to provide at least 25 percent of the DV. We used different criteria for anthocyanins, carotenoids, and omega-3s (see those entries for the details).

Don't be surprised if your mouth starts to water as you read through the recipe lists. These dishes are proof positive that nutrient-rich food does not have to be flavorless and boring. In fact, we'd put them up against the recipes in the best cookbooks. And doesn't it sound a whole lot more appetizing to meet your daily vitamin C needs with a sweet, juicy Tropical Ambrosia Salad (page 71) or to get more than a third of your daily calcium requirement by digging into a plate of Baked Penne with Creamy Swiss Cheese Sauce, Mushrooms, and Asparagus (page 130) than by popping a supplement? We thought you'd agree.

YOUR DAILY DOSE: Not established

TOP SOURCES: Blueberries, red cabbage, eggplant, blackberries, black raspberries, cranberries, red grapes, strawberries, plums, purple potatoes, black currants, black rice, beets, cherries

ANTHOCYANINS

FILLING YOUR CLOSET with neutral shades may be a fail-safe choice when it comes to fashion, but the opposite is true for your diet. It's not just about the occasional "pop of color" either; to get the biggest health bang from food, load up on colorful produce. And the deep blues, purples, and reds are just as important as the oranges and dark greens. They get their jewel tones from anthocyanins, members of the flavonoid family, a group of compounds that occur naturally in produce and have a variety of functions.

Anthocyanins stand out among the thousands of flavonoids because they act as powerful antioxidants, scrubbing away harmful free radicals that can damage cells, causing inflammation and chronic disease. Canadian researchers fed people powdered blueberries and then performed blood tests to measure changes in antioxidant capacity. They discovered that blueberry anthocyanins absorbed during digestion directly resulted in increased antioxidant activity in the body.

But the advantages of anthocyanins include more than antioxidant protection, according to Diane L. McKay, PhD, FACN, assistant professor of nutrition at Tufts University in Boston. "They can signal cells to turn certain biochemical pathways on and others off in order to protect the cells," she says. "They can also prevent damage to DNA, inhibit tumor cells, and have anti-inflammatory properties."

Scientists still don't know enough about these plant pigments to recommend a daily dose. So instead of listing a percentage of your daily anthocyanin needs in the recipe nutrition information, we provide the number of servings of anthocyanin-rich foods (such as the Top Sources listed above) that you'll get in one portion of the recipe. A serving is equal to ½ cup of raw or cooked vegetables and fruits. And after reading about the health-promoting effects of anthocyanin-rich foods, you'll be inspired to fill up on them.

Why you can't live without anthocyanins

They protect the brain.

A review of the existing research on anthocyanins at Tufts University in Boston showed that berries reduce free radical damage and help aging brain cells communicate and stay active. Eating anthocyanin-rich foods like blueberries and strawberries fights inflammation and helps us continue to build new neuronal connections in areas of the brain that affect learning and the sense of smell, which is closely tied to memory, according to study co-author Barbara Shukitt-Hale, PhD, a USDA researcher at the Human Nutrition Research Center on Aging at Tufts. In one study, older adults diagnosed with mild cognitive impairment, a risk factor for Alzheimer's disease, drank blueberry juice daily for 12 weeks, while another group drank a placebo beverage. The juice drinkers performed better on memory and verbal tests, By preventing neuron damage, anthocyanins also fend off Parkinson's disease, according to a study conducted jointly at Harvard University and the University of East Anglia in England. The researchers analyzed the diets of nearly 130,000 people and found a 23 percent lower risk of Parkinson's for participants who ate berries two to four times a week, compared with those who ate less than one serving per month.

Healthier blood pressure, healthier heart.

A recent study in the *American Journal of Clinical Nutrition* showed that eating just one serving of blueberries per week results in a 10 percent lower risk of developing high blood pressure. And anthocyanins may prevent prehypertension from progressing to hypertension, according to researchers at Tufts. People who drank 3 cups of hibiscus tea (the hibiscus plant is rich in anthocyanins and commonly found in herbal teas) every day for 6 weeks lowered systolic blood pressure by 5.9 points compared to the placebo group. Studies have also shown that eating blueberries and strawberries at least once a week significantly reduces the risk of death from cardiovascular disease. Researchers at Oklahoma State University point out that fresh or frozen whole berries are best because the commercial processing required to make juices or extracts can negatively affect the berries' nutritional value.

Anthocyanin-rich fruits help fight diabetes.

Swapping rich desserts for naturally sweet berries can help you control your weight, which protects against diabetes. But their anthocyanins also give you added protection. A large study analyzing dietary questionnaires from more than 200,000 people found that eating anthocyanin-rich produce strongly reduced the risk of developing type 2 diabetes. Benefits were greatest for people who ate two or more servings of blueberries per week compared to those who ate less than one serving a month. This study looked at the various classes of flavonoids individually and found that only the anthocyanins provided significant protection.

They may attack cancer cells.

Test-tube experiments suggest that anthocyanins fight cancer in several ways. They scavenge for cell-damaging free radicals and help cells defend themselves from these substances; they reduce cancer cell growth without interfering with normal cells; they regulate apoptosis, or cell death, which often fails to occur in cancer cells; and they inhibit tumor growth and reduce the invasive abilities of cancer cells. One laboratory study in Portugal showed that blueberry anthocyanins prevented two breast cancer cell lines from multiplying. A Chinese study showed that anthocyanins from black rice significantly inhibited tumor growth in mice. These early studies are promising and researchers have begun to look at the ways anthocyanins can help protect people against cancer.

>>>>

Do I need to buy organic berries?

Berries are packed with anthocyanins, vitamin C, and fiber, but they do have a downside: They have some of the highest pesticide levels compared to other fresh produce. According to the Environmental Working Group (EWG)—which publishes an annual list ranking the 12 fruits and vegetables with the highest likelihood of contamination (the "Dirty Dozen") based on USDA testing—strawberries rank third for potential contamination, and blueberries don't fare much better at number 10. What's a berry lover to do? Buy organic if you can. Berries in season, even the organic ones, can be affordable, and stores often run sales because of the high supply. You can buy organic frozen berries, which are generally cheaper than fresh, year-round. But the most important advice is to eat up: The benefits of berries and other produce outweigh concerns over possible pesticide exposure, according to the EWG.

CALCIUM

CONSIDERING THE FACT that 99 percent of the calcium in your body is stored in the bones and teeth, it's no surprise that this mineral plays an important role in protecting your skeleton. Countless research studies have shown that calcium from milk, as well as other dairy and nondairy foods, is vital to bone health whether you're as young as 6 or as old as 86. Early in life, getting enough calcium helps you maximize your bone stores. As you age, adequate intake of the mineral will slow or stop bone loss, reducing your risk for osteoporosis.

Aside from its role in the constant growth and maintenance of bones throughout your life, calcium is essential to artery, vein, and muscle function. It also regulates hormone secretion and is involved in your body's messaging system, affecting nerves and communication between cells. Although plenty of research supports the benefits of calcium from food, studies show that people tend to eat calcium-poor diets as they get older, while increasing supplement doses. This may have serious negative effects on heart health: A 2010 analysis of data from 11 studies found that the risk of heart attack was 30 percent higher for people taking calcium supplements. Getting your daily dose from diet, on the other hand, does not pose this risk, and it can do even more for your health than just building bones.

Why you can't live without calcium

Low-fat dairy equals low blood pressure.

In a report from the Dietary Approaches to Stop Hypertension (DASH) study, researchers compared the blood pressure effects of different diets in people with hypertension and in healthy people. Although a diet rich in fruits and vegetables but low in calcium (about 534 milligrams per day) reduced blood pressure, adding enough low-fat dairy to supply 1,265 milligrams of calcium per day led to an average 11.4 point decline in systolic blood pressure (the upper number) and 5.5 point drop in diastolic (the lower number) in the people with hypertension. But even those whose blood pressure was already in the healthy range at the beginning of the study saw reductions in blood pressure on the diet rich in low-fat dairy.

It slashes colon cancer risk.

Adding about 1 cup of milk to your daily diet may be all it takes to reduce your risk of colorectal cancer by up to 15 percent, according to a study at Brigham and Women's Hospital and Harvard Medical School in Boston. By analyzing data from thousands of participants in 10 separate studies, the researchers also determined that hitting the recommended daily value for calcium of 1,000 milligrams slashes the cancer risk by 21 percent compared to eating less than 500 milligrams.

Dairy foods slim you down.

Eating fewer calories than you burn is the proven ticket to weight loss, but making sure some of those calories come from fat-free milk, yogurt, and cheese may give you an extra edge. These calcium-rich foods appear to interfere with fat absorption, which translates to less bulk on your body. And even when dairy doesn't help weight loss, it can protect against the build-up of intra-abdominal fat, the kind that raises your odds of diabetes and heart disease. A recent study showed that women who got 1,000 milligrams of calcium each day gained less belly fat over the course of a year than women who got less. Another study that analyzed the diets and health records of more than 3,400 men and women found that eating more dairy lowered the risk of developing metabolic syndrome. Think you'll get the same effect with a pill? A study in the journal *Annals of Internal Medicine* showed that taking a daily 1,500-milligram supplement for 2 years had no effect on weight in overweight people.

PMS will be less of a pain.

One study found that women who reported the highest intake of calcium from food (1,283 milligrams per day on average) were less likely to have PMS than women getting an average of just 529 milligrams per day. In another study that involved 33 women with a history of PMS, 73 percent of those who upped their daily calcium intakes by 1,000 milligrams experienced fewer changes in mood, less water retention, and less pain before their periods.

YOUR DAILY DOSE: Not established

TOP SOURCES: Carrots, winter squash, cantaloupe, sweet potatoes, spinach, kale, apricots, red bell peppers, mangoes, Brussels sprouts, tomatoes, tomato paste, tomato juice, watermelon

CAROTENOIDS

SINCE CARROTS ARE the unofficial mascot of the carotenoid family, you might think that this nutrient is only found in orange produce like pumpkins, cantaloupe, and sweet potatoes. The reality is a lot more colorful: Carotenoids actually encompass an array of bold pigments found in various plant foods. For instance, watermelon, dark leafy greens, and tomatoes are all good sources of carotenoids.

There are hundreds of different carotenoids, but some of the most common ones in our diets are alpha-carotene, beta-carotene, lycopene, lutein, and zeaxanthin. Beta- and alpha-carotene and a few other carotenoids are converted to vitamin A, providing an estimated 26 to 34 percent of the vitamin in our diets. The carotenoids like lycopene that are not turned into vitamin A boost health in other ways, especially as antioxidants fighting cell-damaging free radicals.

Studies have revealed a slew of information about the protective powers of carotenoids, but the jury's still out on what the optimal daily dose should be. When you look at the recipes in this book, you won't find a percent of your daily carotenoid needs, since none has been set. Instead, we provide the number of servings of carotenoid-rich foods (such as the Top Sources listed above) that you'll get in one portion of the recipe. One serving equals ½ cup of raw or cooked vegetables or fruits; 1 cup of raw leafy greens; or 2 tablespoons of tomato paste, which is more concentrated than regular canned tomatoes. As a general guide, the National Institutes of Health recommend at least 5 servings of fruits and vegetables each day, including some orange, red, and green choices to get the health benefits of carotenoids.

Why you can't live without carotenoids

Carotenoids trump cancer.

Whether they analyze individual carotenoids or the whole lot, studies show that these nutrients may protect against a variety of cancers, most likely due to their antioxidant function. Harvard University researchers tracked data from more than 80,000 women and found that consuming more carotenoids lowered breast cancer risk in premenopausal women. Those who ate five or more servings of fruits and vegetables a day cut their odds by 23 percent compared to those who ate less than two. For women with a family history of breast cancer, the risk dropped by 71 percent. In the case of prostate cancer, several studies have shown that lycopene may have protective benefits, especially for the more advanced forms of the disease. In a 6-year study involving more than 47,000 men, those who consumed the most lycopene from tomato products had a 35 percent lower risk compared to those who ate the least, while their risk of advanced prostate cancer was 53 percent lower.

They're cardio-protective.

Lycopene is a weapon against heart disease as well. It lowers LDL cholesterol, the bad type that invades artery walls and leads to plaque buildup that narrows arteries and increases the odds of a heart attack. In one Harvard study, women who ate 10 servings of tomato-based foods a week were 40 percent less likely to have elevated LDL levels compared with those who got less than 1½ servings. Alpha- and beta-carotene also appear to boost heart health: In a Dutch study of more than 500 elderly men, higher consumption of these carotenoids, with carrots as the primary source, was associated with a lower risk of death from cardiovascular disease over 15 years. While researchers aren't sure whether it is due to antioxidant activity or a combination of factors from carotenoid-rich foods, there's mounting evidence that these nutrients are key to a healthy aging heart. When Japanese researchers examined total blood levels of beta- and alpha-carotene and lycopene in more than 3,000 subjects, they observed a lower risk of cardiovascular death over a nearly 12-year period in people with the highest carotenoid levels in their blood.

You'll get sick less often.

The carotenoids that are converted to vitamin A in the body are the stars when it comes to supporting your immune system. Vitamin A is needed for white blood cells to fight off viruses and bacterial infections, and it helps strengthens mucous membranes to keep harmful germs out. It also keeps the linings of the respiratory, intestinal, and urinary tracts healthy.

Sharper vision as you age.

Lutein and zeaxanthin guard against two age-related vision robbers: macular degeneration and cataracts. A review of studies in the *British Journal of Nutrition* concluded that those who got the most of these carotenoids lowered their chances of macular degeneration by 26 percent. People with the highest blood levels of these carotenoids slashed their odds of developing cataracts by about 40 percent, a Finnish study found.

YOUR DAILY DOSE: 25 grams

TOP SOURCES: Barley, pears, black beans
and other beans, oat bran, oatmeal,
apples, lentils, bulgur, artichokes,
raspberries, pumpkin, broccoli, sweet
potatoes

FIBER

WHAT IMAGES COME to mind when you hear the word *fiber*? A bowl of stewed prunes (now called "dried plums")? You at 85 choking down a bowl of oat bran? These foods may be the standard-bearers for fiber's power to, ahem, move things along, but there are plenty of other healthy and great-tasting ways to get your daily dose. Fiber is simply the indigestible parts of plant foods, like fruits, vegetables, legumes, and grains, and it does a lot more than just keep your digestive system on track.

There are two types of fiber, and each has different but equally important functions. Insoluble fiber, the kind that does not dissolve in water and moves through the gut intact, is largely responsible for regularity. Soluble fiber (which turns into a thick, gel-like substance in water) binds with cholesterol in the intestines and helps lower your blood cholesterol levels, reducing the risk of heart disease. By slowing the body's absorption of sugar in foods, it keeps blood glucose levels stable, an important factor in treating and preventing type 2 diabetes. Most natural fiber-rich foods contain both types in various proportions, so there's no need to worry about the technical stuff as long as you focus on variety.

Even though getting enough fiber is easy if you stick to whole, unprocessed foods, it's estimated that Americans only get about 15 grams a day. Since fiber is filling, provides major health gains, and improves your odds for weight loss, think of it as your body's new best friend.

Why you can't live without fiber

It makes fighting heart disease easier to swallow.

When it comes to heart-protective dietary strategies, we often focus on what foods we need to cut back on rather than which ones we can add. While it's still necessary to go easy on the thick rib-eyes, cream sauces, and salty snacks, eating more foods with fiber is good for your heart, according to multiple studies. A University of Minnesota analysis of 10 studies found that for every 10 grams of fiber consumed per day, the risk of a heart attack or stroke drops by 14 percent and the chance of coronary death declines by 27 percent. Another study at Harvard University found a 41 percent reduction in cardiovascular disease risk for men who ate the most fiber compared to men who ate the least. Fiber likely protects your heart by lowering blood cholesterol levels in a number of ways, including slowing the absorption of fat and decreasing the liver's production of cholesterol.

Blood sugar stays steady.

Here's a tale of two breakfasts. A plain bagel with cream cheese gives you a quick burst of energy, but leaves you tired and hungry again within a couple of hours. Eat two slices of whole wheat toast (with that same smear of cream cheese, to keep all things equal) and you'll stay full and wide awake until lunch. That's because fiber-rich foods leave your stomach more slowly, preventing blood sugar (glucose) levels from spiking and then dropping quickly. This effect helps people with type 2 diabetes keep glucose levels in a healthy range, and it may help ward off the disease in healthy people. A study at Boston University found that black women (who have twice the rate of diabetes as whites) who ate at least 6 grams of fiber from cereal had an 18 percent lower risk of developing diabetes than those who ate less. Researchers in New Zealand determined that eating about three daily servings of whole grains (all great sources of fiber) resulted in a 20 to 30 percent decrease in type 2 diabetes risk compared with eating fewer servings per week.

It wards off weight creep.

Study after study has shown that by filling your belly and slowing digestion, fiber keeps you satisfied longer. A large review of studies on fiber and weight regulation determined that eating an additional 14 grams per day translates to a 10 percent reduction in overall calorie intake (the theory is that you'll eat fewer calories without even trying because the fiber fills you up) and an average weight loss of 4 pounds in just under 4 months. A long-term study at Harvard University showed how the nutrient works to our advantage as we age and metabolism slows: Women who increased their fiber intake the most over a 12-year period gained an average of 3.3 pounds less than women who increased their fiber the least. Overall, the researchers determined that the women eating the greatest amount of fiber had a 49 percent lower risk of major weight gain than those eating the least amount.

Your digestive tract will thank you.

Fiber is essential for preventing constipation. One of the ways it does this is by absorbing water, which softens and bulks up stools, so they pass easily through your system. That is why it's good to drink more water when you increase your fiber intake. Scientists once believed that a high-fiber diet protected against colon cancer, but recent studies and large reviews of existing research have shown little evidence to support this. What it does do, however, is fend off diverticulitis—a condition where small pouches form in the wall of the colon and become inflamed. It is very common in older adults, but studies show that a fiber-rich diet effectively prevents and treats the problem. A long-term Harvard study of more than 40,000 men found that eating a lot of fiber, especially the insoluble type, reduced the risk of diverticular disease by 40 percent.

>>>

High-fiber junk food: too good to be true?

Yogurt, chocolate–peanut butter snack bars, and ice cream aren't known as fiber powerhouses, yet suddenly manufacturers are touting these foods as good sources right on the package. If you think this sounds fishy, you're right. With health experts singing the praises of fiber, companies are adding it to their products in the hopes of attracting health-conscious consumers. To do it, they extract undigestible carbohydrates from foods like chicory root, oat hulls, corn, soy, and apple pulp (in some cases, these added fibers are synthesized from sucrose, or sugar), then add them to traditionally fiber-poor foods like yogurt. While these extracted and added fibers are unlikely to hurt you, they don't come with the complex interplay of antioxidants, phytonutrients, and vitamins that make naturally fiber-rich produce and grains so beneficial. The verdict: Processed foods with added fiber aren't inherently bad, but natural whole foods have bigger health advantages.

YOUR DAILY DOSE: 400 micrograms

TOP SOURCES: Broccoli, spinach, asparagus, lentils, avocado, papaya, corn, peanuts

FOLATE

WHILE IT MAY be best known as a nutrient that pregnant women need, this B vitamin is important for everyone's health. Without folate, cells can't divide and multiply properly—it's required to make new DNA and RNA, the building blocks of cells. It also helps the body process homocysteine, an amino acid that may be linked to heart disease.

Any woman who may become pregnant should pay close attention to folate intake because she will need adequate stores just before and just after conception to protect against neural tube defects (like spina bifida) and cleft palate. Evidence supporting folate's role in healthy pregnancies led the FDA to mandate in 1998 that folic acid (the synthetic form of folate) be added to processed foods like flour, bread, pasta, and cereal. A 2001 study reported a 19 percent reduction in neural tube birth defects after the mandate was put into effect. You probably consume synthetic folate if you make your sandwiches on store-bought bread or eat cereal for breakfast, but getting it from natural sources like spinach and broccoli is just as important—the FDA emphasizes getting naturally occurring folate from a varied diet, as well as from fortified foods and supplements.

Why you can't live without folate

You'll have a stronger heart.

A Dutch study found that getting enough folate reduced homocysteine levels in people with stable coronary artery disease by 18 percent. People with high homocysteine levels are often deficient in folate and vitamins B_6 and B_{12}, which help your body convert homocysteine into other amino acids, keeping levels in a healthy range.

Your brain will get a boost.

It turns out that too much homocysteine can not only lead to heart disease, but it is also a risk factor for Alzheimer's disease. Older people with memory problems often lose brain volume, and those who experience a rapid decline tend to be more likely to progress to Alzheimer's disease. British researchers found that getting plenty of folic acid and other B vitamins slowed the rate of brain shrinkage. When mice were fed a diet deficient in folate and the other B vitamins for 10 weeks, their blood levels of homocysteine were elevated and their memory and spatial learning abilities got worse.

Beating the blues is easier.

Depression can be difficult to treat, and many patients need to try various prescription medications before finding one that works best for them. But in the case of some antidepressants, higher folate intake may lead to greater success. A group of 127 men and women diagnosed with depression were treated with an antidepressant for 10 weeks. Half were also given 500 micrograms of folate each day. Only the women in the folate group experienced a significant reduction in symptoms of depression, as well as a reduction in homocysteine levels. Researchers hypothesized that men may require a higher dose of folate to achieve similar results.

YOUR DAILY DOSE: 18 milligrams

TOP SOURCES: Oysters, lentils, beef,
turkey, tuna, chicken, pork, crab, beans,
tofu, fortified cereals, oatmeal

IRON

IF YOU FEAST on spinach (à la Popeye) to satisfy your iron quota, you actually may not be getting enough of this critical nutrient. While spinach does contain iron, it also contains oxalic acid, which prevents most of the leafy green's iron from being absorbed. The idea that it's okay to rely on spinach is just one of the common myths about iron.

Another misconception is that all sources of iron are created equal. In reality, animal and seafood sources not only tend to have the highest levels of iron, but they also provide heme iron, which is the most readily absorbed form of the nutrient. Vegetarian sources provide non-heme iron. The body absorbs 15 to 35 percent of the heme iron you consume, compared to 2 to 20 percent of non-heme iron. To optimize non-heme iron absorption, it should be paired with vitamin C or meat (for non-vegetarians).

Iron is a vital component of many proteins in your body, chiefly hemoglobin, which carries oxygen to tissues. As part of the protein myoglobin, iron helps keep muscles functioning optimally by supplying them with oxygen as well. Iron is also needed to make DNA, regulate cell growth, and produce ATP, the chemical compound that is the body's main energy source.

Consistently missing out on your daily dose of iron reduces the supply of oxygen to your cells and can cause iron deficiency anemia. Symptoms include fatigue, inability to focus, and a weakened immune system. This condition needs to be treated with iron supplements. The other faulty notion about iron is that supplements are safe for healthy people, too. While some individuals (pregnant women, for example) may need extra iron, too much is toxic and can cause oxidative damage that raises the risk of diseases like cancer. While it is essential to work more iron-rich foods into our diets so that we don't become deficient, taking a pill to make up for any shortfall may actually be harmful.

Why you can't live without iron

You'll be fitter.

You carve out gym time even on busy days, put in your best effort, and stick to a consistent workout schedule. But if you're iron deficient, your performance—and the health gains that go with it—could suffer. In a study at Cornell University in New York, 42 women who were iron depleted, but not anemic, took a timed cycling test, and were then given either iron or a placebo for 6 weeks. During the last 4 weeks of the study, they trained for 30 minutes, 5 days a week. When they were tested again at the end, the iron group improved their 15 km times by 3.4 minutes, while the placebo group only shaved 1.6 minutes from their initial times. Iron helps you not only kick butt with your cardio, but also strength train efficiently. A study at the State University of New York at Albany showed that iron supplementation led to greater muscle endurance for iron-depleted women.

Not getting enough can take a toll on emotions.

Getting your daily dose of iron ensures your brain stays sharp and your outlook remains bright. Women of reproductive age have been the focus of study because of their higher risk of iron deficiency due to menstrual blood loss and increased iron needs during pregnancy. One study showed that previously iron-deficient women whose levels increased after receiving supplements for 16 weeks had a five- to sevenfold improvement in cognitive performance compared to women who received a placebo. Another study at Pennsylvania State University documented a 25 percent improvement in depression and stress ratings over the 7-month study period for iron-deficient anemic new mothers who received iron supplements.

It can keep you in your "thin" jeans.

We all have that favorite pair of pants we use to tell if we've been indulging in too many late-night bowls of ice cream or if our waistlines are holding steady. Even if your thin jeans indicate the latter, studies indicate that getting enough iron can help to keep it that way. A large analysis of data showed that as the severity of iron deficiency increased in U.S. women, body mass index increased as well. The researchers found this relationship even after taking into account variables like race, income, and education level.

YOUR DAILY DOSE: 400 milligrams

TOP SOURCES: Pumpkin seeds, edamame, Swiss chard, almonds, spinach, cashews, oatmeal, pinto beans, brown rice

MAGNESIUM

IF THE ONLY time you think about pumpkin seeds is when you're scooping them out of your kid's Halloween jack-o'-lantern, you may want to get to know these tasty morsels better. They're a top source of magnesium, possibly the hardest-working mineral in your body. Essential for more than 300 cell reactions, magnesium keeps your nervous system happily firing messages off to your brain, builds bone, and regulates muscle contraction (reminder: your heart is a muscle!). Despite its importance, it's a nutrient that nearly half of men and women fall short on. So why don't doctors just recommend you take supplements? Two reasons: In high doses, it has a laxative effect and can put stress on your kidneys. But get your magnesium from food and you'll reap all the benefits without having to worry about side effects.

Why you can't live without magnesium

Sleep will come more easily.

Even if you do make the effort to turn off the TV (and the computer and the smartphone) and climb into bed at a reasonable time, it's not always easy to fall asleep and stay that way for 8 solid hours. So how's this for a solution? One study showed that increasing daily magnesium by just 225 milligrams (about the same amount in a serving of our recipe for Pumpkin Seed–Coated Chicken Breasts with Bulgur Pilaf, page 160) helped insomniacs nod off more easily, stay asleep longer, and feel more refreshed in the morning than they did before upping their magnesium.

It makes for a more resilient heart.

Can something as simple as adding an edamame appetizer to your sushi order protect you from a heart attack? Yep. Women who get enough magnesium from food may slash their risk of heart disease in half, according to a Japanese study. It's likely that magnesium helps by keeping arteries clear, but it also regulates heart rhythm and lowers blood pressure. In a review of 22 studies published in the *European Journal of Clinical Nutrition,* researchers determined that getting more than 370 milligrams of magnesium per day was linked with an average 3- to 4-point drop in systolic blood pressure (the upper number) and a 2- to 3-point decline in diastolic blood pressure (the lower number).

It derails major headaches.

A recent study found that migraine sufferers with low magnesium levels experienced these debilitating headaches more often than those with adequate amounts in their bodies. As for the rest of us, pumping up the magnesium may help thwart everyday tension headaches. A German study showed that people who raised their daily magnesium had 40 percent fewer headaches over a 12-week period.

You'll get relief from PMS.

Pre-period bloating, weight gain, breast tenderness—in one study, magnesium helped control all these symptoms. Researchers at the University of Reading in the United Kingdom found that an extra 200 milligrams of magnesium along with vitamin B$_6$ a day can ease anxiety, tension, and irritability, too. One of magnesium's key functions is keeping nerve cells from going into overdrive and sending too many messages to the muscles, so there's reason to believe it also helps combat cramps.

You can sidestep diabetes.

When Harvard University researchers looked at the magnesium intakes of thousands of men and women, they found that people who got the most of the mineral lowered their chances of developing type 2 diabetes by about a third compared to those who ate the least. If you already have type 2 diabetes, magnesium is especially critical: It's been shown to reduce insulin resistance and control blood sugar in patients who were previously deficient in the mineral.

You'll feel powered, not pooped, after a workout.

USDA researchers found that women who ate a diet that contained less than half the daily recommendation for magnesium had faster heartbeats and greater oxygen needs during exercise than they did when they were getting a full daily dose. Translation: They ran out of steam sooner than they otherwise would have. This means that a low-magnesium diet results in exhausting, rather than energizing, workouts and may reduce your ability to do longer or more intense exercise, seriously cutting into your calorie burn.

>>>

The domino effect

When you aren't meeting your magnesium needs, your levels of two other important minerals may suffer. Magnesium plays a crucial role in the absorption of calcium and potassium. Correcting magnesium deficiencies has been shown to raise levels of potassium. Low magnesium intake hinders the body's ability to produce calcium-regulating hormones and process calcium efficiently. This intimately related functioning of nutrients in the body keeps bones healthy as you age. One study showed that a diet high in magnesium may help maintain bone mineral density in older adults, staving off osteoporosis.

YOUR DAILY DOSE: 1,000 milligrams

TOP SOURCES: Salmon, tuna, mackerel, herring, sardines, trout, walnuts, flaxseeds, canola oil, dark leafy greens

O3

OMEGA-3 FATTY ACIDS

YOU'VE HEARD OF good fats (like the mono-unsaturated kind in olive oil) and bad fats (like trans fatty acids in some processed foods), but when it comes to the most important fat for better health, the title goes to omega-3 fatty acids. All of the cell membranes in our bodies rely on fats to function. Omega-3s keep cell membranes fluid and flexible. That enables the cells to let the right amount of good stuff in, flush out waste, and communicate with other cells. These fatty acids are highly concentrated in brain cells and maintain healthy neurons and proper functioning of the central nervous system. They also support the immune system, helping to block the release of inflammatory compounds that can raise your risk of chronic diseases like diabetes.

Like the members of most families, the three main fatty acids in the omega-3 family have a complicated relationship. Alpha-linolenic acid (ALA) is found in plant-based foods and is the only omega-3 considered essential, which is the technical way of saying

our bodies can't make it, so it must come from food. The other two types, eicosapentaenoic acid (EPA) and docosahexaenoic acid (DHA), are marine based and considered to have greater health benefits. Some of the ALA we consume is converted to EPA and DHA, but scientists estimate that it's a small amount, so you can't rely on ALA alone. (Women convert more ALA than men do.) That means the best way to make sure you're getting the optimal dose of omega-3s is to work every type in to your diet. Since the American Heart Association has endorsed the health benefits of getting 1,000 milligrams of omega-3s (primarily from fish) per day for people with established heart disease—and that's a safe level—we've used that amount as the daily dose. If you don't have heart disease, eating two servings of fish a week, along with several foods rich in ALA, is enough to meet your needs. For recipes that provide only ALA, we don't list a percentage of the daily dose but instead note that they're high in ALA.

Why you can't live without omega-3 fatty acids

More omega-3s fortify your heart.

Evidence of the protective powers of a diet rich in omega-3 fatty acids is so convincing that the American Heart Association recommends it for the treatment and prevention of coronary heart disease. A study at the University of Washington in Seattle analyzed the seafood intake of people who experienced cardiac arrest (where the heart suddenly stops beating) for the month prior to the event. Using a control group for comparison, the researchers found that the risk was cut in half for people who ate fatty fish twice a week. A Danish study that followed nearly 50,000 women with an average age of 30 at the start of the study found that those who rarely or never ate omega-3-rich fish had a 91 percent higher chance of cardiovascular disease over an 8-year period than women who ate the fish weekly. Studies also show heart benefits of ALAs, or nonseafood omega-3s. Harvard University researchers found that people who ate the most ALA (a median of 1,360 mg a day) were 45 percent less likely to die from a heart attack than those who ate the least.

They may keep your brain young.

While wrinkles serve as visible signs of aging, there are other signs we can't see. As we age, brain volume declines, whittling away at memory, problem-solving skills, and abstract-thinking abilities. Omega-3 fatty acids, especially DHA, are abundant in brain cells, and studies show a relationship between blood levels of these nutrients and brain function. Healthy middle-age people with the highest amounts of DHA scored better on tests measuring cognitive ability in a recent study in the *Journal of Nutrition.* A study at UCLA measured the brain volume of more than 1,500 people who did not have dementia and found that those with the lowest DHA levels had less brain volume and scored worse on memory and cognition tests than those with the highest levels. Omega-3s may even protect against Alzheimer's disease. One study showed that people who got an estimated 180 milligrams of DHA per day (equal to 3 servings of seafood per week) reduced their odds of developing Alzheimer's by 39 percent and their chance of dementia from any cause by 47 percent.

They're a weapon against breast cancer.

The role of omega-3s in cancer prevention is still uncertain, but there is evidence that they may keep cancer from returning. A recent study in the *Journal of Nutrition* reported that women treated for early-stage breast cancer who consumed the most EPA and DHA from food were 25 percent less likely to have a recurrence compared to the women who got the least. Researchers also noted that the risk of death from any cause was reduced as omega-3 intake increased.

They prevent and treat diabetes.

Adding even moderate amounts of omega-3s to your diet may help you steer clear of metabolic syndrome, the group of risk factors that increases the likelihood of developing type 2 diabetes. A study analyzing the diets of Korean men found a 47 percent lower risk of metabolic syndrome over a 4-year period for those who consumed the most omega-3 fatty acids (a median of 786 milligrams per day) compared to men who consumed the least (37 milligrams per day). And when researchers tested the blood levels of omega-3s in more than 3,000 older adults and followed up to see who developed diabetes over a 10-year period, they found a 43 percent lower risk for the people with the highest levels of ALA, while those with the most EPA and DHA had a 36 percent lower risk.

While prevention is the ultimate goal, it's never too late to take advantage of these protective fats. A recent review of the evidence showed that diabetes patients—who are vulnerable to heart disease—with high intakes of fish and total omega-3s had a 15 to 19 percent reduction in the risk of death from cardiovascular disease.

>>>

The right wine to serve with fish

Most people wouldn't consider trout and merlot an ideal pairing, but a European study found a link between moderate alcohol intake and higher levels of EPA and DHA in the body. Researchers saw the greatest benefit from wine and believe that polyphenols, compounds with antioxidant properties found in the skins of grapes, may be the cause (red wines tend to have more polyphenols than whites because the grape skins are used in the wine making process). Luckily for non-imbibers, polyphenols are also available in a variety of foods. Simply eating grapes, as well as other colorful produce like berries, apples, plums, cherries, and broccoli—along with beans, green tea, and coffee—will provide polyphenols, along with other nutrients you need to stay healthy.

YOUR DAILY DOSE: 3,500 milligrams

TOP SOURCES: Beets, dates, white beans, raisins, lima beans, figs, salmon, mushrooms, chicken breast, clams, sweet potatoes, potatoes, apricots, avocado, cantaloupe, honeydew, nectarines, milk, yogurt, oat bran

POTASSIUM

FIRST, LET'S CLEAR up a myth: Bananas aren't exactly the potassium powerhouses everyone believes they are. For around 120 calories, you can get 487 milligrams from a large banana or 752 milligrams from a small red baked potato. The distinction is important, because while potassium is found in varying amounts in a lot of foods, Americans still aren't getting enough of it. The mineral is a key player in muscle and nerve function and fluid balance. It helps the body use carbohydrates to power our muscles and regulates the amount of sodium in the body, an important job that keeps blood pressure in a healthy range. One reason for the concern about the low intake of fruits and vegetables in the American diet is that they are among the richest sources of potassium (as well as a slew of other disease-fighting nutrients). How's that for an incentive to hit your local farmers' market this weekend?

Why you can't live without potassium

It offsets the blood pressure–raising effects of sodium.

Johns Hopkins researchers put people on a diet low in fruits, vegetables, and dairy products that supplied about 1,752 milligrams of potassium—the amount most Americans get per day. Then they upped the produce and added low-fat dairy, bringing the potassium to 4,415 milligrams a day. On both diets, the sodium intake stayed about the same, but when the potassium was high, systolic blood pressure (the upper number) dropped by 5.5 points and diastolic (the lower number) slid by 3 points.

You'll be protected against stroke.

With high blood pressure comes a greater risk of having a stroke, but potassium can help modify it. In an analysis of several studies, experts at the Karolinska Institute in Stockholm, Sweden, were able to determine that for every 1,000-milligram increase in potassium intake per day (that's the equivalent of 3 ounces of salmon plus a small baked potato), the odds dropped by 11 percent.

You can avoid painful kidney stones.

Potassium keeps the body's acid balance in check. When acid is high, more calcium is excreted in the urine, which can lead to kidney stones. In one Harvard University study of more than 45,000 men, those who got 4,042 milligrams of potassium or more per day were less than half as likely to develop kidney stones as men who took in 2,895 milligrams or less. Potassium was protective for women, too. In another study, women who got 4,099 milligrams a day had 56 percent less risk than those who got 2,407 milligrams.

It's an insurance policy for healthy bones.

A beet and goat cheese salad isn't just a tasty flavor combo. It also supplies the perfect cocktail of nutrients for strong bones. Calcium from the goat cheese ups your body's reserves, while potassium from the beets may help preserve the bone calcium you already have. Here's how it works: Many foods in a typical Western diet can tilt the body's pH balance toward the acidic side of the scale. When that occurs, the body releases calcium (which is alkaline, in case your high school chemistry knowledge is fuzzy) from the bones to restore the balance. Researchers at Tufts University believe that getting your daily dose of potassium, also alkaline, can reset your pH without siphoning the body's calcium stores. The Tufts study found that older men and women with the highest potassium intakes experienced smaller losses in bone mineral density over a 4-year period than those with the lowest.

You may live longer.

Ever heard that an avocado a day keeps the doctor away? Considering the high potassium content of these creamy green fruits (yes, avocados are fruits, and they pack 975 milligrams of potassium each), it might be true. After following more than 12,000 adults for about 15 years, researchers saw a 20 percent decrease in risk of death from any cause for every 1,000 milligrams of potassium people consumed.

YOUR DAILY DOSE: 6 micrograms

TOP SOURCES: Clams, eggs, crab, beef, trout, salmon, tuna, haddock, milk, yogurt

VITAMIN B$_{12}$

IF YOU WANT to age well, you'd do yourself a favor by adding plenty of foods rich in vitamin B$_{12}$ to your diet. It supports metabolism, keeps your nervous system working properly, and helps with the formation of red blood cells, which are needed to move oxygen through your system. Vitamin B$_{12}$ is extracted from food in the stomach, so a healthy digestive system is just as important as your diet when it comes to getting your daily dose. Since vitamin B$_{12}$ is bound to protein in food, seafood and animal products are the best sources. Although some foods, like cereals and grains, are fortified with B$_{12}$, vegans and vegetarians should consider a daily supplement that contains 10 micrograms. This amount is higher than the daily dose of 2.6 micrograms because the body cannot absorb 100 percent of the vitamin when taken in supplement form. With all its benefits, from healthy vision to a stronger brain, missing out on this nutrient is not an option.

Why you can't live without vitamin B$_{12}$

It may ease depression.

More research is needed, but in a study of nearly 4,000 elderly people, those with a deficiency of vitamin B$_{12}$ were about 70 percent more likely to suffer from depression than those with adequate levels. In a Finnish study of middle-age people, high blood levels of the vitamin were linked to better recovery from depression.

It bolsters the aging brain.

Having depression puts you at greater risk of cognitive decline, which can lead to dementia, but one study showed that vitamin B$_{12}$ may help fight this progression. The diets and depression symptoms of more than 3,500 seniors were studied at 3-year intervals. Researchers observed a 2 percent decrease in depression risk per year for every additional 10 micrograms of B$_{12}$ and 10 milligrams of vitamin B$_6$ in their diets. Other studies support the brain-B$_{12}$ connection: British researchers observed faster cognitive decline in people with lower vitamin B$_{12}$ levels, and a 7-year Swedish study found that subjects with higher concentrations of B$_{12}$ in their bodies had lower risks of Alzheimer's disease.

You'll see clearly.

If you picture yourself behind the wheel of a convertible cruising up the coast well into retirement, consider boosting your B$_{12}$ for healthy eyes. A study in the journal *Archives of Internal Medicine* reported a 41 percent reduction in the risk of macular degeneration, a condition that significantly affects vision. More than 5,000 women were given either vitamin B$_{12}$, along with folate and B$_6$, or a placebo and were followed for 7 years. Those who got the B vitamins had a 33 percent less chance of developing age-related macular degeneration than those in the placebo group.

It puts the brakes on migraines.

Together with folic acid and B$_6$, vitamin B$_{12}$ reduced the severity and frequency of migraines for patients in an Australian study. The B vitamins lowered the patients' homocysteine levels by 39 percent, which researchers attribute to the success of the treatment. Elevated homocysteine, an amino acid regulated by B vitamins, has been observed in people who suffer from migraines.

YOUR DAILY DOSE: 60 milligrams

TOP SOURCES: Brussels sprouts, strawberries, red bell peppers, oranges, kiwi, green bell peppers, broccoli, grapefruit, tomato juice, cantaloupe, cabbage

VITAMIN C

WHEN YOU THINK of vitamin C, two things probably come to mind: oranges and cold prevention. But what you should be thinking is red bell peppers and smooth skin. A medium red bell pepper has nearly twice the vitamin C of a medium navel orange. And while loading up on C doesn't prevent colds, it does play an important role in collagen production. This protein is found in connective tissue, like ligaments and tendons, and also in the middle layer of the skin, called the dermis. There it forms a meshlike support system that keeps skin firm. When collagen diminishes, you may notice wrinkles and sagging. In fact, in one study, dermatologists examined the skin of more than 4,000 women between the ages of 40 and 74 and found that those with a high intake of vitamin C were 11 percent less likely to have a wrinkled appearance.

Of course, looking good isn't the only reason to get enough C in your diet. The vitamin is a powerful antioxidant that absorbs free radicals, the toxic substances that can damage cells and lead to inflammation and disease. It also helps the body use other antioxidants, especially vitamin E. Without vitamin C, our bodies couldn't make certain neurotransmitters (chemicals that help nerve and brain cells communicate with each other), heal wounds, or metabolize protein. Unlike most animals, humans can't manufacture vitamin C from the foods we eat, so we need to get a steady supply from our diets.

Why you can't live without vitamin C

It fights inflammation.

Men who got around 100 milligrams of vitamin C a day (about the amount in a cup of sliced strawberries) had less chance of having elevated levels of C-reactive protein, a marker for inflammation that's been linked to a higher risk for heart disease.

You'll protect yourself against diabetes.

People with the highest intake of vitamin C from fruits and vegetables cut their type 2 diabetes risk by 22 percent compared to those with the lowest intake, according to a 12-year study involving more than 21,000 people.

It may help you avoid a stroke.

Getting plenty of vitamin C in your diet was linked to lower incidence of stroke in a study of more than 20,000 people. Those with the highest blood levels of the vitamin (an indication of their fruit and vegetable intake) cut their stroke risk by 42 percent compared to those with the lowest levels.

Colds won't last as long.

Pumping up your vitamin C is unlikely to make any difference once you have cold symptoms. But consistently getting enough while you're healthy might shorten the duration of any cold you do catch. An analysis of data from thousands of patients found an 8 percent decrease in the length of the colds for adults and a 14 percent decrease in children when they were getting about 200 milligrams a day.

>>>

The perfect pairing

When you top a bean burrito with a hefty spoonful of salsa, you're doing more than spicing up your meal. You're making sure that you're going to absorb more of the iron in the beans. Vitamin C, found in this case in tomatoes, makes the iron in plant foods more available to the body.

VITAMIN D

VITAMIN D IS one of the most controversial nutrients today, but its efficacy is not what's in question. As the benefits of vitamin D continue to emerge, the debate has focused on just how much of it we need to thrive. The current recommendation is 400 IU a day, so that's the value we use here. But many experts believe that that amount is too low. A study in the journal *Archives of Internal Medicine* estimates that 77 percent of Americans have inadequate blood levels of the vitamin. The researchers suggest that 1,000 IU or more may be needed to correct and prevent a deficiency. A report from the National Institute of Medicine recommends 600 IU.

Technically a hormone, vitamin D production in our bodies is triggered by sunlight on exposed skin, and it's also found naturally in a few foods. (Milk, soy milk, cereal, and yogurt are often fortified with the vitamin.) Best known for its healthy bone benefits, vitamin D also regulates cell growth, immune function, and neuromuscular activity, and controls inflammation.

Thanks to sunscreen use, Americans aren't getting as much vitamin D as we used to from the sun, and in northern climates during the winter, the sun isn't strong enough to trigger vitamin D production. While you can meet the current daily dose through food, you probably need a supplement to get more than that; you may want to ask your doctor to do a blood test to determine your vitamin D levels. If you take a supplement, look for vitamin D_3; it may be the best-absorbed form.

Why you can't live without Vitamin D

You can't have strong bones without it.

Don't think of milk as a kiddie beverage, but rather the perfect cocktail of calcium and vitamin D. Experts estimate that only 10 to 15 percent of the calcium in our diets is absorbed without adequate vitamin D. Together, these two nutrients prevent osteoporosis. A Tufts University study showed that calcium and vitamin D supplementation reduced bone loss and lowered the chance of nonvertebral fractures over a 3-year period for men and women over age 65. A Swiss study showed that the bone benefits can't be attributed to calcium alone. Researchers gave half of a group of older women calcium plus vitamin D, while the other half received calcium alone. After 3 months, they found that the calcium and vitamin D group had a 60 percent reduction in the rate of falling (which helps prevent broken bones), compared to the calcium group.

It's a cancer fighter.

Scientists have shown that vitamin D has an effect on cancer cell growth and can stop the disease from spreading. A European study calculated a 40 percent lower risk of colorectal cancer in people with the highest concentrations of vitamin D in their bodies compared to people with the lowest. In women, it may protect against breast cancer. Canadian researchers analyzed sun exposure throughout the lives of more than 6,500 women and used the information to estimate vitamin D levels. They found that women who got the most sun had 26 to 50 percent lower odds of developing breast cancer. Vitamin D may also prevent the growth of breast cancer cells in women already battling the disease by producing a tumor-fighting protein, according to researchers at the University of Medicine & Dentistry of New Jersey.

D stands for diabetes protection.

Exercise and maintaining a healthy weight are still the top tools for preventing diabetes, but getting enough vitamin D gives you an extra boost that may reduce your risk even more. In a study of more than 83,000 women, researchers at Tufts University found that the combination of vitamin D and calcium slashed the chances of developing type 2 diabetes by 33 percent over a 20-year period. The protective amount was more than 800 IU of vitamin D and more than 1,200 milligrams of calcium per day. Scientists believe vitamin D helps regulate insulin production in the pancreas, helping the body process glucose efficiently.

You'll burn more fat.

Overweight and obese people with high vitamin D levels were 70 percent more likely to drop pounds than those with the lowest levels, according to a study in *The American Journal of Clinical Nutrition*. Other studies found that vitamin D with calcium slows postmenopausal weight gain. Australian researchers report that having a breakfast high in calcium and vitamin D even helps you eat less during the day. The vitamin helps release leptin, the hormone that makes you feel full, and reduces your production of two other hormones, parathyroid hormone and calcitrol, that cause your body to hang on to fat.

It helps hypertension.

Studies suggest that calcium can treat high blood pressure, but researchers in Germany discovered that adding vitamin D to the mix provides even bigger improvements. Women who got calcium and vitamin D over an 8-week period saw a 9.3 percent drop in systolic blood pressure compared to women who took only calcium. Another connection between vitamin D and heart health has been observed when scientists take into account where you live: Both vitamin D deficiency and blood pressure increase the further away you get from the equator, where sun exposure and, in turn, vitamin D levels are lowest.

You may prevent a serious autoimmune disease.

Australian researchers found that people with more sun damage, and consequently higher blood levels of vitamin D, had a 60 percent lower risk of multiple sclerosis. This is not a free pass to go tanning (note the word *damage*), but the study does suggest that the vitamin is protective. A Harvard study that did not measure sun exposure also found benefits: As vitamin D levels in the body increased, risk of multiple sclerosis decreased in whites, though the benefit did not hold up for African American and Hispanic study participants.

It keeps depression at bay.

Once you've battled depression, it's not uncommon to experience a recurrence. Researchers at the University of Texas Southwestern Medical Center in Dallas found that having adequate vitamin D levels cut the risk of a relapse by 10 percent.

YOUR DAILY DOSE: 30 IU

TOP SOURCES: Peanuts, almonds, kiwi, sunflower seeds, hazelnuts, mango, peanut butter, olive oil, spinach

VITAMIN E

VITAMIN E'S PRIMARY job is to act as an antioxidant in the body. It destroys free radicals, unstable molecules that can damage cells' DNA and lead to disease. Free radicals may be the by-products of natural processes in our bodies, but they also result from exposure to pollution, UV radiation, and cigarette smoke.

The antioxidant power alone is reason to up your intake, but vitamin E has other important roles in your body. It is involved in gene expression, communication between cells, healthy blood vessel function, and immune response. Since vitamin E is fat soluble, fat must be present in the digestive tract for the body to absorb it. Some of the most vitamin E–rich foods, like nuts and seeds, contain healthy fats that may help the uptake of the vitamin. Getting your daily dose is not only delicious, but its antioxidant punch could also make it a lifesaver.

Why you can't live without vitamin E

It could keep your heart going strong.

A review of studies performed by the Department of Biochemistry and Molecular Biology at the University of Bern in Switzerland found that the more vitamins E and C and carotenoids people ate in their diets, the lower the incidence of cardiovascular disease and cancer. Vitamin E may reduce the odds of coronary heart disease by preventing the oxidation of bad LDL cholesterol, which can lead to atherosclerosis, and by preventing blood clots, which can block the arteries and keep blood from reaching the heart, leading to a heart attack.

It protects your brain.

In a Dutch study published in the *Archives of Neurology,* people who had the highest levels of vitamin E had a 25 percent lower risk of being diagnosed with dementia over a 9-year period compared with those who had the lowest levels. Researchers believe the vitamin may counteract oxidative damage to neurons in the brain that can build up over time and lead to cognitive decline. Another trial of patients already suffering from Alzheimer's disease showed that vitamin E slowed the disease's progression, lengthening the time before patients required institutionalization or lost the ability to perform basic activities. A third study evaluated the total vitamin E intake of seniors over a 3-year period. The researchers observed a 36 percent slower rate of mental decline in people with the highest vitamin E consumption. Notably, this effect was seen not only when vitamin E intake came from a combination of food and supplements, but also when it came from food alone.

It may help you beat cancer.

Study results are mixed, but some data points to antioxidants like vitamin E as tools in the arsenal of cancer prevention. A study of more than 35,000 women showed that those who took in about 36 IU of vitamin E a day were less likely to develop colon cancer compared to those who got just about 6 IU a day. The effect was especially strong in those younger than 65. A study of male smokers in Finland found that having high blood levels of vitamin E translated to a 48 percent reduction in the risk of developing pancreatic cancer (smoking is a major risk factor for this disease).

It provides extra protection against the flu.

For vaccinations to work effectively, our bodies must mount an immune response, creating antibodies that destroy the flu virus or whatever disease we're being vaccinated against. In other words, if our immune systems can't get "angry" enough to do something about the offending substance, we may still get sick. Vitamin E has been shown to improve the response to vaccinations in older people whose immune systems may be less feisty.

ANTHOCYANIN-RICH RECIPES

Blueberry-Oatmeal Casserole with Baked Yogurt Topping (p 59)
2 servings

Blueberry-Cornmeal Waffles with Blueberry Sauce (p 60)
2 servings

Grilled Eggplant, Tomato, and Fresh Mozzarella Sandwiches (p 96)
2 servings

Pearl Couscous with Roasted Beets, Lima Beans, and Feta (p 97)
1½ servings

Borscht (p 109)
2 servings

Swiss Chard, Eggplant, and Mushroom Lasagna (p 139)
2 servings

Stuffed Eggplant with Couscous, Roasted Red Peppers, and Goat Cheese (p 147)
2 servings

Roasted Chicken Breasts with Sautéed Cabbage and Apples (p 153)
2½ servings

Roasted Beet and Beet Green Sauté (p 191)
2 servings

Grilled Japanese Eggplant with Miso Glaze (p 201)
4½ servings

Red Cabbage Slaw with Tangy Poppy Seed Dressing (p 204)
1½ servings

Blueberry Fool (p 214)
2 servings

CALCIUM-RICH RECIPES

Blueberry-Oatmeal Casserole with Baked Yogurt Topping (p 59)
27% of your daily dose

Creamy Steel-Cut Oats with Dried Cranberries and Pistachios (p 63)
35% of your daily dose

Sweet Corn Frittata (p 67)
33% of your daily dose

Baked Eggs in Ham Cups (p 68)
26% of your daily dose

Eggs Florentine on English Muffins (p 69)
36% of your daily dose

Chopped Vegetable Salad with Sardines and Toasted Pita Croutons (p 77)
33% of your daily dose

Sardine Baguette Sandwiches with Creamy Avocado Spread (p 78)
33% of your daily dose

Date-Ricotta Crostini and Arugula Salad (p 85)
36% of your daily dose

Ham and White Cheddar Panini with Mango Chutney (p 91)
30% of your daily dose

Roasted Tomato Soup with White Cheddar Grilled Cheese Sandwiches (p 94)
35% of your daily dose

Grilled Brussels Sprout and Tofu Skewers with Balsamic Glaze (p 100)
41% of your daily dose

Turkey-Feta Meatballs with Roasted Red Pepper Dipping Sauce (p 125)
29% of your daily dose

Yogurt-Marinated Chicken Skewers with Cucumber-Yogurt Sauce (p 126)
29% of your daily dose

Baked Penne with Creamy Swiss Cheese Sauce, Mushrooms, and Asparagus (p 130)
38% of your daily dose

Stuffed Shells with Chunky Tomato Sauce (p 134)
41% of your daily dose

Spinach Gnudi with Quick Chunky Tomato Sauce (p 136)
34% of your daily dose

Swiss Chard, Eggplant, and Mushroom Lasagna (p 139)
47% of your daily dose

Linguine with Kale, Olives, and Currants (p 145)
27% of your daily dose

Spaghetti with Sardines, Caramelized Fennel, and Buttery Garlic Bread Crumbs (p 146)
38% of your daily dose

Pizza with Butternut Squash, Spinach, and Fontina (p 149)
26% of your daily dose

Baked Chicken Parmesan with Homemade Tomato Sauce (p 155)
37% of your daily dose

Individual Tuna Casseroles with Peas and Tarragon (p 180)
38% of your daily dose

Braised Kale with Black-Eyed Peas (p 192)
26% of your daily dose

Tuscan Kale Salad with Almonds and Parmesan (p 210)
26% of your daily dose

Dark Chocolate Pudding with Whipped Ricotta (p 217)
26% of your daily dose

Cardamom Yogurt Cheesecake with Caramelized Plums (p 226)
25% of your daily dose

CAROTENOID-RICH RECIPES

Eggs Florentine on English Muffins (p 67)
2 servings

Tropical Ambrosia Salad (p 71)
5 servings

Roasted Sweet Potato and Pumpkin Seed Salad with Warm Bacon-Tomato Vinaigrette (p 74)
3½ servings

Date-Ricotta Crostini and Arugula Salad (p 85)
1 serving

Mediterranean Edamame Patties in Whole Wheat Pita with Tahini Sauce (p 86)
1½ servings

Roasted Tomato Soup with White Cheddar Grilled Cheese Sandwiches (p 94)
1½ servings

Asian Chicken Salad in Lettuce Cups with Peanut Sauce (p 102)
1½ servings

Tuna and Chickpea Salad in Tomato Cups (p 105)
1 serving

Creamy Broccoli-Pea Soup with Bacon and Cheddar (p 110)
5 servings

Curried Red Lentil and Carrot Soup (p 112)
2 servings

Swiss Chard and White Bean Soup (p 113)
2½ servings

CAROTENOID-RICH RECIPES—CONTINUED

Lemony Chicken, Spinach and Orzo Soup (p 115)
1 serving

Brussels Sprout Poppers with Orange–Poppy Seed Dipping Sauce (p 118)
1½ servings

Stuffed Shells with Chunky Tomato Sauce (p 134)
1 serving

Spinach Gnudi with Quick Chunky Tomato Sauce (p 136)
2 servings

Swiss Chard, Eggplant, and Mushroom Lasagna (p 139)
5 servings

Fettuccine with Lentil Bolognese (p 142)
2 servings

Linguine with Kale, Olives, and Currants (p 145)
2 servings

Pizza with Butternut Squash, Spinach, and Fontina (p 149)
2 servings

Picadillo-Stuffed Red Bell Peppers (p 150)
3 servings

Wild Rice–Stuffed Acorn Squash (p 151)
2 servings

Baked Chicken Parmesan with Homemade Tomato Sauce (p 155)
2 servings

Roast Chicken with Brussels Sprouts, Roasted Grapes, and Hazelnuts (p 158)
2 servings

Black Bean–Turkey Chili with Butternut Squash (p 162)
3½ servings

Beef Stew with Root Vegetables (p 166)
1 serving

Beef and Broccoli with Brown Rice (p 168)
4 servings

Grilled Steak au Poivre with Sautéed Broccoli Rabe (p 170)
1 serving

Shrimp and Asparagus Stir-Fry with Rice Noodles (p 184)
2½ servings

Broiled Asparagus with Sun-Dried Tomato Vinaigrette (p 189)
3 servings

Sweet and Tangy Baked Beans and Tomatoes (p 190)
1 serving

Roasted Beet and Beet Green Sauté (p 191)
3 servings

Braised Kale with Black-Eyed Peas (p 192)
3 servings

Carrot Gratin with Creamy Goat Cheese Sauce (p 195)
2 servings

Braised Spinach and Potatoes with Indian Spices (p 198)
2 servings

Honey-Lime Glazed Carrots (p 199)
2 servings

Shredded Carrot and Chickpea Salad (p 199)
2 servings

Red Cabbage Slaw with Tangy Poppy Seed Dressing (p 204)
1 serving

Fingerling Potato Salad with Creamy Mustard-Anchovy Dressing (p 208)
2 servings

Tuscan Kale Salad with Almonds and Parmesan (p 210)
1 serving

FIBER-RICH RECIPES

Barley-Banana Pancakes (p 58)
44% of your daily dose

Blueberry-Cornmeal Waffles with Blueberry Sauce (p 60)
36% of your daily dose

Creamy Steel-Cut Oats with Dried Cranberries and Pistachios (p 63)
28% of your daily dose

Pear–Oat Bran Quick Bread (p 64)
25% of your daily dose

Eggs Florentine on English Muffins (p 69)
40% of your daily dose

Tropical Ambrosia Salad (p 71)
44% of your daily dose

Sardine Baguette Sandwiches with Creamy Avocado Spread (p 78)
28% of your daily dose

Steak Salad with Pickled Pears and Blue Cheese (p 79)
32% of your daily dose

Turkey, Pear, and Grilled Radicchio Baguette Sandwiches (p 80)
32% of your daily dose

Date-Ricotta Crostini and Arugula Salad (p 85)
40% of your daily dose

Mediterranean Edamame Patties in Whole Wheat Pita with Tahini Sauce (p 86)
44% of your daily dose

Fish Tacos with Black Bean–Papaya Salsa (p 88)
32% of your daily dose

Flaxseed-Coated Cod Sandwiches (p 90)
52% of your daily dose

Roasted Tomato Soup with White Cheddar Grilled Cheese Sandwiches (p 94)
32% of your daily dose

Grilled Eggplant, Tomato, and Fresh Mozzarella Sandwiches (p 96)
40% of your daily dose

Pearl Couscous with Roasted Beets, Lima Beans, and Feta (p 97)
36% of your daily dose

Grilled Brussels Sprout and Tofu Skewers with Balsamic Glaze (p 100)
44% of your daily dose

Asian Chicken Salad in Lettuce Cups with Peanut Sauce (p 102)
32% of your daily dose

Borscht (p 109)
36% of your daily dose

Creamy Broccoli-Pea Soup with Bacon and Cheddar (p 110)
40% of your daily dose

Curried Red Lentil and Carrot Soup (p 112)
56% of your daily dose

Swiss Chard and White Bean Soup (p 113)
36% of your daily dose

Baked Penne with Creamy Swiss Cheese Sauce, Mushrooms, and Asparagus (p 130)
28% of your daily dose

Pearled Barley Risotto with Peas, Pancetta, and Sun-Dried Tomatoes (p 133)
52% of your daily dose

Swiss Chard, Eggplant, and Mushroom Lasagna (p 139)
48% of your daily dose

Fettuccine with Lentil Bolognese (p 142)
80% of your daily dose

Linguine with Kale, Olives, and Currants (p 145)
44% of your daily dose

Spaghetti with Sardines, Caramelized Fennel, and Buttery Garlic Bread Crumbs (p 146)
52% of your daily dose

Stuffed Eggplant with Couscous, Roasted Red Peppers, and Goat Cheese (p 147)
56% of your daily dose

Pizza with Butternut Squash, Spinach, and Fontina (p 149)
52% of your daily dose

Wild Rice-Stuffed Acorn Squash (p 151)
52% of your daily dose

Roast Chicken with Brussels Sprouts, Roasted Grapes, and Hazelnuts (p 158)
32% of your daily dose

Pumpkin Seed-Coated Chicken Breasts with Bulgur Pilaf (p 160)
36% of your daily dose

Black Bean-Turkey Chili with Butternut Squash (p 162)
60% of your daily dose

Beef Stew with Root Vegetables (p 166)
44% of your daily dose

Beef and Broccoli with Brown Rice (p 168)
28% of your daily dose

Grilled Steak au Poivre with Sautéed Broccoli Rabe (p 170)
28% of your daily dose

Roast Pork Tenderloin with Edamame Succotash (p 173)
28% of your daily dose

Pork Braised in Kiwi-Coconut Sauce with White Beans (p 174)
36% of your daily dose

Pan-Roasted Salmon with Lentil Pilaf (p 179)
40% of your daily dose

Sweet and Tangy Baked Beans and Tomatoes (p 190)
44% of your daily dose

Roasted Beet and Beet Green Sauté (p 191)
28% of your daily dose

Braised Kale with Black-Eyed Peas (p 192)
36% of your daily dose

Red Potatoes with Edamame Pesto (p 196)
28% of your daily dose

Shredded Carrot and Chickpeas Salad (p 199)
32% of your daily dose

Grilled Japanese Eggplant with Miso Glaze (p 201)
40% of your daily dose

Quinoa with Black Beans, Tomatoes, Corn, and Feta (p 203)
28% of your daily dose

Curried Roasted Cauliflower with Flaxseeds (p 207)
28% of your daily dose

Kiwi-Banana Smoothie with Sunflower Seeds (p 225)
44% of your daily dose

Date Squares with Easy Banana "Ice Cream" (p 229)
32% of your daily dose

Cocoa-Roasted Peanuts with Cayenne (p 230)
28% of your daily dose

FOLATE-RICH RECIPES

Poached Eggs with Steamed Asparagus and Asiago Cheese (p 65)
28% of your daily dose

Eggs Florentine on English Muffins (p 69)
48% of your daily dose

Tropical Ambrosia Salad (p 71)
26% of your daily dose

Mediterranean Edamame Patties in Whole Wheat Pita with Tahini Sauce (p 86)
70% of your daily dose

Fish Tacos with Black Bean-Papaya Salsa (p 88)
26% of your daily dose

Flaxseed-Coated Cod Sandwiches (p 90)
121% of your daily dose

Pearl Couscous with Roasted Beets, Lima Beans, and Feta (p 97)
44% of your daily dose

Grilled Brussels Sprout and Tofu Skewers with Balsamic Glaze (p 100)
32% of your daily dose

Asian Chicken Salad in Lettuce Cups with Peanut Sauce (p 102)
29% of your daily dose

Borscht (p 109)
42% of your daily dose

Creamy Broccoli-Pea Soup with Bacon and Cheddar (p 110)
32% of your daily dose

Lemony Chicken, Spinach, and Orzo Soup (p 115)
42% of your daily dose

Crab Cocktail with Mango (p 121)
31% of your daily dose

Spinach Gnudi with Quick Chunky Tomato Sauce (p 136)
31% of your daily dose

Fettuccine with Lentil Bolognese (p 142)
48% of your daily dose

Wild Rice-Stuffed Acorn Squash (p 151)
31% of your daily dose

Roast Chicken with Brussels Sprouts, Roasted Grapes, and Hazelnuts (p 158)
28% of your daily dose

Beef Stew with Root Vegetables (p 166)
31% of your daily dose

Beef and Broccoli with Brown Rice (p 168)
35% of your daily dose

Grilled Steak au Poivre with Sautéed Broccoli Rabe (p 170)
40% of your daily dose

Roast Pork Tenderloin with Edamame Succotash (p 173)
78% of your daily dose

Seafood Paella (p 183)
43% of your daily dose

Shrimp and Asparagus Stir-Fry with Rice Noodles (p 184)
28% of your daily dose

Broiled Asparagus with Sun-Dried Tomato Vinaigrette (p 189)
26% of your daily dose

Sweet and Tangy Baked Beans and Tomatoes (p 190)
36% of your daily dose

Roasted Beet and Beet Green Sauté (p 191)
31% of your daily dose

Red Potatoes with Edamame Pesto (p 196)
56% of your daily dose

Braised Spinach and Potatoes with Indian Spices (p 198)
33 percent of your daily dose

Cocoa-Roasted Peanuts with Cayenne (p 230)
36% of your daily dose

IRON-RICH RECIPES

Poached Eggs with Steamed Asparagus and Asiago Cheese (p 65)
25% of your daily dose

Grass-Fed Beef Burgers with Blue Cheese Sauce (p 82)
28% of your daily dose

Mediterranean Edamame Patties in Whole Wheat Pita with Tahini Sauce (p 86)
28% of your daily dose

Flaxseed-Coated Cod Sandwiches (p 90)
28% of your daily dose

Oyster Po'Boys with Quick Remoulade Sauce (p 92)
39% of your daily dose

Grilled Brussels Sprout and Tofu Skewers with Balsamic Glaze (p 100)
39% of your daily dose

Curried Red Lentil and Carrot Soup (p 112)
28% of your daily dose

Baked Oysters with Leeks and Buttery Bread Crumbs (p 116)
33% of your daily dose

Fettuccine with Lentil Bolognese (p 142)
26% of your daily dose

Spaghetti with Sardines, Caramelized Fennel, and Buttery Garlic Bread Crumbs (p 146)
33% of your daily dose

Pizza with Butternut Squash, Spinach, and Fontina (p 149)
28% of your daily dose

Wild Rice-Stuffed Acorn Squash (p 151)
28% of your daily dose

Roast Chicken with Brussels Sprouts, Roasted Grapes, and Hazelnuts (p 158)
28% of your daily dose

Pumpkin Seed-Coated Chicken Breasts with Bulgur Pilaf (p 160)
28% of your daily dose

Black Bean-Turkey Chili with Butternut Squash (p 162)
39% of your daily dose

Beef Stew with Root Vegetables (p 166)
33% of your daily dose

Beef and Broccoli with Brown Rice (p 168)
28% of your daily dose

Grilled Steak au Poivre with Sautéed Broccoli Rabe (p 170)
33% of your daily dose

Pan-Roasted Salmon with Lentil Pilaf (p 179)
28% of your daily dose

Steamed Clams and Chickpeas in Tomato-Leek Broth (p 181)
83% of your daily dose

Seafood Paella (p 183)
83% of your daily dose

Shrimp and Asparagus Stir-Fry with Rice Noodles (p 184)
33% of your daily dose

Braised Kale with Black-Eyed Peas (p 192)
28% of your daily dose

MAGNESIUM-RICH RECIPES

Blueberry-Oatmeal Casserole with Baked Yogurt Topping (p 59)
26% of your daily dose

Roasted Sweet Potato and Pumpkin Seed Salad with Warm Bacon-Tomato Vinaigrette (p 74)
35% of your daily dose

Mediterranean Edamame Patties in Whole Wheat Pita with Tahini Sauce (p 86)
28% of your daily dose

Flaxseed-Coated Cod Sandwiches (p 90)
60% of your daily dose

Swiss Chard and White Bean Soup (p 113)
35% of your daily dose

Pumpkin Seed Dip (p 122)
27% of your daily dose

Swiss Chard, Eggplant, and Mushroom Lasagna (p 130)
39% of your daily dose

Wild Rice-Stuffed Acorn Squash (p 151)
37% of your daily dose

Braised Chicken with Dates, Ginger, and Almonds (p 154)
26% of your daily dose

Pumpkin Seed-Coated Chicken Breasts with Bulgur Pilaf (p 160)
55% of your daily dose

Beef Stew with Root Vegetables (p 166)
29% of your daily dose

Beef and Broccoli with Brown Rice (p 168)
36% of your daily dose

Roast Pork Tenderloin with Edamame Succotash (p 173)
27% of your daily dose

Red Potatoes with Edamame Pesto (p 196)
26% of your daily dose

Kiwi-Banana Smoothie with Sunflower Seeds (p 225)
26% of your daily dose

Cocoa-Roasted Peanuts with Cayenne (p 230)
25% of your daily dose

OMEGA-3-RICH RECIPES

Blueberry-Cornmeal Waffles with Blueberry Sauce (p 60)
ALA

Pear-Oat Bran Quick Bread (p 64)
ALA

Eggs Florentine on English Muffins (p 69)
63% of your daily dose

Chopped Vegetable Salad with Sardines and Toasted Pita Croutons (p 77)
114% of your daily dose

Sardine Baguette Sandwiches with Creamy Avocado Spread (p 78)
124% of your daily dose

Fish Tacos with Black Bean-Papaya Salsa (p 88)
34% of your daily dose

Flaxseed-Coated Cod Sandwiches (p 90)
423% of your daily dose

Oyster Po'Boys with Quick Remoulade Sauce (p 92)
29% of your daily dose

Tuna and Chickpea Salad in Tomato Cups (p 105)
34% of your daily dose

Baked Oysters with Leeks and Buttery Bread Crumbs (p 116)
49% of your daily dose

Crab Cocktail with Mango (p 121)
35% of your daily dose

Salmon Cakes with Dill Yogurt (p 123)
116% of your daily dose

Spaghetti with Sardines, Caramelized Fennel, and Buttery Garlic Bread Crumbs (p 146)
104% of your daily dose

Stuffed Eggplant with Couscous, Roasted Red Peppers, and Goat Cheese (p 147)
ALA

Roast Chicken with Brussels Sprouts, Roasted Grapes, and Hazelnuts (p 158)
ALA

Beef and Broccoli with Brown Rice (p 168)
ALA

Roasted Cedar-Plank Salmon with Mustard-Maple Glaze (p 176)
180% of your daily dose

Pan-Roasted Salmon with Lentil Pilaf (p 179)
180% of your daily dose

Individual Tuna Casseroles with Peas and Tarragon (p 180)
28% of your daily dose

Seafood Paella (p 183)
75% of your daily dose

Sweet and Tangy Baked Beans and Tomatoes (p 190)
ALA

Braised Kale with Black-Eyed Peas (p 192)
ALA

Curried Roasted Cauliflower with Flaxseeds (p 207)
ALA

Crab Fried Rice with Tofu (p 211)
44% of your daily dose

Baked Apples with Walnuts, Cinnamon, and Raisins (p 221)
ALA

Dark Chocolate Walnut Brownies (p 222)
ALA

Spiced Walnuts with Orange Zest and Rosemary (p 231)
ALA

POTASSIUM-RICH RECIPES

Tropical Ambrosia Salad (p 71)
31% of your daily dose

Date-Ricotta Crostini and Arugula Salad (p 85)
25% of your daily dose

Flaxseed-Coated Cod Sandwiches (p 90)
63% of your daily dose

Pearl Couscous with Roasted Beets, Lima Beans, and Feta (p 97)
25% of your daily dose

Borscht (p 109)
39% of your daily dose

Curried Red Lentil and Carrot Soup (p 112)
31% of your daily dose

Swiss Chard and White Bean Soup (p 113)
27% of your daily dose

Lemony Chicken, Spinach, and Orzo Soup (p 115)
29% of your daily dose

Baked Potato Skins with Bacon and Cheddar (p 117)
26% of your daily dose

Swiss Chard, Eggplant, and Mushroom Lasagna (p 139)
35% of your daily dose

Fettuccine with Lentil Bolognese (p 142)
28% of your daily dose

Spaghetti with Sardines, Caramelized Fennel, and Buttery Garlic Bread Crumbs (p 146)
33% of your daily dose

Wild Rice–Stuffed Acorn Squash (p 151)
48% of your daily dose

Roasted Chicken Breasts with Sautéed Cabbage and Apples (p 153)
39% of your daily dose

Braised Chicken with Dates, Ginger, and Almonds (p 154)
42% of your daily dose

Roast Chicken with Brussels Sprouts, Roasted Grapes, and Hazelnuts (p 158)
33% of your daily dose

Pumpkin Seed–Coated Chicken Breasts with Bulgur Pilaf (p 160)
31% of your daily dose

Black Bean–Turkey Chili with Butternut Squash (p 162)
32% of your daily dose

Grilled Steak with Peperonata Sauce (p 164)
29% of your daily dose

Beef Stew with Root Vegetables (p 166)
53% of your daily dose

Beef and Broccoli with Brown Rice (p 168)
37% of your daily dose

Grilled Steak au Poivre with Sautéed Broccoli Rabe (p 170)
27% of your daily dose

Roast Pork Tenderloin with Edamame Succotash (p 173)
36% of your daily dose

Pork Braised in Kiwi-Coconut Sauce with White Beans (p 174)
30% of your daily dose

Pan-Roasted Salmon with Lentil Pilaf (p 179)
34% of your daily dose

Roasted Beet and Beet Green Sauté (p 191)
28% of your daily dose

Braised Kale with Black-Eyed Peas (p 192)
25% of your daily dose

Red Potatoes with Edamame Pesto (p 196)
32% of your daily dose

Fingerling Potato Salad with Creamy Mustard-Anchovy Dressing (p 208)
25% of your daily dose

Kiwi-Banana Smoothie with Sunflower Seeds (p 225)
32% of your daily dose

Date Squares with Easy Banana "Ice Cream" (p 229)
26% of your daily dose

VITAMIN B$_{12}$-RICH RECIPES

Sweet Corn Frittata (p 67)
33% of your daily dose

Baked Eggs in Ham Cups (p 68)
33% of your daily dose

Eggs Florentine on English Muffins (p 69)
27% of your daily dose

Chopped Vegetable Salad with Sardines and Toasted Pita Croutons (p 77)
100% of your daily dose

Sardine Baguette Sandwiches with Creamy Avocado Spread (p 78)
117% of your daily dose

Grass-Fed Beef Burgers with Blue Cheese Sauce (p 82)
50% of your daily dose

Flaxseed-Coated Cod Sandwiches (p 90)
167% of your daily dose

Oyster Po'Boys with Quick Remoulade Sauce (p 92)
150% of your daily dose

Tuna and Chickpea Salad in Tomato Cups (p 105)
50% of your daily dose

Crab Cocktail with Mango (p 121)
67% of your daily dose

VITAMIN B₁₂–RICH RECIPES—CONTINUED

Spaghetti with Sardines, Caramelized Fennel, and Buttery Garlic Bread Crumbs (p 146)
100% of your daily dose

Grilled Steak with Peperonata Sauce (p 164)
33% of your daily dose

Beef Stew with Root Vegetables (p 166)
100% of your daily dose

Beef and Broccoli with Brown Rice (p 168)
33% of your daily dose

Grilled Steak au Poivre with Sautéed Broccoli Rabe (p 170)
28% of your daily dose

Roasted Cedar-Plank Salmon with Mustard-Maple Glaze (p 176)
133% of your daily dose

Pan-Roasted Salmon with Lentil Pilaf (p 179)
116% of your daily dose

Individual Tuna Casseroles with Peas and Tarragon (p 180)
43% of your daily dose

Steamed Clams and Chickpeas in Tomato-Leek Broth (p 181)
717% of your daily dose

Seafood Paella (p 183)
500% of your daily dose

Crab Fried Rice with Tofu (p 211)
50% of your daily dose

VITAMIN C–RICH RECIPES

Blueberry-Cornmeal Waffles with Blueberry Sauce (p 60)
30% of your daily dose

Sweet Corn Frittata (p 67)
30% of your daily dose

Eggs Florentine on English Muffins (p 69)
37% of your daily dose

Tropical Ambrosia Salad (p 71)
480% of your daily dose

Roasted Sweet Potato and Pumpkin Seed Salad with Warm Bacon-Tomato Vinaigrette (p 74)
47% of your daily dose

Chopped Vegetable Salad with Sardines and Toasted Pita Croutons (p 77)
53% of your daily dose

Sardine Baguette Sandwiches with Creamy Avocado Spread (p 78)
37% of your daily dose

Date-Ricotta Crostini and Arugula Salad (p 85)
32% of your daily dose

Mediterranean Edamame Patties in Whole Wheat Pita with Tahini Sauce (p 86)
60% of your daily dose

Fish Tacos with Black Bean–Papaya Salsa (p 88)
67% of your daily dose

Flaxseed-Coated Cod Sandwiches (p 90)
128% of your daily dose

Roasted Tomato Soup with White Cheddar Grilled Cheese Sandwiches (p 94)
185% of your daily dose

Pearl Couscous with Roasted Beets, Lima Beans, and Feta (p 97)
55% of your daily dose

Soba Noodles with Almond Sauce and Shredded Chicken (p 99)
80% of your daily dose

Grilled Brussels Sprout and Tofu Skewers with Balsamic Glaze (p 100)
298% of your daily dose

Asian Chicken Salad in Lettuce Cups with Peanut Sauce (p 102)
123% of your daily dose

Tuna and Chickpea Salad in Tomato Cups (p 105)
75% of your daily dose

Borscht (p 109)
45% of your daily dose

Creamy Broccoli-Pea Soup with Bacon and Cheddar (p 110)
278% of your daily dose

Curried Red Lentil and Carrot Soup (p 112)
47% of your daily dose

Swiss Chard and White Bean Soup (p 113)
80% of your daily dose

Lemony Chicken, Spinach, and Orzo Soup (p 115)
40% of your daily dose

Baked Potato Skins with Bacon and Cheddar (p 117)
43% of your daily dose

Brussels Sprout Poppers with Orange–Poppy Seed Dipping Sauce (p 118)
202% of your daily dose

Pumpkin Seed Dip (p 122)
25% of your daily dose

Turkey-Feta Meatballs with Roasted Red Pepper Dipping Sauce (p 125)
60% of your daily dose

Stuffed Shells with Chunky Tomato Sauce (p 134)
43% of your daily dose

Spinach Gnudi with Quick Chunky Tomato Sauce (p 136)
42% of your daily dose

Swiss Chard, Eggplant, and Mushroom Lasagna (p 139)
87% of your daily dose

Fettuccine with Lentil Bolognese (p 142)
63% of your daily dose

Linguine with Kale, Olives, and Currants (p 145)
233% of your daily dose

Spaghetti with Sardines, Caramelized Fennel, and Buttery Garlic Bread Crumbs (p 146)
50% of your daily dose

Stuffed Eggplant with Couscous, Roasted Red Peppers, and Goat Cheese (p 147)
110% of your daily dose

Pizza with Butternut Squash, Spinach, and Fontina (p 149)
35% of your daily dose

Picadillo-Stuffed Red Bell Peppers (p 150)
382% of your daily dose

Wild Rice–Stuffed Acorn Squash (p 151)
90% of your daily dose

Roasted Chicken Breasts with Sautéed Cabbage and Apples (p 153)
112% of your daily dose

Braised Chicken with Dates, Ginger, and Almonds (p 154)
42% of your daily dose

Baked Chicken Parmesan with Homemade Tomato Sauce (p 155)
62% of your daily dose

Roast Chicken with Brussels Sprouts, Roasted Grapes, and Hazelnuts (p 158)
242% of your daily dose

Black Bean–Turkey Chili with Butternut Squash (p 162)
138% of your daily dose

Grilled Steak with
Peperonata Sauce (p 164)
465% of your daily dose

Beef Stew with Root
Vegetables (p 166)
85% of your daily dose

Beef and Broccoli with
Brown Rice (p 168)
258% of your daily dose

Grilled Steak au Poivre with
Sautéed Broccoli Rabe (p 170)
47% of your daily dose

Roast Pork Tenderloin with
Edamame Succotash (p 173)
123% of your daily dose

Pork Braised in Kiwi-Coconut
Sauce with White Beans
(p 174)
268% of your daily dose

Steamed Clams and
Chickpeas in Tomato-Leek
Broth (p 181)
67% of your daily dose

Seafood Paella (p 183)
173% of your daily dose

Shrimp and Asparagus
Stir-Fry with Rice Noodles
(p 184)
38% of your daily dose

Roasted Beet and Beet Green
Sauté (p 191)
57% of your daily dose

Braised Kale with Black-Eyed
Peas (p 192)
355% of your daily dose

Red Potatoes with Edamame
Pesto (p 196)
48% of your daily dose

Braised Spinach and Potatoes
with Indian Spices (p 198)
47% of your daily dose

Shredded Carrot and
Chickpea Salad (p 199)
40% of your daily dose

Red Cabbage Slaw with Tangy
Poppy Seed Dressing (p 204)
190% of your daily dose

Curried Roasted Cauliflower
with Flaxseeds (p 207)
191% of your daily dose

Fingerling Potato Salad with
Creamy Mustard-Anchovy
Dressing (p 208)
97% of your daily dose

Tuscan Kale Salad with
Almonds and Parmesan
(p 210)
137% of your daily dose

Crab Fried Rice with Tofu
(p 211)
50% of your daily dose

Blueberry Fool (p 214)
33% of your daily dose

Strawberry-Ricotta Crepes
(p 219)
87% of your daily dose

Strawberry Cocoa Shortcakes
with Amaretto Whipped
Cream (p 224)
82% of your daily dose

Strawberry-Mango Smoothie
(p 225)
207% of your daily dose

Kiwi-Banana Smoothie with
Sunflower Seeds (p 225)
328% of your daily dose

VITAMIN D-RICH RECIPES

Creamy Steel-Cut Oats
with Dried Cranberries
and Pistachios (p 63)
29% of your daily dose

Chopped Vegetable Salad
with Sardines and Toasted
Pita Croutons (p 77)
33% of your daily dose

Sardine Baguette Sandwiches
with Creamy Avocado Spread
(p 78)
39% of your daily dose

Tuna and Chickpea Salad
in Tomato Cups (p 105)
45% of your daily dose

Spaghetti with Sardines,
Caramelized Fennel, and
Buttery Garlic Bread Crumbs
(p 146)
34% of your daily dose

Roasted Cedar-Plank Salmon
with Mustard-Maple Glaze
(p 176)
330% of your daily dose

Pan-Roasted Salmon
with Lentil Pilaf (p 179)
258% of your daily dose

Individual Tuna Casseroles
with Peas and Tarragon
(p 180)
34% of your daily dose

VITAMIN E-RICH RECIPES

Almond-Apricot Scones (p 56)
30% of your daily dose

Tropical Ambrosia Salad
(p 71)
25% of your daily dose

Soba Noodles with Almond
Sauce and Shredded
Chicken (p 99)
33% of your daily dose

Asian Chicken Salad in
Lettuce Cups with Peanut
Sauce (p 102)
27% of your daily dose

Pork Braised in Kiwi-Coconut
Sauce with White Beans
(p 174)
27% of your daily dose

Kiwi-Banana Smoothie
with Sunflower Seeds (p 225)
27% of your daily dose

Cocoa-Roasted Peanuts
with Cayenne (p 230)
25% of your daily dose

BREAKFAST 3

Blueberries : **ANTHOCYANINS**
Eggs : **VITAMIN B$_{12}$**
Kiwi : **VITAMIN E**

Almond-Apricot Scones

Almond meal not only contributes vitamin E, but also makes these scones incredibly moist and tender. In addition, the healthy fats in the nuts replace some of the butter typically used in scone recipes, keeping the saturated fat content low.

PREP TIME: 20 MINUTES **/ TOTAL TIME:** 40 MINUTES **/ SERVINGS:** 8

1½ cups almond meal

¾ cup white whole wheat flour

1 tablespoon plus 1 teaspoon granulated sugar

2 teaspoons baking powder

1 teaspoon ground ginger

3 tablespoons butter, frozen

1 cup dried apricots, chopped

¼ cup 2% milk

3 tablespoons honey

1 teaspoon vanilla extract

2 large eggs

2 teaspoons turbinado or other coarse sugar

2 tablespoons sliced almonds, toasted

Jam, for serving (optional)

1 **HEAT** the oven to 375°F and line a baking sheet with parchment paper. Whisk together the almond meal, flour, granulated sugar, baking powder, ginger, and ½ teaspoon salt in a large bowl. Grate the butter on the large holes of a box grater and add to the bowl. Stir to combine. Stir in the apricots.

2 **WHISK** together the milk, honey, vanilla extract, and one of the eggs in a small bowl. Add to the almond meal mixture and stir until just combined. Transfer to a floured cutting board, sprinkle with flour, and form into a thick disk. Roll into a 7" to 8" circle, about ¾" thick, sprinkling flour over the dough and board as needed. Cut into 8 wedges.

3 **WHISK** together the remaining egg and 1 tablespoon water in a small bowl. Lightly brush over the dough. Sprinkle with the turbinado sugar and almonds, pressing lightly to adhere. Transfer scones to the prepared baking sheet, arranging them about 1" apart. Bake until tops and bottoms are golden brown and a toothpick inserted in the center comes out clean, 14 to 16 minutes. Cool on the baking sheet 5 minutes and serve, or transfer to a rack and cool completely. Serve with jam, if desired.

NUTRITION *(per serving)* 298 calories, 8 g protein, 35 g carbs, 16 g fat, 4 g saturated fat, 284 mg sodium

VE 30% (9 IU) daily vitamin E

Barley-Banana Pancakes

Barley makes these pancakes especially filling and tender. To cut prep time, make the barley up to 2 days ahead, or plan to make extra the next time you serve barley as a side dish.

PREP TIME: 5 MINUTES **/ TOTAL TIME:** 1 HOUR 20 MINUTES **/ SERVINGS:** 4

½ cup hulled barley

1¼ cups white whole wheat flour

1 tablespoon sugar

2 teaspoons baking powder

½ teaspoon baking soda

1 teaspoon cinnamon

¼ teaspoon nutmeg

1 cup low-fat milk

2 large egg whites

2 tablespoons butter, melted and cooled

2 medium bananas, sliced

Maple syrup(optional)

1 **BRING** 1¼ cups water to a boil on high heat in a small saucepan. Stir in the barley and reduce the heat to low. Cover and simmer until the barley is tender and the liquid is absorbed, about 50 minutes. Remove from the heat and rest, covered, 10 minutes. (May be made up to 2 days ahead. Cool at room temperature and refrigerate.)

2 **WHISK** together the flour, sugar, baking powder, baking soda, cinnamon, nutmeg, and ¼ teaspoon salt in a large bowl. Whisk together the milk, egg whites, and butter in a medium bowl. Add to the flour mixture. Add the barley and stir until just combined.

3 **HEAT** a nonstick skillet or griddle on medium heat. For each pancake, coat the skillet with cooking spray. Place 3 to 4 banana slices close together in the skillet and cook without moving until the bottom sides are golden brown, about 1 minute. Pour ¼ cup of the barley mixture over the bananas and quickly spread to cover them completely. Cook until the edges are set and bubbles form in the center, 1½ to 2 minutes. Flip and cook until the bottom side is golden brown, 1 to 1½ minutes longer. Serve with maple syrup, if desired.

NUTRITION *(per serving: three 4" pancakes)* 390 calories, 14 g protein, 68 g carbs, 7 g fat, 4 g saturated fat, 721 mg sodium

Fi **44% (11 g) daily fiber**

Blueberry-Oatmeal Casserole with Baked Yogurt Topping

A layer of thick Greek yogurt is spread on this berry-packed casserole and baked, adding a hefty dose of calcium. The oven's heat quickly turns the yogurt thick and dense, almost like a soft cheese, creating a rich-tasting topping.

PREP TIME: 10 MINUTES / **TOTAL TIME:** 1 HOUR 10 MINUTES / **SERVINGS:** 4

4 cups fresh or frozen blueberries

1½ cups rolled ("old fashioned") oats

¼ cup light brown sugar

1½ teaspoons cinnamon

¾ teaspoon baking powder

1⅓ cups fat-free milk

1 large egg

2 teaspoons vanilla extract

1½ cups fat-free plain Greek yogurt

2 tablespoons honey

1 **HEAT** the oven to 400°F. Add 3 cups of the blueberries to an 8" × 8" baking dish. (If using frozen berries, thaw the remaining berries on a paper towel–lined plate to soak up excess water.) Whisk together the oats, brown sugar, cinnamon, baking powder, and ½ teaspoon salt in a large bowl. Scatter over the blueberries.

2 **WHISK** together the milk, egg, and vanilla extract in a medium bowl. Pour evenly over the oats. Bake until the liquid is bubbling at the edges and the oats are nearly set, 30 minutes. Remove from the oven.

3 **COMBINE** the yogurt and honey in a medium bowl. Spread evenly over the oats and sprinkle with the remaining berries. Return to the oven and bake until the yogurt is firm, 20 minutes. Cool 10 minutes and serve.

NUTRITION *(per serving: 1¾ cups)* 358 calories, 17 g protein, 64 g carbs, 4 g fat, 1 g saturated fat, 439 mg sodium

Ca **27% (266 mg) daily calcium**   Mg **26% (105 mg) daily magnesium**   An **2 servings anthocyanin-rich food (blueberries)**

Blueberry-Cornmeal Waffles with Blueberry Sauce

Swapping fresh blueberry sauce for the usual maple syrup cuts down on sugar since the berries are naturally sweet, saving you calories. The cornstarch in the batter helps produce crisp waffles. You can just as easily use this recipe for pancakes if you don't have a waffle iron.

PREP TIME: 10 MINUTES **/ TOTAL TIME:** 40 MINUTES **/ SERVINGS:** 6

6 cups fresh blueberries

7 tablespoons granulated sugar

Juice of 1 lemon (about 3 tablespoons)

1 cup white whole wheat flour

1 cup cornmeal

¼ cup cornstarch

1½ teaspoons baking powder

½ teaspoon baking soda

1½ cups buttermilk

2 large eggs, separated

3 tablespoons canola oil

Zest of 1 lemon (about 2 teaspoons), plus extra for garnish (optional)

Confectioner's sugar (optional)

1 **COMBINE** 4½ cups of the blueberries, 5 tablespoons of the granulated sugar, and the lemon juice in a large saucepan and bring to a simmer on medium-high heat. Reduce the heat to medium-low and simmer, stirring frequently, until the berries break down and the mixture thickens, 6 to 8 minutes. Cover and set aside.

2 **WHISK** together the flour, cornmeal, cornstarch, baking powder, baking soda, ½ teaspoon salt, and the remaining granulated sugar in a large bowl. Whisk together the buttermilk, egg yolks, oil, and 2 teaspoons zest in a medium bowl.

3 **HEAT** a waffle iron. Beat the egg whites with an electric mixer on high speed until stiff peaks form, 3 to 4 minutes. Add the buttermilk mixture to the flour mixture and gently stir until just moistened. Add half the egg whites and gently fold until just combined. Fold in the remaining egg whites and the remaining 1½ cups of blueberries.

4 **COAT** the hot waffle iron with cooking spray. Cook the waffles according to the manufacturer's instructions, misting the iron with cooking spray before adding batter each time. Warm the blueberry sauce on low heat if necessary and serve with the waffles. Garnish with lemon zest and dust with confectioner's sugar, if desired.

NUTRITION *(per serving: 1 regular waffle, 7" to 8", and ½ cup sauce)* 395 calories, 9 g protein, 71 g carbs, 10 g fat, 1 g saturated fat, 499 mg sodium

Fi	36% (9 g) daily fiber	O₃	ALA omega-3s	An	2 servings anthocyanin-rich food (blueberries)
Vc	30% (18 mg) daily vitamin C				

Creamy Steel-Cut Oats with Dried Cranberries and Pistachios

If you've never tried steel-cut oats, they're nothing like the "old-fashioned" type that have been rolled or flattened to speed up cooking time. They have a chewy, creamy texture, making them especially stick-to-your-ribs satisfying. They do take longer to cook, but we've nixed that concern with an overnight method that takes just minutes of active time.

PREP TIME: 10 MINUTES / **TOTAL TIME:** 20 MINUTES + STANDING TIME / **SERVINGS:** 4

4 cups fat-free milk

1 cup steel-cut oats

½ teaspoon cinnamon

½ teaspoon ground ginger

½ cup dried cranberries, chopped

6 tablespoons chopped shelled pistachios

2 tablespoons plus 2 teaspoons maple syrup

1 **BRING** the milk to a simmer in a medium saucepan on medium-high heat, stirring occasionally to keep the milk from sticking to the bottom of the pan, about 10 minutes. Add the oats, cinnamon, ginger, and ⅛ teaspoon salt. Return to a simmer, reduce the heat to medium low, and cook, stirring constantly, 1 minute. Cover and remove from the heat. Cool at room temperature 30 minutes to 1 hour, using the shorter time if room temperature is warm. Place the covered saucepan in the refrigerator; chill overnight.

2 **HEAT** the oats on low heat, stirring frequently, until thickened and tender, 10 to 15 minutes. Divide among 4 bowls and top evenly with the cranberries, pistachios, and maple syrup.

NUTRITION (per serving: 1¼ cups) 385 calories, 18 g protein, 65 g carbs, 8 g fat, 1 g saturated fat, 168 mg sodium

Ca **35% (354 mg) daily calcium**   VD **29% (115 IU) daily vitamin D**   Fi **28% (7 g) daily fiber**

Pear–Oat Bran Quick Bread

A thick slice of this bread makes a hearty on-the-go breakfast. It also freezes well, so you can wrap individual slices in a double layer of plastic wrap, freeze them all in a large zip-top bag, and grab a slice on your way out the door.

PREP TIME: 25 MINUTES / **TOTAL TIME:** 1 HOUR 20 MINUTES / **SERVINGS:** 8

1½ cups white whole wheat flour
¾ cup oat bran
⅔ cup light brown sugar
2 teaspoons baking powder
½ teaspoon ground ginger
½ teaspoon cinnamon
½ teaspoon baking soda
2 large eggs
1 cup buttermilk
3 tablespoons canola oil
3 cups diced pears (skin on)
½ cup chopped dried plums
¼ cup pecans, toasted and chopped
1 tablespoon turbinado or other coarse sugar

1 **HEAT** the oven to 350°F. Lightly coat a 9" × 5" bread pan with cooking spray.

2 **WHISK** together the flour, oat bran, brown sugar, baking powder, ginger, cinnamon, baking soda, and ½ teaspoon salt in a large bowl. Whisk together the eggs, buttermilk, and oil in a medium bowl. Pour into the flour mixture and stir until just combined. Gently stir in the pears, plums, and pecans.

3 **TRANSFER** the batter to the prepared pan and sprinkle the turbinado sugar over the top. Bake until the sides begin pulling away from the pan, the top is lightly browned, and a wooden pick inserted in the center comes out clean, 55 to 65 minutes. Cool in the pan 10 minutes, then remove from the pan, and transfer to a rack. Let cool completely before slicing.

NUTRITION *(per serving: 1 slice 1" thick)* 334 calories, 8 g protein, 59 g carbs, 10 g fat, 2 g saturated fat, 371 mg sodium
Fi 25% (6.25 g) daily fiber   O3 ALA omega-3s

Poached Eggs with Steamed Asparagus and Asiago Cheese

Despite having just four ingredients, this simple dish is elegant and flavorful. It could just as easily work for lunch—or pair it with whole grain bread for an easy dinner. If you prefer grilled or roasted asparagus, feel free to do that instead of steaming.

PREP TIME: 5 MINUTES / **TOTAL TIME:** 25 MINUTES / **SERVINGS:** 4

2 pounds asparagus, tough ends trimmed

4 large eggs

4 teaspoons olive oil

2 ounces Asiago cheese, thinly shaved with a vegetable peeler (about ⅔ cup)

1 **FILL** a large pot with about ½" of water, insert a steamer basket, cover, and bring to a boil on high heat. Reduce heat to medium, add the asparagus, cover, and steam until just tender, 5 to 7 minutes. Divide among 4 plates and season with salt and freshly ground black pepper to taste.

2 **FILL** a large saucepan with about 5" of water and bring to a boil on high heat. Crack 1 egg into a small bowl or ramekin, keeping the yolk intact. Reduce the heat to low. Hold the bowl directly over the water and gently tip the egg into the water. Repeat with the remaining eggs, quickly cracking them into the bowl and adding them to the water. Cook the eggs at a bare simmer (you should see just one or two bubbles rising to the surface at a time) until the whites are firm and the yolks feel slightly firm to the touch, 4½ minutes for soft-set, slightly runny yolks.

3 **TRANSFER** the eggs one at a time with a slotted spoon to a plate lined with 2 layers of paper towel to drain. Top each plate of asparagus with 1 egg. Drizzle each plate with 1 teaspoon of the oil. Season to taste with salt and freshly ground pepper and sprinkle with the cheese.

NUTRITION *(per serving)* 201 calories, 14 g protein, 8 g carbs, 14 g fat, 5 g saturated fat, 238 mg sodium

Fo **28% (112 mcg) daily folate**　　Fe **25% (5 mg) daily iron**

Sweet Corn Frittata

We call for omega-3 eggs in this recipe because they have significantly more vitamin B$_{12}$ than regular eggs. Plus you get 230 milligrams of this healthy fat per serving, some of it the more protective kind found in fish.

PREP TIME: 10 MINUTES / **TOTAL TIME:** 30 MINUTES / **SERVINGS:** 4

8 large omega-3 eggs
4 ounces low-fat Swiss cheese, grated (about 1 cup)
1½ cups frozen corn
1½ cups grape tomatoes, halved
6 scallions, chopped (about ⅓ cup)
Pinch of dried thyme

1 **WHISK** the eggs in a large bowl. Whisk in the cheese and season with ½ teaspoon salt and freshly ground black pepper. Heat the broiler and position a rack in the center of the oven.

2 **COAT** a 10" cast-iron or ovenproof nonstick skillet thoroughly with cooking spray and heat on medium-high heat. Add the corn and tomatoes and cook, stirring occasionally, until the tomatoes soften, about 4 minutes. Add the scallions and thyme and continue cooking until any liquid in the skillet evaporates, about 4 minutes. Season to taste with salt and freshly ground black pepper.

3 **REDUCE** the heat to medium and add the eggs. Cook until the bottom and edges start to set, about 2 minutes. Lift the edges with a spatula and tilt the skillet, allowing any uncooked egg to run underneath. Transfer to the oven and broil until the center is puffed and set, and the top is lightly browned, 4 to 5 minutes. Run a knife along the edges to loosen the frittata and cool in the skillet 5 minutes. Slice and serve directly from the skillet, or hold a large plate over the skillet and quickly flip, transferring the frittata to the plate. Put a second plate over the frittata and flip again, so the frittata is right side up. Slice and serve.

NUTRITION (per serving) 260 calories, 22 g protein, 17 g carbs, 10 g fat, 3 g saturated fat, 455 mg sodium
Ca 33% (331 mg) daily calcium   B$_{12}$ 33% (2 mcg) daily vitamin B$_{12}$ Vc 30% (18 mg) daily vitamin C

Baked Eggs in Ham Cups

This dish is so simple and quick to prepare, you'll hardly believe the deliciously adorable results. It's also a great recipe to have in your back pocket when you need to make breakfast for a lot of people at once and don't want to stand around flipping omelets all morning.

PREP TIME: 15 MINUTES **/ TOTAL TIME:** 30 MINUTES **/ SERVINGS:** 6

24 thin slices reduced sodium deli ham (about 6 ounces)

6 ounces Swiss cheese, grated (about 1½ cups)

12 large omega-3 eggs

¼ cup chopped fresh chives

1 **HEAT** the oven to 400°F. Coat a 12 cup muffin tin with cooking spray. Press 2 ham slices into each muffin cup, overlapping them. Sprinkle about half the cheese evenly into the ham cups.

2 **CRACK** 1 egg in a small bowl or ramekin and gently tip it into one of the ham cups, keeping the yolk intact. Repeat with the remaining eggs. Top evenly with the remaining cheese and season with freshly ground black pepper. Loosely cover muffin tin with foil. Bake until the whites are set and yolks are soft to firm, according to preference, 12 to 14 minutes.

3 **COOL** in the muffin tin 5 minutes. Lift by the edges of the ham and place on individual plates. Sprinkle evenly with the chives and serve.

NUTRITION (per serving: 2 ham cups) 301 calories, 29 g protein, 6 g carbs, 16 g fat, 7 g saturated fat, 1,046 mg sodium

B₁₂ 33% (2 mcg) daily vitamin B₁₂   Ca 26% (259 mg) daily calcium

Eggs Florentine on English Muffins

Scallions, garlic, and a dab of reduced-fat cream cheese make spinach flavorful and creamy, while nutmeg, often added to cooked greens, adds a hint of spice. This breakfast is sophisticated enough to work as dinner, if you're in the mood for a change of pace.

PREP TIME: 10 MINUTES **/ TOTAL TIME:** 35 MINUTES **/ SERVINGS:** 4

1 tablespoon canola oil

4 scallions, white and light green parts, chopped (about ¼ cup)

2 cloves garlic, chopped

10 cups spinach leaves, chopped (about 10 ounces)

2 ounces reduced-fat cream cheese (Neufchâtel), about ¼ cup

2 tablespoons low-fat milk

Pinch of nutmeg

8 large omega-3 eggs

4 light multigrain English muffins, split and toasted (we used Thomas')

2 ounces low-fat Swiss cheese, grated (about ½ cup)

1 **HEAT** the oil in a large skillet on medium heat. Add the scallions and cook, stirring frequently, until soft, about 2 minutes. Add the garlic and cook, stirring constantly, until softened, 1 minute. Add the spinach in batches and cook, stirring frequently, until just wilted, about 3 minutes. Add the cream cheese, milk, and nutmeg and cook, stirring constantly to combine, until the mixture is creamy, about 3 minutes. Season to taste with salt and freshly ground black pepper. Cover and keep warm.

2 **FILL** a large saucepan with about 5" of water and bring to a boil on high heat. Crack 1 egg into a small bowl or ramekin, keeping the yolk intact. Reduce the heat to low. Hold the bowl directly over the water and gently tip the egg into the water. Repeat with 3 more eggs, quickly cracking them into the bowl and adding them to the water. Cook the eggs at a bare simmer (you should see just one or two bubbles rising to the surface at a time) until the whites are firm and the yolks feel slightly firm to the touch, 4½ minutes for soft-set, slightly runny yolks, or up to 7 minutes for firm yolks.

3 **TRANSFER** the eggs one at a time with a slotted spoon to a plate lined with 2 layers of paper towel to drain. Repeat with the 4 remaining eggs. Divide the spinach mixture among the toasted English muffin halves. Top each half with 1 egg and sprinkle evenly with the Swiss cheese.

NUTRITION (per serving: 2 English muffin halves) 362 calories, 27 g protein, 32 g carbs, 17 g fat, 5 g saturated fat, 468 mg sodium

Fo 48% (191 mcg) daily folate	Ca 36% (355 mg) daily calcium	Cr 2 servings carotenoid-rich food (spinach)
Fi 40% (10 g) daily fiber	B₁₂ 27% (1.6 mcg) daily vitamin B₁₂	
Vc 37% (22 mg) daily vitamin C		O₃ ALA omega-3s

Tropical Ambrosia Salad

The mint syrup used to sweeten this fruit salad is so flavorful because you use whole sprigs instead of just the leaves. For the best results, make sure the stems look fresh and unbruised and smell fragrant.

PREP TIME: 30 MINUTES / **TOTAL TIME:** 30 MINUTES / **SERVINGS:** 4

5 tablespoons sugar

5 whole mint sprigs, plus 3 tablespoons chopped mint leaves

15 kiwi, peeled and cut into quarters (about 5 cups)

2 mangos, halved, pitted, peeled, and cut into ¾" chunks (about 2½ cups)

½ medium papaya, halved, pitted, peeled, and cut into ¾" chunks (about 2½ cups)

3 tablespoons unsweetened coconut flakes, toasted

1 **BRING** the sugar and 5 tablespoons water to a simmer in a small saucepan on medium-high heat, stirring occasionally. Reduce the heat to low, add the mint sprigs, and simmer until fragrant, about 4 minutes. Discard the sprigs. Place the saucepan in a larger bowl or baking dish filled with ice water, stirring occasionally, until cold, about 10 minutes. Alternatively, cool at room temperature and refrigerate until chilled, about 1 hour.

2 **COMBINE** the kiwi, mango, and papaya in a large serving bowl. Add the cold mint syrup and stir to combine. Sprinkle with the coconut and mint leaves and serve immediately.

NUTRITION *(per serving: 2½ cups)* 304 calories, 4 g protein, 71 g carbs, 4 g fat, 3 g saturated fat, 13 mg sodium

Vc 480% (288 mg) daily vitamin C	**K** 31% (1,083 mg) daily potassium	**VE** 25% (7.5 IU) daily vitamin E
Fi 44% (11 g) daily fiber	**Fo** 26% (104 mcg) daily folate	**Cr** 5 servings carotenoid-rich food (mango)

Sardines : **VITAMIN D**
Pears : **FIBER**
Edamame : **MAGNESIUM**

LUNCH

4

Roasted Sweet Potato and Pumpkin Seed Salad with Warm Bacon-Tomato Vinaigrette

The sautéed tomato dressing goes straight from the pan to the salad, so it slightly wilts the spinach while coating every leaf with flavor. To keep it healthy, we used just enough bacon to make it tasty, relying on roasted sweet potatoes and toasted pumpkin seeds to keep the dish satisfying.

PREP TIME: 15 MINUTES **/ TOTAL TIME:** 35 MINUTES **/ SERVINGS:** 4

5 cups baby spinach leaves (5 ounces)

1½ pounds sweet potatoes, peeled and cut into ¾" chunks

4 strips lower-sodium bacon, halved crosswise

1½ cups grape tomatoes, halved

2 cloves garlic, chopped

3 tablespoons red wine vinegar

2 tablespoons honey

½ cup pumpkin seeds, toasted

1 **HEAT** the oven to 425°F. Place the spinach in a large serving bowl. Lightly coat a baking sheet with cooking spray. Add the potatoes and season with ¼ teaspoon salt and freshly ground black pepper. Mist with cooking spray, toss to combine, and spread in a single layer. Roast, turning halfway through, until tender and golden brown, 25 to 30 minutes.

2 **PLACE** the bacon in a large nonstick skillet on medium heat. Cook until browned and crisp, turning halfway through, 8 to 10 minutes. Transfer the bacon to a paper towel–lined plate, cover with additional paper towels, and press lightly to remove excess fat. Crumble when cool enough to handle.

3 **DISCARD** all but 1½ tablespoons of the bacon fat from the skillet. Heat on medium-low heat and add the tomatoes and garlic. Cook, stirring occasionally, until tomatoes soften, 2 to 3 minutes. Stir in the vinegar and honey.

4 **DRIZZLE** the hot tomato mixture over the spinach and toss to coat. Add the pumpkin seeds, sweet potatoes, and bacon and toss. Season to taste with salt and black pepper.

NUTRITION (per serving: 1½ cups) 285 calories, 10 g protein, 41 g carbs, 10 g fat, 3 g saturated fat, 305 mg sodium

Vc 47% (28 mg) daily vitamin C

Mg 35% (141 mg) daily magnesium

Cr 3½ servings carotenoid-rich foods (spinach, sweet potatoes, grape tomatoes)

Chopped Vegetable Salad with Sardines and Toasted Pita Croutons

This dish is inspired by a Middle Eastern salad called fattoush that makes use of day-old pita by toasting it and breaking it into shards to create rustic croutons. Using whole wheat pitas adds not only texture, but also fiber to this fresh-tasting main course salad.

PREP TIME: 20 MINUTES / **TOTAL TIME:** 35 MINUTES / **SERVINGS:** 4

2 whole wheat pitas (6" each)

2 cups chopped green leaf or romaine lettuce

2 plum tomatoes, chopped (about 1 cup)

1 cup chopped English cucumber

8 radishes, thinly sliced (about 1 cup)

6 scallions, chopped (about ⅓ cup)

¼ cup chopped fresh parsley

¼ cup chopped fresh mint

2 tablespoons olive oil

Juice of 1 lemon (about 3 tablespoons)

1 tablespoon ground sumac

3 cans (3.75 ounces each) sardines packed in olive oil, drained

Lemon wedges

1 **HEAT** the oven to 400°F. Place the pitas on a baking sheet and toast until lightly browned and crisp, about 5 minutes per side. Break into 1" pieces when cool enough to handle.

2 **COMBINE** the lettuce, tomatoes, cucumber, radishes, scallions, parsley, and mint in a large bowl. Add the olive oil and lemon juice and toss. Add the sumac and the pita croutons and toss to combine. Season to taste with salt and freshly ground black pepper. Divide among 4 plates and top evenly with sardines. Serve with lemon wedges.

NUTRITION (per serving: 2½ cups) 323 calories, 22 g protein, 25 g carbs, 16 g fat, 2 g saturated fat, 541 mg sodium

O3 114% (1,140 mg) daily omega-3s	Vc 53% (32 mg) daily vitamin C	Vd 33% (133 IU) daily vitamin D
B12 100% (6 mcg) daily vitamin B12	Ca 33% (332 mg) daily calcium	

Sardine Baguette Sandwiches with Creamy Avocado Spread

You won't believe that the smooth avocado spread only requires three ingredients and a quick whirl in the blender. Plenty of fresh lemon juice makes it the perfect complement to the sardines in this quick and easy lunch, but it would also be a good addition to chicken sandwiches, turkey wraps, or fish tacos.

PREP TIME: 15 MINUTES **/ TOTAL TIME:** 15 MINUTES **/ SERVINGS:** 4

1 ripe avocado, halved, pitted, peeled, and coarsely chopped

¼ cup fat-free plain Greek yogurt

Juice of 1 lemon (about 3 tablespoons)

1 whole grain baguette, cut crosswise into 4" pieces

3 cans (3.75 ounces each) olive oil–packed sardines, drained

2 medium tomatoes, sliced

1 large shallot, thinly sliced (about ¼ cup)

½ cup fresh flat-leaf parsley leaves

1 **PUT** the avocado, yogurt, and lemon juice in a blender. Blend on high speed until smooth, scraping down the sides as needed. Season to taste with salt and freshly ground black pepper.

2 **HALVE** each piece of baguette lengthwise. Spread about 1 tablespoon of the avocado mixture on each piece of bread (top and bottom halves). Divide the sardines among the bottom halves of the bread. Top evenly with the tomatoes, shallots, and parsley. Cover with the top halves of the bread and serve.

NUTRITION (per serving) 455 calories, 28 g protein, 47 g carbs, 17 g fat, 2 g saturated fat, 842 mg sodium

O₃	124% (1,240 mg) daily omega-3s	V_D	39% (154 IU) daily vitamin D	Ca	33% (334 mg) daily calcium
B₁₂	117% (7 mcg) daily vitamin B₁₂	V_C	37% (22 mg) daily vitamin C	Fi	28% (7 g) daily fiber

Steak Salad with Pickled Pears and Blue Cheese

A light pickling infuses the pears with flavor, without making them overly vinegary, and mellows the bite of the onions. Together they make an addictive addition to this salad. Try to use thick steaks for this recipe; otherwise, reduce the oven time to avoid overcooking.

PREP TIME: 15 MINUTES **/ TOTAL TIME:** 45 MINUTES + PICKLING TIME **/ SERVINGS:** 4

1 cup white vinegar

⅓ cup sugar

1 cinnamon stick

½ teaspoon mustard seeds

½ teaspoon black peppercorns

1 teaspoon ground ginger

½ teaspoon allspice

3 large Bartlett pears, halved, cored, and thinly sliced

½ large red onion, thinly sliced (about ¾ cup)

14 ounces beef tenderloin steaks, about 1½" thick

¼ teaspoon dried thyme

2 teaspoons Dijon mustard

3 tablespoons olive oil

6 cups mixed baby greens or spring mix

½ cup chopped pecans, toasted

2 ounces reduced-fat blue cheese, crumbled (about ½ cup)

1 **COMBINE** the vinegar, sugar, cinnamon, mustard seeds, peppercorns, ginger, allspice, and 1 cup water in a medium saucepan. Bring to a boil on high heat. Reduce the heat to medium-low and simmer, stirring occasionally, until the sugar dissolves and the flavors blend, about 5 minutes. Place the pears and onion in a wide, shallow bowl. Pour the hot vinegar mixture through a fine mesh strainer over the pears and onion. Refrigerate, stirring once or twice, for 1 hour.

2 **HEAT** the oven to 400°F. Heat a large ovenproof skillet on medium-high heat and coat with cooking spray. Season the beef with the thyme, ¼ teaspoon salt, and freshly ground black pepper. Place in the skillet and cook without moving until the bottom sides are deeply browned, 3 to 4 minutes. Turn and repeat on opposite sides. Transfer to the oven and cook according to preference, turning steaks about halfway through, 9 to 11 minutes for medium-rare to medium. Transfer to a cutting board and rest 5 minutes. Thinly slice.

3 **RESERVE** 3 tablespoons of the vinegar mixture in a large bowl, then drain the pears and onion in a colander. Whisk the mustard, oil, and ⅛ teaspoon of salt into the vinegar. Add the baby greens, pecans, and cheese and toss to combine. Divide among 4 large plates. Top evenly with the pears, onions, and steak and serve.

NUTRITION *(per serving: 2 cups)* 514 calories, 28 g protein, 37 g carbs, 30 g fat, 7 g saturated fat, 506 mg sodium

Fi **32% (8 g) daily fiber**

Turkey, Pear, and Grilled Radicchio Baguette Sandwiches

Radicchio has a naturally bitter taste, but caramelizing it slightly under the broiler brings out its sweetness. The warm, smoky radicchio is also a unique contrast to the juicy pears and tangy goat cheese. This sandwich is equally good made ahead of time and wrapped to go.

PREP TIME: 10 MINUTES **/ TOTAL TIME:** 20 MINUTES **/ SERVINGS:** 4

1 head radicchio, quartered and cored

2 teaspoons olive oil

¼ cup honey

7 teaspoons Dijon mustard

1 whole grain baguette, cut crosswise into four 4" pieces

8 ounces thinly sliced low-sodium deli turkey breast

3 medium green or red pears, halved, cored, and thinly sliced

2 ounces goat cheese, crumbled (about ½ cup)

1 cup baby spinach leaves

1 **HEAT** the broiler and coat a baking sheet with cooking spray. Lightly brush the radicchio with oil and place on the prepared baking sheet cut side up. Broil about 6" from the heat until lightly browned and crisp at the edges, 3 to 4 minutes. Turn and broil until the opposite side is lightly browned, about 2 minutes. Separate the leaves when cool enough to handle and season to taste with salt and freshly ground black pepper.

2 **COMBINE** the honey and mustard in a small bowl. Split each baguette piece horizontally and spread each side with about 1 teaspoon of the honey-mustard mixture. Layer one-quarter of the radicchio leaves on the bottom half of each baguette and drizzle evenly with the remaining honey mustard. Layer the turkey, pears, goat cheese, and spinach evenly over the radicchio. Cover with the baguette tops and serve.

NUTRITION (per serving) 445 calories, 23 g protein, 80 g carbs, 6 g fat, 3 g saturated fat, 1,045 mg sodium

Fi **32% (8 g) daily fiber**

Grass-Fed Beef Burgers with Blue Cheese Sauce

Thick, rich Greek yogurt is a boon to the healthy cook, adding a creamy quality to sauces and dressings. Here it forms the base of a cheese sauce—all you'll need to top the simply seasoned burgers.

PREP TIME: 10 MINUTES / **TOTAL TIME:** 45 MINUTES / SERVINGS 4

2 teaspoons olive oil

1 medium red onion, halved lengthwise and sliced

1¼ pounds lean grass-fed ground beef or 90% lean ground beef

1 tablespoon plus 2 teaspoons Worcestershire sauce

1 teaspoon onion powder

¼ teaspoon garlic powder

5 tablespoons chopped fresh flat-leaf parsley

½ cup low-fat plain Greek yogurt

1½ ounces blue cheese, crumbled (about ⅓ cup)

1 teaspoon Dijon mustard

4 whole wheat hamburger buns

4 leaves green leaf lettuce

1 medium tomato, sliced

1 **HEAT** the broiler and coat a baking sheet with cooking spray. Heat the oil in a medium skillet on medium-high heat. Add the onion and cook, stirring occasionally, until tender and lightly browned, about 8 minutes. Season to taste with salt and freshly ground black pepper.

2 **COMBINE** the beef, Worcestershire sauce, onion powder, garlic powder, 4 tablespoons of the parsley, ¼ teaspoon salt, and freshly ground black pepper in a large bowl. Form into 4 patties, about 3" wide and ½" thick. Place on the prepared baking sheet and broil 6" from the heat until the patties feel firm and the centers are no longer pink, turning halfway through, about 12 minutes.

3 **MIX** the yogurt, blue cheese, mustard, and the remaining 1 tablespoon parsley in a small bowl. Spread the top halves of the buns with the yogurt mixture. Top the bottom half of each bun with a patty, lettuce leaf, one-quarter of the onions, and a slice of tomato. Cover with the top halves of the buns and serve.

NUTRITION (per serving) 436 calories, 36 g protein, 31 g carbs, 19 g fat, 7 g saturated fat, 661 mg sodium

B₁₂ 50% (3 mcg) daily vitamin B₁₂   Fe 28% (5 mg) daily iron

Date-Ricotta Crostini and Arugula Salad

In this recipe, dates and pistachios are blended to create a creamy vinaigrette and also combined with ricotta cheese to top toasted slices of baguette.

PREP TIME: 20 MINUTES / **TOTAL TIME:** 30 MINUTES / **SERVINGS:** 6

2 tablespoons olive oil

2 tablespoons white wine or cider vinegar

1 teaspoon Dijon mustard

Juice of 2 oranges (about ⅔ cup)

1¼ cups chopped pitted Medjool dates

¾ cup chopped shelled pistachios

6 cups arugula (about 6 ounces)

1 can (15 ounces) chickpeas, rinsed and drained

½ medium red onion, thinly sliced (about ½ cup)

16 ounces part-skim ricotta

1 whole grain baguette, cut on the diagonal into 18 slices (each ⅓" thick)

1 **HEAT** the oven to 400°F. Combine the oil, vinegar, mustard, orange juice, ¼ cup of the dates, and 1 tablespoon of the pistachios in a blender and puree until smooth. Blend in a small amount of water if necessary to achieve a thick, pourable consistency. Alternatively, puree using an immersion blender and the accompanying blending cup.

2 **COMBINE** the arugula, chickpeas, onion, and ⅓ cup of the pistachios. Set aside 3 tablespoons of the dressing. Add the remaining dressing to the arugula mixture and toss well.

3 **COMBINE** the ricotta and the remaining dates and pistachios in a medium bowl. Season with freshly ground black pepper.

4 **ARRANGE** the bread on a baking sheet in a single layer. Bake, rotating the baking sheet about halfway through, until lightly browned and crisp, 5 to 8 minutes. Spread each of the bread slices with 2 to 3 tablespoons of the ricotta mixture. Divide the salad among 6 plates. Stack 3 of the ricotta-topped bread slices on each plate. Drizzle evenly with the reserved dressing and serve immediately.

NUTRITION (per serving: 1½ cups salad and 3 crostini) 533 calories, 23 g protein, 65 g carbs, 22 g fat, 6 g saturated fat, 319 mg sodium

Fi 40% (10 g) daily fiber

Ca 36% (364 mg) daily calcium

Vc 32% (19 mg) daily vitamin C

K 25% (886 mg) daily potassium

  Cr 1 serving carotenoid-rich food (arugula)

Mediterranean Edamame Patties in Whole Wheat Pita with Tahini Sauce

This baked-not-fried take on falafel stars shelled edamame instead of chickpeas. A generous amount of fresh herbs add flavor, as do the spices, which are typically found in Middle Eastern dishes. To turn this recipe into a healthy appetizer, make the patties smaller and serve them with the tahini sauce for dipping.

PREP TIME: 30 MINUTES **/ TOTAL TIME:** 45 MINUTES **/ SERVINGS:** 4

PATTIES

2 cups frozen shelled edamame, thawed and patted dry

½ medium red onion, chopped (about ½ cup)

4 scallions, white and some green, sliced (about ¼ cup)

¼ cup chopped fresh parsley

¼ cup chopped cilantro

2 tablespoons chopped dill

Juice of ½ lemon (1 tablespoon plus 2 teaspoons)

2 cloves garlic, chopped

Zest of ½ lemon (about 1 teaspoon)

1 tablespoon all-purpose flour

1 teaspoon ground cumin

½ teaspoon ground coriander

⅛ teaspoon cayenne

1 **PREPARE PATTIES:** Heat the oven to 400°F and coat a baking sheet with cooking spray. Combine all of the ingredients for the patties, ½ teaspoon salt, and freshly ground black pepper in a food processor and process to a slightly chunky paste, scraping down the sides of the bowl as needed. Form into 16 patties, about 1¾" wide and ¼" thick. Spray tops with cooking spray. Place on the prepared baking sheet and bake, turning halfway through, until lightly browned and slightly firm to the touch, 12 to 14 minutes.

SAUCE AND PITAS

¼ cup low-fat plain Greek yogurt

Juice of 1 lemon (about 3 tablespoons)

3½ tablespoons tahini

2 cups chopped romaine or green leaf lettuce

2 large tomatoes, thinly sliced (16 slices)

4 whole wheat pitas (6" each), halved

2 PREPARE SAUCE AND PITAS: Whisk together the yogurt, lemon juice, tahini, and ⅓ cup water in a small bowl.

3 TUCK 2 patties, ¼ cup lettuce, and 2 tomato slices into each pita half. Drizzle each half with 1½ tablespoons of the sauce and serve.

NUTRITION *(per serving: 1 whole pita)* 366 calories, 18 g protein, 54 g carbs, 12 g fat, 1 g saturated fat, 605 mg sodium

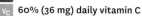 **Fo** 70% (279 mcg) daily folate

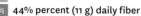 **Vc** 60% (36 mg) daily vitamin C

Fi 44% percent (11 g) daily fiber

Fe 28% (5 mg) daily iron

Mg 28% (110 mg) daily magnesium

Cr 1½ servings carotenoid-rich foods (tomato, Romaine lettuce)

Fish Tacos with Black Bean–Papaya Salsa

This colorful dish is also versatile: Use mango or peaches if papaya is unavailable, or swap the cod for catfish or tilapia. We chose corn over flour tortillas because they have more fiber and are easy to find in the "taco" (6") size.

PREP TIME: 15 MINUTES **/ TOTAL TIME:** 25 MINUTES **/ SERVES:** 4

1 pound skinless cod fillet

½ teaspoon chili powder

1 can (15 ounces) black beans, drained and rinsed

¼ medium papaya, halved, seeded, peeled, and chopped (about 1¼ cups)

1 large fresh jalapeño, seeded and chopped (about ¼ cup)

¼ medium red onion, chopped (about ¼ cup)

½ cup cilantro, chopped

Juice of 1 lime (about 2 tablespoons)

1½ teaspoons olive oil

8 corn tortillas (6" each)

1½ cups chopped Romaine or green leaf lettuce

8 teaspoons reduced-fat (light) sour cream

1 **HEAT** the broiler and coat a baking sheet with cooking spray. Place the cod on the baking sheet and season with chili powder, ⅛ teaspoon salt, and black pepper. Broil 6" from the heat until opaque in the thickest part, 3 to 5 minutes per side. Flake into bite-size pieces when cool enough to handle.

2 **COMBINE** the beans, papaya, jalapeño, onion, cilantro, lime juice, and oil in a medium bowl. Season to taste with salt and pepper.

3 **HEAT** a large skillet on medium heat. Add the tortillas in batches of two or three and cook until warmed through, 1 to 2 minutes per side. Wrap in a kitchen towel to keep warm until all tortillas are done. Divide the lettuce, cod, and black bean salsa evenly among the tortillas. Top each with about 1 teaspoon sour cream and serve immediately.

NUTRITION (per serving: 2 tacos) 339 calories, 29 g protein, 44 g carbs, 6 g fat, 1 g saturated fat, 487 mg sodium

Vc 67% (40 mg) daily vitamin C   Fi 32% (8 g) daily fiber   Fo 26% (102 mcg) daily folate

O3 34% (340 mg) daily omega-3s

Flaxseed-Coated Cod Sandwiches

Ground flaxseeds make a good coating for delicate fish like cod because they are fine enough to adhere well, yet still add a bit of crunch. The creamy topping is a healthier take on tartar sauce that keeps the briny zip of capers but cuts the fat.

PREP TIME: 20 MINUTES / **TOTAL TIME:** 40 MINUTES / **SERVINGS:** 4

½ cup all-purpose flour

1 large egg

½ cup ground flaxseeds

½ teaspoon dried tarragon

1 pound skinless cod fillet, cut into 4 portions

2 tablespoons reduced-fat mayonnaise

2 tablespoons low-fat plain Greek yogurt

2 teaspoons Dijon mustard

2 teaspoons dill pickle relish

1 tablespoon capers, rinsed, drained, and chopped

1 tablespoon chopped fresh parsley

1¼ cups finely sliced red or green cabbage

2 teaspoons olive oil

Juice of ½ lemon (1 tablespoon plus 2 teaspoons)

4 whole wheat hamburger buns

½ cup baby spinach leaves

1 medium tomato, cut into 4 thick slices

1 **HEAT** the oven to 425°F. Coat a baking sheet with cooking spray. Place 3 wide, shallow bowls in front of you. Add the flour to the first bowl. Crack the egg into the second bowl, beat, and season with ⅛ teaspoon salt and freshly ground black pepper. Add the flaxseeds, ¼ teaspoon of the tarragon, ⅛ teaspoon salt, and freshly ground black pepper to the third bowl. Dip the cod in the flour, shaking off the excess. Dip it in the egg, then press it into the flaxseeds so the mixture adheres to the cod. Place on the prepared baking sheet. Bake until opaque in the thickest part, 14 to 18 minutes.

2 **WHISK** together the mayonnaise, yogurt, mustard, relish, capers, parsley, and the remaining tarragon in a small bowl. Combine the cabbage, oil, and lemon juice in a medium bowl.

3 **SPLIT** the buns and top the bottom halves with one-quarter of the spinach, 1 tomato slice, 1 cod fillet, 1 tablespoon of the mayonnaise mixture, and ¼ cup of the cabbage mixture. Cover with the top halves of the buns and serve.

NUTRITION (per serving) 499 calories, 34 g protein, 48 g carbs, 20 g fat, 2 g saturated fat, 654 mg sodium

O3 **423% (4,230 mg) daily omega-3s**	Fo **121% (484 mcg) daily folate**	Fi **52% (13 g) daily fiber**
B12 **167% (10 mcg) daily vitamin B12**	K **63% (2,205 mg) daily potassium**	Fe **28% (5 mg) daily iron**
Vc **128% (77 mg) daily vitamin C**	Mg **60% (242 mg) daily magnesium**	

Ham and White Cheddar Panini with Mango Chutney

A substantial bakery loaf with a dense, chewy interior is ideal for panini. Unlike soft, prepackaged sandwich bread, the heartier slices hold up to the pressing that gives this sandwich its characteristic crispy exterior. Instructions are given for a countertop grill and stove-top cooking, but you can use a panini press if you have one.

PREP TIME: 10 MINUTES / **TOTAL TIME:** 20 MINUTES / **SERVINGS:** 4

1 tablespoon plus 1 teaspoon olive oil

8 slices (⅓" thick) crusty whole grain bread

4 ounces reduced-fat white Cheddar, sliced thin

4 ounces thinly sliced low-sodium deli ham

4 tablespoons mango chutney

2 cups arugula

1 **HEAT** a countertop grill or heat a large skillet on medium heat. Brush oil on one side of each bread slice. Flip the slices over so the oil-free sides are facing up and arrange the cheese evenly over all 8 slices. Top evenly with the ham. Put 2 slices together to form a sandwich.

2 **COAT** the grill or skillet with cooking spray and add 2 of the sandwiches. If using the grill, close the top and cook until the bread is deep golden brown and crisp and the cheese is melted, turning the sandwiches 180 degrees about halfway through, 4 to 5 minutes. If using the skillet, place another skillet directly on top of the sandwiches to weigh them down. Cook until the bread is deep golden brown and crisp on the bottom and the cheese is melted, flipping the sandwiches halfway through, 5 to 6 minutes. Quickly open each sandwich and add 1 tablespoon chutney and ½ cup arugula. Repeat with remaining sandwiches and serve.

NUTRITION (per serving) 417 calories, 28 g protein, 46 g carbs, 13 g fat, 4 g saturated fat, 1,044 mg sodium

Ca 30% (298 mg) daily calcium

Oyster Po' Boys with Quick Remoulade Sauce

Freshly shucked oysters (ask your fishmonger to do the job, if possible) are great in this New Orleans favorite, but good-quality, preshucked ones, often sold at the fish counter, also work well (don't use canned or smoked oysters). Deep-frying is traditional, but we got a crispy coating by pan-frying the oysters in a small amount of oil.

PREP TIME: 20 MINUTES / **TOTAL TIME:** 30 MINUTES / **SERVINGS:** 4

3 tablespoons reduced-fat mayonnaise

3 tablespoons low-fat plain Greek yogurt

2 tablespoons grainy mustard

1 tablespoon plus 1 teaspoon dill pickle relish

1 tablespoon fresh lemon juice

1½ teaspoons hot sauce

2 large eggs

⅓ cup finely ground cornmeal

¼ cup all-purpose flour

⅛ teaspoon cayenne

16 medium or 12 large oysters, shucked

2 tablespoons safflower or canola oil

4 French sandwich rolls or hoagie rolls (about 5" long), toasted

1½ cups shredded romaine lettuce

2 plum tomatoes, sliced

Lemon wedges

1 **WHISK** together the mayonnaise, yogurt, mustard, relish, lemon juice, and hot sauce in a small bowl.

2 **COAT** a baking sheet with cooking spray. Lightly beat the eggs in a medium bowl and season with ⅛ teaspoon salt and freshly ground black pepper. Combine the cornmeal, flour, and cayenne in another medium bowl. Dip the oysters in the eggs, shaking off the excess. Press into the cornmeal mixture, coating completely, and transfer to the prepared baking sheet.

3 **HEAT** 1 tablespoon of the oil in a large skillet on medium-high heat. Add half of the oysters (do not overcrowd the skillet) and cook until the bottom sides are deep golden brown, 3 to 4 minutes. Turn and cook until the opposite sides are deep golden brown, 2 to 3 minutes more. Transfer to a paper towel–lined plate and repeat with the remaining oil and oysters.

4 **SPLIT** the rolls open like a book. Spread evenly with the sauce, covering both sides. Arrange the lettuce and tomato slices over the bottom sides of the rolls and top evenly with oysters. Close rolls and serve with lemon wedges.

NUTRITION (per serving) 425 calories, 16 g protein, 58 g carbs, 15 g fat, 2 g saturated fat, 926 mg sodium

B_{12} 150% (9 mcg) daily vitamin B_{12} Fe 39% (7 mg) daily iron   O3 29% (290 mg) daily omega-3s

Roasted Tomato Soup with White Cheddar Grilled Cheese Sandwiches

The sweetness from the orange juice in the soup slightly mellows the acidity of the tomatoes and adds a new flavor twist to this comfort food favorite.

PREP TIME: 20 MINUTES **/ TOTAL TIME:** 1 HOUR, 5 MINUTES **/ SERVINGS:** 4

SOUP

1 tablespoon olive oil

1 medium onion, chopped (about 1 cup)

¼ teaspoon red-pepper flakes

¼ teaspoon dried oregano

2 cloves garlic, chopped

2 tablespoons balsamic vinegar

2 cans (14 ounces each) fire-roasted diced tomatoes

2 cans (14 ounces each) no-salt-added diced tomatoes

2 cups orange juice

2 tablespoons chopped fresh mint or basil

SANDWICHES

8 thin slices whole grain bread

1 tablespoon olive oil

4 ounces reduced-fat sharp white Cheddar, thinly sliced

½ cup baby spinach or arugula

1 **PREPARE SOUP:** Heat the oil in a large pot or Dutch oven on medium heat. Add the onion, pepper flakes (to taste), and oregano and cook until the onion is tender and lightly browned, about 7 minutes. Add the garlic and cook, stirring constantly, 1 minute. Add the balsamic vinegar and simmer, stirring constantly, until reduced by about half, 30 seconds to 1 minute. Add the tomatoes and orange juice. Raise the heat to high, cover, and bring to a boil. Reduce the heat to medium and simmer, uncovered, until slightly thickened, 10 to 12 minutes. Remove from the heat.

2 **PUREE** the soup with an immersion blender or in batches in a regular blender (be careful when blending hot liquids). Return to the pot and reheat on medium-low, if necessary. Season to taste with salt and freshly ground black pepper. When ready to serve, divide the soup among 4 bowls and sprinkle with the mint or basil.

Herbal Medicine

Move over echinacea and St. John's wort—the herbs and spices you find in the produce and baking aisles of the supermarket can have just as many health benefits as those in the supplement aisle. Of the top 50 dietary sources of disease-fighting antioxidants, 13 are herbs and spices, according to an analysis by researchers at the University of Oslo. Fresh or dried, seasonings don't pack just a flavor punch, but a health one as well.

3 PREPARE SANDWICHES: Heat the oven to 250°F. Place 4 slices of bread in front of you. Brush lightly with half of the oil. Turn the slices over and top evenly with the cheese and spinach or arugula. Cover with the remaining slices and brush with the remaining oil (olive oil should be on the outside of the sandwiches). Heat a large skillet coated with cooking spray over medium heat. Add 2 of the sandwiches, cover, and cook until the bottoms are golden brown and crisp, 4 to 5 minutes. Turn, cover, and cook until the opposite sides are golden brown and crisp and the cheese is melted, about 3 minutes. Transfer to a baking sheet and place in the oven to keep warm. Coat the skillet with more cooking spray and repeat with the remaining sandwiches. Serve with the soup.

NUTRITION *(per serving: 1½ cups soup and 1 sandwich)* 465 calories, 19 g protein, 62 g carbs, 16 g fat, 6 g saturated fat, 937 mg sodium

Vc 185% (111 mg) daily vitamin C

Ca 35% (349 mg) daily calcium

Fi 32% (8 g) daily fiber

Cr 1½ servings carotenoid-rich food (tomatoes)

Grilled Eggplant, Tomato, and Fresh Mozzarella Sandwiches

Anytime you're firing up the grill for dinner, make some extra veggies, like this eggplant, for another meal. Cool at room temperature, cover, and refrigerate up to 2 days. That way, this sandwich becomes an easy brown-bag lunch that you put together in 5 minutes.

PREP TIME: 10 MINUTES **/ TOTAL TIME:** 25 MINUTES **/ SERVINGS:** 4

2 large eggplants (about 1¼ pounds each), trimmed and sliced lengthwise ⅓" thick (about 12 slices)

2 tablespoons olive oil

2 medium tomatoes, sliced

12 fresh basil leaves

4 ounces fresh mozzarella, cut into 8 (¼"-thick) slices

4 ciabatta rolls, split lengthwise

2 tablespoons balsamic vinegar

1 **BRUSH** a grill rack with vegetable oil and heat the grill to medium-high heat. Brush both sides of the eggplant slices lightly with the olive oil and season with ½ teaspoon salt and freshly ground black pepper. Place the eggplant over direct heat. Cook until grill marks form and the eggplant is lightly browned and tender, 5 to 7 minutes per side.

2 **LAYER** 3 slices of the eggplant, 2 slices of tomato, 3 basil leaves, and 2 slices of mozzarella on the bottom half of each ciabatta roll. Drizzle with balsamic vinegar to taste. Cover with the tops of the rolls and serve.

NUTRITION *(per serving)* 341 calories, 10 g protein, 50 g carbs, 12 g fat, 3 g saturated fat, 622 mg sodium

 Fi 40% (10 g) daily fiber

An 2 servings anthocyanin-rich food (eggplant)

Pearl Couscous with Roasted Beets, Lima Beans, and Feta

Pearl couscous should be cooked until it is slightly chewy (like al dente pasta), not soft. If you can't find it, this colorful dish would also work well with quinoa or barley. Regular couscous is a bit too delicate to pair with the chopped beets and firm lima beans.

PREP TIME: 10 MINUTES / **TOTAL TIME:** 1 HOUR 25 MINUTES / **SERVINGS:** 4

5 medium beets

1 tablespoon olive oil

¾ cup Israeli (also called Mediterranean or pearl) couscous

4 medium shallots, chopped (about ½ cup)

1½ cups frozen lima beans

2 ounces reduced-fat feta cheese, crumbled (about ½ cup)

¼ cup chopped fresh parsley or mint

Juice of 1 lemon (about 3 tablespoons)

1 **HEAT** the oven to 425°F. Trim the beet stems and roots, leaving about 1" attached to the beets. Wrap the beets together tightly in foil, place on a baking sheet, and roast until a paring knife inserted into the beets goes in and out with minimal resistance, 55 to 65 minutes. When they're cool enough to handle, remove from foil, trim the root and stem ends. Slip the skin off the beets with your fingers and chop. (May be done up to 1 day ahead, then cover and refrigerate.)

2 **HEAT** the oil in a medium saucepan on medium-low heat. Add the couscous and shallots and cook, stirring frequently, until the shallots are soft and couscous is lightly browned, 3 to 4 minutes. Raise the heat to high, add 1 cup water, and bring to a boil. Stir in the lima beans and ¼ teaspoon salt and return to a boil. Reduce the heat to low, cover, and simmer until the couscous is tender and the liquid is absorbed, 12 to 14 minutes. Remove from the heat and let stand, covered, 5 minutes. Transfer to a large serving bowl.

3 **ADD** the feta, parsley, lemon juice, and chopped beets. Stir gently to combine. Season to taste with salt and freshly ground black pepper.

NUTRITION (*per serving: 2 cups*) 312 calories, 14 g protein, 53 g carbs, 6 g fat, 2 g saturated fat, 463 mg sodium

Vc 55% (33 mg) daily vitamin C

Fo 44% (174 mcg) daily folate

Fi 36% (9 g) daily fiber

K 25% (884 mg) daily potassium

An 1½ servings anthocyanin-rich food (beets)

Soba Noodles with Almond Sauce and Shredded Chicken

This easy-to-transport noodle bowl is delicious eaten right away at room temperature or straight out of the office fridge. It makes good use of leftover grilled or poached chicken, but a purchased rotisserie bird works just as well.

PREP TIME: 20 MINUTES / **TOTAL TIME:** 30 MINUTES / **SERVINGS:** 4

¼ cup almond butter

2 tablespoons honey

2 teaspoons reduced-sodium soy sauce

2 teaspoons rice vinegar

6 ounces soba noodles

2 cups shredded cooked chicken breast

¾ cup grated carrots

½ yellow bell pepper, very thinly sliced (about ⅔ cup)

¼ cup sliced almonds, toasted

8 scallions, white and some green, thinly sliced (about ½ cup)

2 or 3 radishes, very thinly sliced (about ⅓ cup)

2 tablespoons chopped cilantro

1 **WHISK** together the almond butter, honey, soy sauce, vinegar, and 2 tablespoons water in a small bowl.

2 **BRING** a large pot of water to a boil on high heat. Add the noodles and cook per package directions. Place in a colander, rinse with cold water, and drain thoroughly.

3 **COMBINE** the noodles and the almond butter mixture in a large bowl, tossing to coat. Stir in the chicken, carrots, bell pepper, almonds, scallions, radishes, and cilantro. Divide among 4 bowls and serve.

NUTRITION (per serving: 1½ cups) 437 calories, 27 g protein, 50 g carbs, 16 g fat, 2 g saturated fat, 232 mg sodium

VC 80% (48 mg) daily vitamin C   VE 33% (10 IU) daily vitamin E

Grilled Brussels Sprout and Tofu Skewers with Balsamic Glaze

Since Brussels sprouts require a longer cooking time than tofu, we blanch them before grilling. Pressing the tofu removes a good deal of its water so the flavorful marinade isn't diluted and the texture stays firm. Performing these extra steps ensures a finished product that's so hearty even meat eaters will approve.

PREP TIME: 20 MINUTES / **TOTAL TIME:** 45 MINUTES + MARINATING AND RESTING TIMES / **SERVINGS:** 4

2 packages (14 ounces each) extra-firm tofu, drained

¾ cup balsamic vinegar

Juice of 1 lemon (about 3 tablespoons)

1 tablespoon plus 2 teaspoons olive oil

2 cloves garlic, finely chopped

1 teaspoon dried thyme

2 pounds Brussels sprouts, trimmed

2 ounces Parmesan, grated (about ½ cup)

1 **PLACE** each block of tofu on a plate lined with four layers of paper towel. Top each one with four more layers of paper towel. Cover each one with a heavy skillet or 2 to 3 plates, and let sit until a good deal of water is extracted from the tofu and the paper towels are very wet, 30 minutes. Cut each block of tofu into 12 cubes. Transfer to a large zip-top bag.

2 **WHISK** together the balsamic vinegar, lemon juice, oil, garlic, and thyme in a small bowl. Add to the bag with the tofu, seal, and turn the bag over gently a few times to coat the tofu with the mixture. Refrigerate 2 to 4 hours, turning the bag once or twice.

3 **BRING** a large pot of water to a boil on high heat. Add the Brussels sprouts and simmer until tender enough to eat, but still somewhat resistant when pierced with a fork, 4 to 6 minutes. Drain and pat dry with paper towels.

Kebab Know-How

Bamboo skewers are easier to work with than metal ones, but they must be soaked before you use them or they'll catch fire on the grill. Fill a shallow pan with warm water, add the skewers, and soak 20 to 30 minutes, depending on skewer size. For this recipe, you'll want a thick skewer so it slides easily through the sprouts; use a thin skewer for delicate foods, like the Yogurt-Marinated Chicken Skewers with Cucumber-Yogurt Sauce (page 126).

4 **BRUSH** a grill rack with vegetable oil and heat the grill to medium-high heat. Remove the tofu from the bag, reserving the balsamic mixture. Thread the tofu and Brussels sprouts evenly onto 8 skewers and place on a large plate or baking sheet. Season with ½ teaspoon salt and freshly ground black pepper.

5 **ADD** the reserved balsamic mixture to a small saucepan and bring to a simmer on high heat. Reduce heat to medium low and simmer until reduced by about half and slightly thickened, 2 to 3 minutes.

6 **PLACE** the skewers on the grill over direct heat. Cook, turning once or twice, until deeply browned, 8 to 9 minutes. Brush tofu and sprouts with balsamic mixture and continue cooking 1 minute longer. Transfer to a serving platter and sprinkle with the cheese.

NUTRITION (per serving: 2 skewers) 430 calories, 32 g protein, 34 g carbs, 11 g fiber, 20 g fat, 5 g saturated fat, 506 mg sodium

| Vc | 298% (179 mg) daily vitamin C | Ca | 41% (410 mg) daily calcium | Fo | 32% (127 mcg) daily folate |
| Fi | 44% (11 g) daily fiber | Fe | 39% (7 mg) daily iron | | |

Asian Chicken Salad in Lettuce Cups with Peanut Sauce

Sriracha, a Thai sun-ripened chile sauce with garlic, adds heat and flavor to the salty-sweet peanut dip and can be found in large supermarkets and Asian markets. Regular hot sauce, such as Tabasco, may be substituted.

PREP TIME: 20 MINUTES / **TOTAL TIME:** 35 MINUTES / **SERVES:** 4

¼ cup smooth peanut butter

5 tablespoons light coconut milk

2 teaspoons unseasoned rice vinegar

2 teaspoons honey

1 teaspoon Sriracha or hot sauce

3 tablespoons reduced-sodium soy sauce

1 cup roasted unsalted peanuts

1 tablespoon canola oil

1 red bell pepper, chopped (about 1¼ cups)

½ large red onion, chopped (about ¾ cup)

1½ pounds ground chicken breast

2 fresh jalapeños, seeded amd chopped (about ⅓ cup)

2 tablespoons peeled and chopped fresh ginger (2" piece)

2 cups shredded carrot

Juice of 2 limes (about ¼ cup)

½ cup chopped cilantro

2 small heads Bibb lettuce, stem ends trimmed, leaves separated

1 **COMBINE** the peanut butter, coconut milk, vinegar, honey, Sriracha, and 1 tablespoon of the soy sauce in a small bowl. Finely chop ¼ cup of the peanuts and stir into the sauce. Coarsely chop the remaining peanuts for filling.

2 **HEAT** the oil in a large skillet on medium-high heat. Add the bell pepper and onion and cook, stirring frequently, until lightly browned, about 7 minutes. Add the chicken, jalapeños, and ginger and cook, crumbling the chicken as you stir, until it is no longer pink, about 6 minutes. Add the carrot, lime juice, and the remaining 2 tablespoons soy sauce. Cook until the carrot is tender and the liquid is reduced by about half, 2 to 3 minutes. Stir in the cilantro and the coarsely chopped peanuts. Remove from the heat.

3 **DIVIDE** the lettuce leaves and chicken mixture among 4 plates. Serve with the sauce.

NUTRITION (per serving: 1¾ cups chicken and 2½ tablespoons sauce) 586 calories, 52 g protein, 30 g carbs, 32 g fat, 5 g saturated fat, 707 mg sodium

| Vc | 123% (74 mg) daily vitamin C | Fo | 29% (115 mcg) daily folate | | 1½ servings carotenoid-rich foods (red bell pepper, carrots) |
| Fi | 32% (8 g) daily fiber | VE | 27% (8 IU) daily vitamin E | | |

Tuna and Chickpea Salad in Tomato Cups

Chickpeas are filling and they add texture to this protein-packed tuna salad. Smoked paprika lends savory flavor, but if you don't have any, mild chili powder or regular paprika are good substitutes. Since the chickpeas are also a healthy, fiber-rich starch, you won't miss the bread in this low-cal lunch.

PREP TIME: 25 MINUTES **/ TOTAL TIME:** 25 MINUTES **/ SERVES:** 4

1 cup rinsed, drained chickpeas

2 pouches (6.4 ounces each) chunk light tuna in water, drained

⅓ cup chopped jarred Peppadew peppers or roasted red peppers

¼ cup chopped fresh parsley, dill, cilantro, or chives, or a combination

½ teaspoon smoked paprika

3 large omega-3 eggs, hard-boiled, yolks and whites separated

⅔ cup low-fat plain Greek yogurt

4 large beefsteak tomatoes

1 **MASH** the chickpeas coarsely with a fork in a large bowl, leaving some whole. Add the tuna, peppers, herbs, and paprika. Chop the egg whites and add to the bowl. Stir to combine.

2 **MASH** the egg yolks with a fork in a small bowl. Add the yogurt and stir well to combine. Add to the tuna mixture and stir to combine. Season to taste with salt and freshly ground black pepper.

3 **SLICE** the top (stem end) off of each tomato and hollow out the centers with a paring knife. Fill each with 1 cup of the tuna mixture and serve.

NUTRITION (per serving) 281 calories, 32 g protein, 26 g carbs, 5 g fat, 1 g saturated fat, 544 mg sodium

V_C 75% (45 mg) daily vitamin C	V_D 45% (178 IU) daily vitamin D	Cr 1 serving carotenoid-rich food (tomatoes)
B_12 50% (3 mcg) daily vitamin B_12	O_3 34% (340 mg) daily omega-3s	

Beets : **POTASSIUM**
Spinach : **FOLATE**
Pumpkin Seeds : **MAGNESIUM**

SOUPS AND STARTERS

5

Borscht

This eastern European soup is chock-full of vegetables, although the vibrant ruby red from the beets overtakes all other colors. Half of the soup is pureed, creating a thick, rich texture that doesn't weigh you down.

PREP TIME: 25 MINUTES **/ TOTAL TIME:** 1 HOUR 15 MINUTES **/ SERVINGS:** 4

1 tablespoon olive oil

1 large onion, sliced (about 1½ cups)

2 medium carrots, thickly sliced (about 1 cup)

1 celery stalk, sliced (about ½ cup)

½ teaspoon fennel seeds

½ teaspoon caraway seeds

2 tablespoons tomato paste

2 cloves garlic, chopped

4 cups low-sodium vegetable broth

1½ pounds red beets, peeled and chopped (about 4 cups)

1 fennel bulb, trimmed and cored

1 pound red potatoes, chopped (about 2¾ cups)

¼ cup reduced-fat (light) sour cream

Fresh dill sprigs

1 **HEAT** the oil in a large pot or Dutch oven on medium heat. Add the onion and cook, stirring occasionally, until lightly browned, about 5 minutes. Add carrots, celery, fennel seeds, and caraway seeds and cook until the onion is tender and carrots are lightly browned, 7 to 8 minutes. Add the tomato paste and garlic and cook, stirring constantly, 1 minute. Add the broth and 1 cup water. Cover and bring to a boil on high heat. Add the beets and reduce the heat to medium low. Simmer, covered, until the beets are partially cooked, 20 minutes.

2 **SHAVE** about ¼ of the fennel bulb with a vegetable peeler. Set strips aside. Chop the rest of the fennel. Add the potatoes and chopped fennel to the pot and simmer, covered, until the potatoes and beets are tender, 10 to 15 minutes.

3 **TRANSFER** about half of the soup to a blender, working in batches if necessary. Puree (be careful when blending hot liquids) until smooth and return to the soup pot. Season to taste with salt and freshly ground black pepper. Divide among 4 bowls and top evenly with sour cream, dill, and the reserved shaved fennel.

NUTRITION *(per serving: about 2 cups)* 252 calories, 6 g protein, 47 g carbs, 6 g fat, 2 g saturated fat, 550 mg sodium

Vc 45% (27 mg) daily vitamin C

Fo 42% (168 mcg) daily folate

 K 39% (1,358 mg) daily potassium

Fi 36% (9 g) daily fiber

 An 2 servings anthocyanin-rich food (beets)

Creamy Broccoli-Pea Soup with Bacon and Cheddar

Cooked broccoli is quite mild in flavor, so we punched things up with sweet frozen peas and added potatoes for a creamy texture. Topped with bacon, Cheddar, sour cream, and chives, it's like eating a veggie-stuffed baked potato in soup form. Pair any leftovers with half a sandwich for a filling, nutrient-packed lunch.

PREP TIME: 20 MINUTES / **TOTAL TIME:** 50 MINUTES / **SERVES:** 4

1 tablespoon olive oil

1 large onion, chopped (about 1¼ cups)

2 cloves garlic, chopped

⅛ teaspoon red-pepper flakes

2 pounds broccoli, trimmed, florets chopped

1 small Russet potato, peeled and chopped (about 1½ cups)

2 cups frozen peas

3 strips lower-sodium bacon, halved crosswise

3 tablespoons cider vinegar

4 tablespoons reduced-fat (light) sour cream

2 ounces reduced-fat Cheddar, grated (about ½ cup)

1 tablespoon chopped fresh chives

1 **HEAT** the oil in a large pot or Dutch oven on medium heat. Add the onion and cook, stirring occasionally, until soft and translucent, about 6 minutes. Add the garlic and pepper flakes and cook, stirring constantly, 1 minute. Add 5 cups water, raise the heat to high, cover, and bring to a boil.

2 **ADD** the broccoli and potato and return to a boil. Reduce the heat to medium and simmer, uncovered, until the vegetables are very tender, 12 to 15 minutes. Add the peas and simmer until heated through, about 2 minutes. Remove from the heat. Working in batches, transfer the soup to a blender (or use an immersion blender) and puree until smooth (be careful when blending hot liquids). Return the soup to the pot.

3 **COOK** the bacon in a large skillet on medium heat until browned and crisp, turning once, about 8 minutes. Transfer to a paper towel–lined plate and press with more paper towels to drain. Crumble when cool enough to handle and set aside.

4 **REHEAT** the soup on medium-low heat. Stir in the vinegar and season with ½ teaspoon salt and freshly ground black pepper to taste. Ladle into 4 bowls and top evenly with the sour cream, cheese, reserved bacon, and chives.

NUTRITION (per serving: 1½ cups) 279 calories, 16 g protein, 35 g carbs, 11 g fat, 4 g saturated fat, 611 mg sodium

VC 278% (167 mg) daily vitamin C

Fi 40% (10 g) daily fiber

Fo 32% (129 mcg) daily folate

Cr 5 servings carotenoid-rich foods (broccoli, peas)

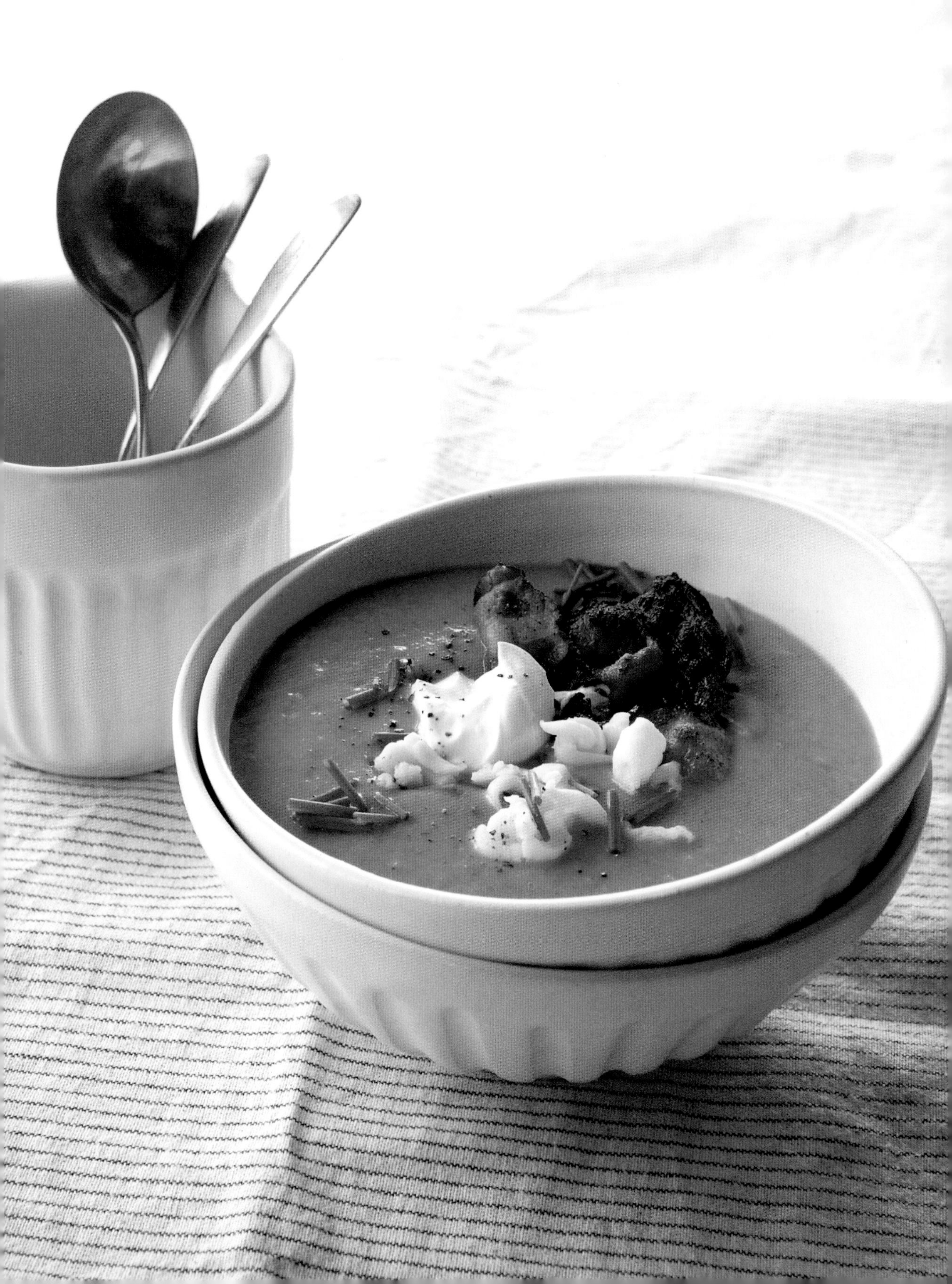

Curried Red Lentil and Carrot Soup

Adding fresh lime juice at the very end gives this soup a zip of acidity. Don't skip this finishing touch. It boosts the flavor so that you may not need as much salt as you usually would.

PREP TIME: 10 MINUTES **/ TOTAL TIME:** 45 MINUTES **/ SERVINGS:** 4

1 tablespoon canola or safflower oil

1 medium onion, chopped (about 1 cup)

2 tablespoons fresh ginger, peeled and finely chopped (2" piece)

1 tablespoon curry powder

1 can (14 ounces) light coconut milk

1⅓ cups red lentils

5 medium carrots, sliced (about 2½ cups)

1 can (14 ounces) fire-roasted diced tomatoes

Juice of 1 to 2 limes (2 to 4 tablespoons)

¾ cup low-fat plain yogurt

¼ cup chopped cilantro

1 **HEAT** the oil in a large pot or Dutch oven on medium heat. Add the onion and cook, stirring occasionally, until tender and lightly browned, 6 to 7 minutes. Add the ginger and curry powder and cook, stirring constantly, until the ginger softens, 1 minute. Add 4½ cups water and the coconut milk. Cover and bring to a simmer on high heat.

2 **ADD** the lentils and carrots, reduce the heat to medium-low, and simmer, uncovered, stirring every few minutes, until the lentils and carrots are tender, 25 to 30 minutes. Add the tomatoes and simmer until heated through, about 2 minutes. Remove from the heat. Add the lime juice. Taste, then season with salt and freshly ground black pepper. Divide among 4 bowls and top evenly with the yogurt and cilantro.

NUTRITION (per serving: 1¼ cups) 428 calories, 23 g protein, 60 g carbs, 11 g fat, 6 g saturated fat, 344 mg sodium

Fi	56% (14 mg) daily fiber
Vc	47% (28 mg) daily vitamin C
K	31% (1,074 mg) daily potassium
Fe	28% (5 mg) daily iron
Cr	2 servings carotenoid-rich foods (carrots and tomatoes)

Swiss Chard and White Bean Soup

Swiss chard cooks a lot faster than other hearty greens like kale and collards, making this the perfect weeknight soup. The olive topping is similar to tapenade but takes just 2 minutes to make and doesn't require a food processor, which means less cleanup.

PREP TIME: 20 MINUTES / **TOTAL TIME:** 35 MINUTES / **SERVINGS:** 6

2 pounds Swiss chard (about 2 bunches)

1 tablespoon olive oil

1 medium onion, chopped (about 1 cup)

3 cloves garlic, chopped

¼ teaspoon red-pepper flakes

2 cans (14 ounces each) basil, garlic, and oregano-flavored diced tomatoes

2 cans (15 ounces) cannellini beans, drained and rinsed

12 green olives, finely chopped

Zest of 2 lemons (about 4 teaspoons)

¼ cup finely chopped fresh parsley

1½ ounces Parmesan, grated (about ⅓ cup)

1 **TRIM** and discard the thick stem ends from the Swiss chard, but reserve any thin stems (⅓" wide or less) and cut into 1½" lengths. Chop the chard leaves.

2 **HEAT** the oil in a large pot or Dutch oven on medium. Add the onion and cook until tender and lightly browned, 6 to 7 minutes. Add the garlic and pepper flakes and cook 1 minute. Add the tomatoes and 4 cups water. Cover and bring to a boil on high.

3 **ADD** the chard stems to the pot, reduce the heat to medium, and simmer, covered, until the stems are partially tender, about 1 minute. Add the chard leaves and simmer, covered, until the leaves and stems are tender, 3 to 5 minutes. Stir in the beans and heat through, about 1 minute. Remove from the heat.

4 **COMBINE** the olives, zest, parsley, and Parmesan in a small bowl. Divide the soup among 6 bowls and top with the olive mixture.

NUTRITION (per serving: about 1¼ cups) 220 calories, 11 g protein, 32 g carbs, 7 g fat, 1 g saturated fat, 673 mg sodium

Vc 80% (48 mg) daily vitamin C	Mg 35% (140 mg) daily magnesium
Fi 36% (9 g) daily fiber	K 27% (929 mg) daily potassium

Cr 2½ servings carotenoid-rich foods (Swiss chard and tomatoes)

Lemony Chicken, Spinach, and Orzo Soup

Tempering the egg yolks with a small amount of hot soup before adding them to the pot keeps them from cooking too quickly and scrambling. If this does happen, the soup will still taste great—it just won't have the rich, creamy mouthfeel we're after.

PREP TIME: 15 MINUTES **/ TOTAL TIME:** 50 MINUTES **/ SERVINGS:** 4

1 tablespoon olive oil

½ medium onion, chopped (about ½ cup)

1 large carrot, chopped (about ½ cup)

1 large rib celery, chopped (about ½ cup)

2 cloves garlic, chopped

¼ teaspoon red-pepper flakes

4 cups reduced-sodium chicken broth

12 ounces boneless, skinless chicken breast halves

¾ cup orzo

Juice of 2 lemons (about 6 tablespoons)

2 large egg yolks

5 cups baby spinach leaves (5 ounces)

1 **HEAT** the oil in a large pot or Dutch oven over medium heat. Add the onion, carrot, and celery and cook until lightly browned, about 8 minutes. Season with salt and freshly ground black pepper. Add the garlic and pepper flakes and cook 1 minute. Add the broth and 1 cup water, raise the heat to high, cover, and bring to a boil.

2 **ADD** the chicken, reduce the heat to medium low, and simmer, covered, until the chicken is no longer pink in the thickest part, 12 to 14 minutes. Transfer the chicken to a cutting board and let it rest until it's cool enough to handle. Shred or chop the chicken into bite-size pieces. Set aside. Add the orzo to the pot and simmer, covered, until al dente according to package directions. Reduce the heat to low.

3 **WHISK** the lemon juice and egg yolks together in a medium bowl. Scoop about ½ cup of the broth out of the pot and slowly drizzle into the lemon mixture, whisking constantly. Immediately add to the soup, pouring in a slow, steady stream as you whisk. Raise the heat to medium low, add the spinach and shredded chicken, and simmer until the spinach is just wilted and the soup is heated through, 1 to 2 minutes. Ladle into 4 bowls and serve.

NUTRITION (per serving: 1¾ cups) 365 calories, 32 g protein, 40 g carbs, 9 g fat, 2 g saturated fat, 585 mg sodium

| Fo | 42% (166 mcg) daily folate | K | 29% (1,015 mg) daily potassium | Cr | 1 serving carotenoid-rich foods (spinach and carrots) |
| Vc | 40% (24 mg) daily vitamin C |

Baked Oysters with Leeks and Buttery Bread Crumbs

Sautéed leeks and tarragon create a licorice-like flavor and add a fresh, herbaceous taste to briny oysters. Since the bivalves are fully cooked, this light appetizer is ideal for anyone worried about eating raw shellfish.

PREP TIME: 30 MINUTES (IF YOU SHUCK THE OYSTERS YOURSELF) **/ TOTAL TIME:** 50 MINUTES **/ SERVINGS:** 4

2 cups kosher salt

20 fresh shucked oysters (on the half shell)

2 leeks, white and light green parts

1 tablespoon plus 2 teaspoons unsalted butter

3 cloves garlic, finely chopped

½ cup whole wheat panko

¼ cup chopped fresh tarragon

Lemon wedges

1 **HEAT** the oven to 400°F. Spread the salt over the bottom of a 9" × 13" baking dish. Nestle the oyster shells into the salt so they sit upright.

2 **QUARTER** the leeks lengthwise and thinly slice. Wash well in a bowl of cold water and let stand. Lift leeks out of the water with a slotted spoon and transfer to a colander to drain.

3 **HEAT** the butter in a medium skillet on medium heat. Add the leeks and cook, stirring frequently, until soft, about 4 minutes. Add the garlic and panko and stir to combine. Cook, stirring occasionally, until the panko is lightly toasted, 2 to 3 minutes. Season to taste with salt and freshly ground black pepper. Transfer to a small bowl and stir in the tarragon.

4 **SPRINKLE** the panko mixture evenly over the oysters. Bake until the topping is browned and the edges of the oysters curl slightly (the oysters should still feel slightly soft to the touch, not firm), 8 to 9 minutes. Rest 5 minutes and serve with the lemon wedges.

NUTRITION (per serving: 5 oysters) 160 calories, 8 g protein, 18 g carbs, 7 g fat, 4 g saturated fat, 170 mg sodium

O3 49% (490 mg) daily omega-3s   Fe 33% (6 mg) daily iron

Baked Potato Skins with Bacon and Cheddar

Peeling potatoes is tedious, but what's worse is that you're throwing away a wealth of nutrients. This recipe lets you enjoy both parts of the tuber, and baking the skins to a crisp instead of deep frying makes this favorite restaurant appetizer guilt-free.

PREP TIME: 15 MINUTES / **TOTAL TIME:** 2 HOURS 10 MINUTES / **SERVINGS:** 4

4 large Russet potatoes (about 12 ounces each)

2 teaspoons olive oil

6 slices lower-sodium bacon

3 ounces low-fat Cheddar, grated (about ¾ cup)

½ cup reduced-fat (light) sour cream

6 scallions, white and light green parts, sliced (about ⅓ cup)

1 large tomato, seeded and chopped (about 1 cup)

1 **HEAT** the oven to 350°F and coat a baking sheet with cooking spray. Poke a few holes in the potatoes with a fork, then rub the oil evenly over the potatoes. Place on the baking sheet and sprinkle evenly with ¼ teaspoon salt. Bake the potatoes, turning about halfway through, until they feel tender when squeezed gently, about 1 hour 15 minutes. Raise the oven temperature to 450°F.

2 **HALVE** the potatoes lengthwise when they're cool enough to handle. Scoop out the flesh (save it for another use), leaving about ⅓" still attached to the skin. Mist the flesh side of the potatoes with cooking spray and season with ¼ teaspoon salt and freshly ground black pepper. Coat the baking sheet with cooking spray and place the potatoes on it flesh side down. Return to the oven and bake 8 minutes. Turn the potatoes and bake until the edges are golden brown and crisp, about 8 minutes longer.

3 **HEAT** a large skillet on medium heat while the potatoes bake and coat with cooking spray. Add the bacon and cook, turning halfway through, until browned and crisp, about 8 minutes. Transfer to a paper towel–lined plate and press lightly with another layer of paper towel. Crumble when cool enough to handle.

4 **DIVIDE** the cheese and bacon evenly among the potato skins. Return to the oven until the cheese is melted, about 1 minute. Top the potato skins evenly with the sour cream (about 1 tablespoon per half), scallions, and tomato and serve.

NUTRITION (per serving: 2 halves) 298 calories, 14 g protein, 35 g carb, 11 g fat, 5 g saturated fat, 541 mg sodium

Vc 43% (26 mg) daily vitamin C   K 26% (923 mg) daily potassium

Brussels Sprout Poppers with Orange–Poppy Seed Dipping Sauce

Already bite-size, Brussels sprouts were tailor-made for easy party fare like this. Roasting creates an addictive caramelized flavor, and wooden picks are the only utensils you'll need for serving these healthy appetizers.

PREP TIME: 15 MINUTES / **TOTAL TIME:** 50 MINUTES / **SERVINGS:** 6

2 pounds Brussels sprouts, washed and thoroughly dried

1 tablespoon canola oil

½ cup low-fat plain Greek yogurt

¼ cup fresh orange juice

1 tablespoon honey

1 tablespoon poppy seeds

1 teaspoon orange zest

1 **HEAT** the oven to 400°F. Trim the Brussels sprout stems, leaving the sprouts intact, and discard any damaged outer leaves. Place on a baking sheet and toss with the oil, ½ teaspoon salt, and freshly ground black pepper. Roast in the lower third of the oven, turning once or twice, until deep golden brown, 32 to 36 minutes.

2 **WHISK** together the yogurt, orange juice, honey, poppy seeds, and zest in a small bowl. Serve with the Brussels sprouts and provide wooden picks for dipping.

NUTRITION *(per serving: about 7 sprouts)* 110 calories, 6 g protein, 17 g carbs, 4 g fat, 0 g saturated fat, 199 mg sodium

Vc **202% (121 mg) daily vitamin C**

 1½ servings carotenoid-rich food (Brussels sprouts)

Crab Cocktail with Mango

Canned crabmeat works well in this recipe and makes for quick assembly. Drain excess liquid in a fine mesh sieve and pick over to remove any small bits of shell.

PREP TIME: 15 MINUTES / **TOTAL TIME:** 15 MINUTES / **SERVINGS:** 4

8 ounces crabmeat (about 1½ cups)

2 medium mangoes, halved, pitted, peeled, and chopped (about 2 cups)

1 avocado, halved, pitted, peeled, and chopped (about 1 cup)

⅓ cup chopped cilantro

Juice of 2 limes (about ¼ cup)

1½ teaspoons prepared horseradish

COMBINE the crabmeat, mangoes, avocado, cilantro, lime juice, and horseradish in a large bowl. Divide among 4 small bowls or appetizer plates and serve.

NUTRITION *(per serving: about 1 cup)* 134 calories, 13 g protein, 7 g carbs, 7 g fat, 1 g saturated fat, 169 mg sodium

B₁₂ 67% (4 mcg) daily vitamin B₁₂   O₃ 35% (350 mg) daily omega-3s   Fo 31% (123 mcg) daily folate

Pumpkin Seed Dip

Serve this easy-to-make appetizer with a colorful plate of cut veggies (carrots, jicama, broccoli, cauliflower, bell peppers, endive leaves, summer squash, and cherry tomatoes are all good choices). It also makes a great spread for sandwiches and wraps.

PREP TIME: 10 MINUTES **/ TOTAL TIME:** 15 MINUTES **/ SERVINGS:** 8

1¼ cups hulled pumpkin seeds, toasted

¾ cup frozen peas, thawed

½ cup low-fat plain Greek yogurt

½ cup fresh flat-leaf parsley (leaves and thin stems)

6 scallions, white and light green parts, chopped (about ⅓ cup)

2 fresh jalapeños, seeded and chopped

Juice of 2 lemons (about 6 tablespoons)

½ teaspoon smoked paprika

½ teaspoon garlic powder

COMBINE all of the ingredients in a food processor. Process until a slightly chunky puree forms, scraping down the sides of the bowl as needed. Season to taste with salt and freshly ground black pepper.

NUTRITION *(per serving: ¼ cup)* 133 calories, 8 g protein, 7 g carbs, 9 g fat, 2 g saturated fat, 25 mg sodium

Mg **27% (109 mg) daily magnesium**   Vc **25% (15 mg) daily vitamin C**

Salmon Cakes with Dill Yogurt

From an environmental and nutritional standpoint, wild-caught salmon is preferred over farm-raised. But that doesn't always mean spending a lot on fresh Alaskan fillets—all salmon sold in cans and pouches is the wild-caught "pink" variety.

PREP TIME: 20 MINUTES / **TOTAL TIME:** 45 MINUTES + CHILLING TIME / **SERVINGS:** 5

2 pouches (6 ounces each) salmon, drained well

⅔ cup whole wheat panko

4 scallions, thinly sliced (about ⅓ cup)

1 tablespoon capers, rinsed and drained

1 tablespoon Dijon mustard

1½ teaspoons hot sauce

4 tablespoons chopped fresh dill

1 large egg

1 large egg white

⅓ cup all-purpose flour

2 tablespoons canola oil

1 cup low-fat plain Greek yogurt

1 **COMBINE** the salmon, panko, scallions, capers, mustard, hot sauce, and 2 tablespoons of the dill in a large bowl. Season to taste with salt and freshly ground black pepper. Add the egg and egg white and stir to combine. Form 2-tablespoon-size scoops of salmon mixture into 16 patties, about 1½" wide and ½" thick. Transfer to a large plate.

2 **ADD** the flour to a wide, shallow bowl. Coat the patties one at a time in the flour, shaking off the excess. Return to the plate, cover, and refrigerate 30 minutes or up to 4 hours.

3 **HEAT** 1 tablespoon of the oil in a large skillet on medium-low heat. Add 8 patties and cook, turning about halfway through, until deep golden brown, 11 to 13 minutes. Transfer to a plate and cover with foil to keep warm. Repeat with the remaining oil and patties.

4 **COMBINE** the yogurt and the remaining 2 tablespoons dill in a small bowl. Serve with the patties.

NUTRITION (per serving: 3 salmon cakes and 3 tablespoons yogurt) 240 calories, 21 g protein, 17 g carbs, 9 g fat, 2 g saturated fat, 547 mg sodium

O3 **116% (1,160 mg) daily omega-3s**

Turkey-Feta Meatballs with Roasted Red Pepper Dipping Sauce

The tahini, sesame seeds, and feta cheese in these cocktail meatballs add moisture and flavor to lean ground turkey as well as a sizable amount of protein. Sumac, used to season the yogurt dip, is a deep red spice with a slightly sour tang common in Middle Eastern dishes.

PREP TIME: 25 MINUTES **/ TOTAL TIME:** 55 MINUTES **/ SERVINGS:** 8

2 tablespoons sesame seeds, toasted

1 tablespoon dried thyme

1 tablespoon dried oregano

1¼ pounds ground turkey breast (92%-93% lean)

7 ounces reduced-fat feta cheese, crumbled (about 1¾ cups)

8 tablespoons tahini

¼ cup finely chopped onion

¼ cup chopped fresh flat-leaf parsley

2 cups fat-free plain yogurt

2 cups drained roasted red bell peppers from a jar

Juice of 2 lemons (about 6 tablespoons)

2 cloves garlic, finely chopped

2 teaspoons ground sumac

1 **HEAT** the oven to 400°F and coat a baking sheet with cooking spray. Combine the sesame seeds, thyme, and oregano in a small bowl.

2 **COMBINE** the turkey, 1¼ cups of the feta, 5 tablespoons of the tahini, the onion, the parsley, and 2½ tablespoons of the sesame seed mixture in a large bowl. Season with freshly ground black pepper. Form into 40 (1¼") balls and place on the prepared baking sheet. Bake until the outsides are golden brown and the centers are no longer pink, 15 to 18 minutes. Cool 5 minutes, transfer to a serving plate.

3 **COMBINE** the yogurt, bell peppers, lemon juice, garlic, and the remaining ½ cup of feta and 3 tablespoons tahini in a blender and puree until smooth. Transfer to a serving bowl. Stir the sumac into the remaining 1½ tablespoons sesame seed mixture and sprinkle over the yogurt mixture. Serve with the meatballs.

NUTRITION (per serving: 5 meatballs, ⅔ cup yogurt) 307 calories, 24 g protein, 14 g carbs, 18 g fat, 5 g saturated fat, 503 mg sodium

Vc 60% (36 mg) daily vitamin C   Ca 29% (288 mg) daily calcium

Yogurt-Marinated Chicken Skewers with Cucumber-Yogurt Sauce

Yogurt is ideal for marinating because it breaks down proteins without making the meat mushy or tough. Here we also use it to make a sauce modeled on Indian raita, or spiced yogurt, which is often used as a cooling counterpoint to fiery dishes.

PREP TIME: 25 MINUTES **/ TOTAL TIME:** 1 HOUR + MARINATING TIME **/ SERVINGS:** 6

1¼ pounds boneless, skinless chicken breasts

5 scallions, white and light and green parts, sliced (about ⅓ cup)

1 fresh jalapeño, seeded and chopped

2 cloves garlic, chopped

1 teaspoon ground cumin

1 teaspoon turmeric

½ teaspoon ground coriander

½ teaspoon ground ginger

3¾ cups fat-free plain yogurt

1 large cucumber, peeled, halved lengthwise, and seeded

½ cup chopped fresh dill

Juice of 2 lemons (6 tablespoons)

1 **CUT** the chicken into slices, about ⅓" thick and 3" long. Place in a large zip-top bag. Combine the scallions, jalapeño, garlic, cumin, turmeric, coriander, ginger, and ¾ cup yogurt in the bowl of a food processor. Process until a chunky puree forms, scraping down the sides of the bowl as needed. Add to the bag with the chicken and seal the bag. Massage the bag a few times to thoroughly coat the chicken with the marinade. Refrigerate 2 to 4 hours.

2 **GRATE** the cucumber in a food processor or on the large holes of a box grater. Squeeze between several layers of paper towel to remove excess water. Transfer to a large bowl. Add the dill, lemon juice, ½ teaspoon salt, and remaining 3 cups yogurt. Stir to combine. Cover and refrigerate until ready to serve.

A Very Versatile Sauce

While shredded cucumber is one of the most common ingredients in raita, this cooling sauce can actually be made with just about any vegetable or fruit. Indian cooks might use pineapples, onions, tomatoes, or coconut along with herbs and spices. For a twist on these chicken skewers and a pretty burst of color, try a version made with beets. Replace the cucumber, dill, and lemon juice with 1 large peeled and grated beet, 6 tablespoons orange juice, and ¾ teaspoon ground coriander. Season with ½ teaspoon salt and chill. Raita is even better when the flavors have time to blend, so make this a few hours in advance.

3 HEAT the broiler to high and coat a slotted broiler pan with cooking spray (you can also use an ovenproof wire rack on top of a rimmed baking sheet). Shake the excess marinade off the chicken and thread onto skewers. Place on the prepared pan. Season with ½ teaspoon salt and freshly ground black pepper. Broil 6" to 8" from the heat until the top of the chicken is lightly browned and no longer appears wet, 5 to 7 minutes. Turn the skewers and broil until the opposite sides are lightly browned and the chicken is no longer pink in the center, 2 to 3 minutes. Serve with the yogurt-cucumber sauce.

NUTRITION *(per serving: 2 skewers and ½ cup yogurt sauce)* 199 calories, 28 g protein, 14 g carbs, 3 g fat, <1 g saturated fat, 535 mg sodium
Ca **29% (288 mg) daily calcium**

6 DINNER

Baked Penne with Creamy Swiss Cheese Sauce, Mushrooms, and Asparagus

This dish has the creaminess of traditional mac 'n' cheese, but far less calories and fat. That's because the sauce is thickened by combining fat-free milk with a small amount of flour, not by adding a pound (and sometimes more) of melted cheese.

PREP TIME: 20 MINUTES **/ TOTAL TIME:** 1 HOUR 40 MINUTES **/ SERVINGS:** 8

1 pound whole wheat penne

1 pound asparagus spears, tough ends trimmed, cut into 1½" pieces

10 teaspoons olive oil

8 ounces white mushrooms, thinly sliced

5 ounces shiitake mushrooms, thinly sliced

¼ teaspoon dried thyme

2 cloves garlic, finely chopped

1 medium onion, halved lengthwise and sliced (about 1 cup)

⅓ cup all-purpose flour

5 cups fat-free milk

1½ cups grated reduced-fat Swiss or Gruyere cheese (about 5 ounces)

¼ cup chopped fresh mint, basil, or chives

1 **BRING** a large pot of water to a boil on high heat. Add the penne and cook until not quite al dente according to package directions (penne will finish cooking in the oven). Transfer the penne to a colander using a metal strainer or large slotted spoon, reserving the cooking water in the pot. Return the pot to high heat and bring the pasta water to a boil. Add the asparagus and cook until crisp-tender, 2 to 3 minutes. Drain by pouring the asparagus and cooking water into the colander with the pasta.

2 **HEAT** the oven to 350°F and spray a 9" × 13" baking dish with cooking spray.

3 **HEAT** 2 teaspoons of the oil in a large skillet on medium-high heat. Add the mushrooms and thyme and cook until the liquid released by the mushrooms evaporates, 4 to 5 minutes. Reduce the heat to medium-low and cook until tender and lightly browned, about 2 minutes. Add the garlic and cook, stirring constantly, 1 minute. Transfer to a bowl and set aside.

4 **HEAT** 2 teaspoons of the oil in the same skillet, still on medium-low heat. Add the onion and cook, stirring occasionally until very tender and lightly browned, about 20 minutes. Season to taste with salt and freshly ground black pepper and set aside.

Pick the Perfect Pasta

With the variety of pasta shapes to choose from, a little pasta- and sauce-pairing know-how can take a bowl of noodles from homey to restaurant worthy. Smooth, creamy sauces like this one need textured types like penne rigate to cling to. To get the flavor of chunky vegetable and bean-filled sauces in every bite, look for pastas with crevices, such as shells, fusilli, and rigatoni. Oil-based pestos are ideal for coating long, thin spaghetti while hefty ragus are often matched up with thicker fettucine and tagliatelle, as well as sturdier shapes like farfalle and cavatappi (corkscrews). Tomato sauce, however, goes with anything!

5 **DRY** the inside of the pot you used to cook the pasta. Heat the remaining 6 teaspoons oil in the pot on medium heat. Add the flour and cook, stirring constantly, until lightly toasted, about 2 minutes. Whisk in the milk in a slow, steady stream. Raise the heat to high and, whisking constantly to prevent a skin from forming, bring the milk to a simmer. Reduce the heat to medium low and simmer, whisking constantly, until slightly thickened, 3 to 4 minutes. Reduce the heat to low and whisk in 1 cup of the cheese until melted. Remove from the heat.

6 **ADD** the pasta, asparagus, mushrooms, and mint to the milk mixture. Stir well to combine. Season to taste with salt and freshly ground black pepper. Transfer to the prepared baking dish. Add the onions and the remaining ¼ cup cheese to a small bowl and stir to combine. Spread evenly over the pasta mixture. Cover with foil and bake 20 minutes. Remove the foil and continue baking until the cheese is melted and the milk mixture is bubbling around the edges, 5 to 10 minutes. Rest 10 minutes and serve.

NUTRITION (per serving: 1¾ cups) 415 calories, 20 g protein, 59 g carbs, 12 g fat, 4 g saturated fat, 101 mg sodium

Ca 38% (381 mg) daily calcium   Fi 28% (7 g) daily fiber

Pearled Barley Risotto with Peas, Pancetta, and Sun-Dried Tomatoes

Sometimes referred to as "Italian bacon," pancetta is not smoked but rather cured in spices. Look for it in Italian markets and butcher shops, or presliced near the deli meats in large supermarkets. If you can't find it, substitute an equal amount of regular bacon.

PREP TIME: 10 MINUTES / **TOTAL TIME:** 1 HOUR / **SERVINGS:** 4

4 cups low-sodium chicken or vegetable broth

1 slice (⅓" thick) pancetta (about 1½ ounces), diced

1 teaspoon olive oil

2 large shallots, chopped (about ½ cup)

3 cloves garlic, chopped

1⅓ cups pearled barley

1¼ cups frozen peas

½ cup chopped sun-dried tomatoes (not oil packed)

1 ounce Parmesan, shaved

1 **HEAT** the broth and 2½ cups water in a medium saucepan on medium-high heat until the liquid is steaming (do not boil). Reduce the heat to medium low to keep warm. Heat a large pot or Dutch oven on medium-low heat. Add the pancetta and cook, stirring frequently, until lightly browned and crisp, 6 to 8 minutes. Transfer to a paper towel–lined plate with a slotted spoon.

2 **ADD** as much of the olive oil as needed to the rendered fat in the pot to equal approximately 2 teaspoons. Add the shallots and cook on medium low until soft, 2 to 3 minutes. Add the garlic and barley and cook, stirring frequently, until the barley is slightly toasted and fragrant, about 2 minutes. Add 1 cup of the broth mixture and simmer, stirring occasionally, until the liquid is nearly absorbed, 7 to 8 minutes. Repeat with the remaining broth, adding 1 cup at a time and simmering until nearly absorbed, until the barley is tender, about 35 minutes total. (You will use between 5½ and 6½ cups broth mixture, so you may have some leftover.)

3 **STIR** in the peas and tomatoes and cook until heated through, about 2 minutes. Stir in the pancetta. Season to taste with salt and freshly ground black pepper. Divide among 4 bowls and top with the Parmesan.

NUTRITION (per serving: about 1 ⅓ cups) 398 calories, 19 g protein, 66 g carbs, 7 g fat, 2 g saturated fat, 966 mg sodium

Fi 52% (13 g) daily fiber

Stuffed Shells with Chunky Tomato Sauce

Paired with salad and a whole grain baguette, these stuffed shells make a hearty meatless meal. The homemade chunky tomato sauce is quick and easy, and so versatile that you could also use it as a topping for grilled fish or a simple bowl of spaghetti.

PREP TIME: 20 MINUTES / **TOTAL TIME:** 1 HOUR 20 MINUTES / **SERVINGS:** 6

12 ounces large shell pasta

1 tablespoon olive oil

½ medium onion, chopped (about ½ cup)

3 cloves garlic, chopped

½ teaspoon dried oregano

¼ teaspoon red-pepper flakes

2 cans (14.5 ounces each) no-salt-added diced tomatoes

2 tablespoons balsamic vinegar

2 teaspoons sugar

1½ cups part-skim ricotta cheese

1½ cups frozen peas, thawed and patted dry

1 ounce Parmesan, grated (about ¼ cup)

1 large egg white

¼ cup plus 1 tablespoon chopped fresh mint

2 ounces part-skim mozzarella cheese, grated (about ½ cup)

1 **BRING** a large pot of water to a boil and cook the pasta according to package directions to just short of al dente (pasta will continue cooking in the oven).

2 **HEAT** the oil in a large saucepan on medium heat. Add the onion and cook, stirring occasionally, until tender and lightly browned, about 5 minutes. Add the garlic, oregano, and pepper flakes and cook 1 minute. Add the tomatoes and bring to a simmer. Reduce the heat to medium low and simmer, stirring occasionally, until about three-quarters of the liquid evaporates, about 10 minutes. Add the vinegar and sugar and simmer, about 1 minute. Season to taste with salt and freshly ground black pepper.

3 **HEAT** the oven to 350°F. Combine the ricotta, peas, Parmesan, and egg white in a large bowl. Stir in ¼ cup of the mint and season to taste with freshly ground black pepper.

4 **SPREAD** about ¾ cup of the sauce in a 9" × 13" baking dish. Stuff 24 pasta shells with about 1 rounded tablespoon of the ricotta mixture each. Place in the baking dish. Top with the remaining sauce and mozzarella. Cover with foil and bake 25 minutes. Remove the foil and continue baking until the cheese is melted, about 5 minutes. Rest 5 minutes and sprinkle with the remaining 1 tablespoon of mint.

NUTRITION *(per serving: 4 shells)* 371 calories, 20 g protein, 47 g carbs, 12 g fat, 6 g saturated fat, 312 mg sodium

Vc 43% (26 mg) daily vitamin C   Ca 41% (409 mg) daily calcium   Cr 1 serving carotenoid-rich food (tomatoes)

Spinach Gnudi with Quick Chunky Tomato Sauce

Frozen spinach is a nutritious staple to keep on hand. You can add it to omelets, pizzas, meat loaf, and more. Unless you are adding it to soup, though, be sure to squeeze it dry using the method we describe below. Otherwise your dish will be watery.

PREP TIME: 35 MINUTES / **TOTAL TIME:** 45 MINUTES / **SERVINGS:** 4

8 tablespoons all-purpose flour

⅛ teaspoon nutmeg

1 package (10 ounces) frozen chopped spinach, thawed

½ cup part-skim ricotta cheese

2 ounces Parmesan cheese, grated (about ½ cup)

2 large eggs

2 teaspoons olive oil

¼ medium onion, chopped (about ¼ cup)

2 cloves garlic, chopped

¼ teaspoon dried oregano

⅛ teaspoon red-pepper flakes

1 can (14 ounces) no-salt-added diced tomatoes

1 tablespoon balsamic vinegar

3 cups fresh baby spinach leaves (about 3 ounces)

2 tablespoons chopped fresh basil

1 **WHISK** together 5 tablespoons of the flour, the nutmeg, and ⅛ teaspoon freshly ground black pepper in a small bowl.

2 **WRAP** the spinach tightly in a clean kitchen towel, squeeze hard to remove excess moisture, and finely chop. Mix with the ricotta, Parmesan, eggs, and flour mixture in a medium bowl until well combined. Put the remaining 3 tablespoons of flour in a shallow bowl. With wet hands, form the spinach mixture into 24 to 28 round dumplings (about ¾ to 1 inch in diameter). Roll in the flour to coat and arrange on a platter in a single layer. Refrigerate until ready to cook.

3 **HEAT** the oil in a large skillet on medium heat. Add the onion and cook, stirring occasionally, until tender and lightly browned, about 5 minutes. Add the garlic, oregano, and pepper flakes and cook 1 minute. Add the tomatoes and bring to a simmer. Reduce the heat to medium low and simmer, stirring occasionally, until the liquid evaporates by about three-quarters, about 10 minutes.

Ravioli without the Wrappers

Gnudi (pronounced nu-dee) is derived from the Italian word for naked. You get all the cheesy goodness of ravioli without the carbs or calories from the pasta. They'd be ideal for people on a gluten-free diet, except they need flour to bind the cheese so the dumplings hold their shape. Solution? Try using chickpea flour instead of the all-purpose flour called for here.

Add the vinegar and simmer about 1 minute. Add the fresh spinach and cook until just wilted, about 2 minutes. Season to taste with salt and freshly ground black pepper.

4 **BRING** a large pot of water to a boil. Add the dumplings in batches to the pot and cook at a good simmer, about 7 minutes. Transfer with a slotted spoon to a bowl and keep warm.

5 **DIVIDE** the gnudi and sauce among 4 bowls. Sprinkle with basil and Parmesan, if desired.

NUTRITION *(per serving: 6 or 7 gnudi and ½ cup sauce)* 265 calories, 17 g protein, 25 g carbs, 11 g fat, 5 g saturated fat, 489 mg sodium

Vc **42% (25 mg) daily vitamin C**

Ca **34% (340 mg) daily calcium**

Fo **32% (126 mcg) daily folate**

Cr **2 servings carotenoid-rich foods (spinach and tomatoes)**

Swiss Chard, Eggplant, and Mushroom Lasagna

This recipe calls for a lot of vegetables since they lose volume when cooked. To break up the cooking time, you can prep and cook the eggplant, Swiss chard, and mushrooms (steps 1 through 3) in advance. Cover and refrigerate up to 1 day.

PREP TIME: 30 MINUTES **/ TOTAL TIME:** 1 HOUR 55 MINUTES + RESTING TIME **/ SERVES:** 10

3 medium eggplant, trimmed (3 pounds)

3½ pounds Swiss chard, thick stems trimmed, chopped

12 ounces mushrooms, chopped (about 3 cups)

3 cloves garlic, chopped

¼ teaspoon red-pepper flakes

3 cups part-skim ricotta, drained

1 large egg

2 large egg whites

4 cups prepared reduced-sodium marinara sauce

1 package (9 ounces) no-boil lasagna noodles, preferably whole wheat

1½ cups grated part-skim mozzarella cheese (about 6 ounces)

¼ cup grated Parmesan (about 1 ounce)

1 **HEAT** the broiler. Slice the eggplant lengthwise, ⅓" thick. Coat the slices on both sides with cooking spray and season with salt and freshly ground black pepper. Arrange in a single layer on a baking sheet, working in two batches, and broil 6" from the heat until browned, 4 to 5 minutes. Flip and broil until the opposite sides are browned and the flesh is very tender, 2 to 3 minutes.

2 **FILL** a large pot with about ½" of water and place a steamer basket inside. Bring the water to a boil over high heat and add the Swiss chard, working in two batches. Reduce the heat to medium low, cover, and simmer until tender, 4 to 6 minutes. Transfer to a colander and drain thoroughly. When cool enough to handle, squeeze the chard tightly with your hands to extract as much water as possible and blot the chard dry with a clean kitchen towel.

3 **HEAT** the oven to 400°F. Coat a large skillet with cooking spray and heat over medium-high heat. Add the mushrooms and cook, stirring occasionally, until lightly browned and liquid has evaporated, 6 minutes. Reduce the heat to medium low, add the garlic and pepper flakes, and cook 1 minute. Add the Swiss chard and cook until heated through and any liquid has evaporated, 3 minutes. Season to taste with salt and freshly ground black pepper.

(continued)

A Note on Sodium

Even when your diet is made up of fresh unprocessed foods, sticking to the daily recommendation of 2,300 milligrams or less of sodium can be a challenge. That's because sodium is in nutrient-dense whole foods like cheese, canned or jarred tomato products, canned beans, bread, and deli meats—even if you choose low-sodium versions. A few of our recipes, like this lasagna, come in on the high side; when you eat one of these, just make sure to watch your sodium intake the rest of the day. You can cut some of the sodium out of this dish by replacing the store-bought marinara with a double batch of the sauce featured in Baked Chicken Parmesan with Homemade Tomato Sauce (page 155).

4 **COMBINE** the ricotta, egg, and egg whites in a large bowl and season with freshly ground black pepper.

5 **SPREAD** 1 cup of the marinara sauce over the bottom of a deep-dish, 9" × 13" baking dish. Add 4 noodles and cover with half of the ricotta, then half of the eggplant, then half of the Swiss chard-mushroom mixture, then ½ cup of the mozzarella, and then 1 cup of the sauce. Repeat the layers again, starting with the noodles and ending with 1 cup sauce. Top with a third layer of noodles (you may have some leftover), the remaining 1 cup sauce, and ½ cup mozzarella. Top with the Parmesan.

6 **COVER** with foil and bake 35 minutes. Remove the foil and continue baking until the sauce is bubbly and the cheese is lightly browned, 15 minutes longer. Rest 30 minutes, slice into 10 pieces, and serve.

NUTRITION *(per serving)* 401 calories, 26 g protein, 44 g carbs, 16 g fat, 7 g saturated fat, 791 mg sodium

 87% (52 mg) daily vitamin C

Fi 48% (12 g) daily fiber

Ca 47% (466 mg) daily calcium

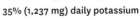 39% (155 mg) daily magnesium

K 35% (1,237 mg) daily potassium

Cr 5 servings carotenoid-rich foods (Swiss chard, marinara sauce)

An 2 servings anthocyanin-rich food (eggplant)

Fettuccine with Lentil Bolognese

This vegetarian Bolognese has the same rich flavor and hearty texture as the classic meat-based sauce, but far less saturated fat. Bolognese is usually finished with a bit of dairy to pull the flavors of the sauce together, but if you prefer a vegan dish you can easily skip the milk and Parmesan and still have a delicious meal.

PREP TIME: 25 MINUTES / **TOTAL TIME:** 1 HOUR 15 MINUTES / **SERVINGS:** 6

1 leek, white and light green parts

1 tablespoon olive oil

2 medium carrots, diced (about 1 cup)

1 rib celery, diced (about ½ cup)

3 cloves garlic, chopped

¼ teaspoon dried thyme

¼ teaspoon dried marjoram or oregano

¼ teaspoon red-pepper flakes

1 can (28 ounces) whole peeled tomatoes

1 can (14 ounces) no-salt-added tomato sauce

1 cup brown lentils, rinsed and picked over

¾ cup 2% milk

16 ounces white mushrooms, diced (about 2 cups)

1 tablespoon balsamic vinegar

12 ounces whole wheat fettuccine

1 ounce Parmesan, grated (about ¼ cup)

3 tablespoons chopped fresh flat-leaf parsley

1 **TRIM** the leek, halve it lengthwise, and slice it thinly. Wash well in a bowl of cold water and let stand. Lift the leek out of the water with a slotted spoon and transfer to a colander to drain.

2 **HEAT** the oil in a Dutch oven or large saucepan with a lid on medium heat. Add the leek, carrots, and celery and cook, stirring occasionally, until lightly browned and crisp-tender, 8 to 9 minutes. Add the garlic, thyme, marjoram, and pepper flakes and cook, stirring constantly, about 1 minute.

3 **DRAIN** the liquid from the whole tomatoes into the pan, then add the tomatoes, crushing and breaking them up with your hands as you add them. Add the tomato sauce and 3 cups water and stir to combine.

4 **ADD** the lentils, cover, and bring to a simmer. Reduce the heat to medium low and simmer, stirring occasionally, until the lentils are tender but still firm to the bite and the mixture reaches a thick but not dry consistency, 35 to 40 minutes. If the liquid evaporates before the lentils finish cooking, add more water, ¼ to ½ cup at a time. Uncover the pan and stir in the milk. Simmer, stirring constantly, until well combined and heated through, about 2 minutes.

Why We Love Lentils

These little discs come in all sorts of pretty colors—from green to yellow to red—and they cook faster than any other dried legume. No presoaking is necessary and they're done in 30 minutes or less, depending on type. Not only that, lentils are among the legumes highest in fiber and iron and the only one to provide a significant amount of folate.

5 **COAT** a large skillet with cooking spray and heat on medium-high heat while the lentils cook. Add the mushrooms and cook, stirring occasionally, until the liquid evaporates, 4 to 5 minutes. Reduce heat to medium low, add the vinegar, and cook until the mushrooms are tender and lightly browned, 3 to 5 minutes. Stir into the lentil mixture and remove from the heat. Season to taste with salt and freshly ground black pepper.

6 **BRING** a large pot of water to a boil over high heat. Cook the fettuccine to al dente according to package directions. Drain and divide among 6 bowls. Top evenly with the lentil mixture, Parmesan, and parsley and serve.

NUTRITION *(per serving: 1 cup fettuccine, ⅔ cup lentils)* 452 calories, 25 g protein, 74 g carbs, 6 g fat, 1 g saturated fat, 415 mg sodium

Fi 80% (20 g) daily fiber	K 28% (973 mg) daily potassium
Vc 63% (38 mg) daily vitamin C	Fe 28% (5 mg) daily iron
Fo 48% (193 mcg) daily folate	Cr 2 servings carotenoid-rich foods (carrots, tomatoes)

Linguine with Kale, Olives, and Currants

Sweet dried currants paired with salty olives is a delicious combination in this earthy pasta. Currants are widely available in large supermarkets and natural food stores (check the bulk bins), but if you can't find them, golden raisins, which are milder than the dark ones, are a good substitute.

PREP TIME: 15 MINUTES **/ TOTAL TIME:** 25 MINUTES **/ SERVINGS:** 4

8 ounces whole wheat linguine

2 teaspoons olive oil

2 cloves garlic, chopped

1¼ pounds Tuscan kale, thick ribs trimmed, chopped

12 pitted kalamata olives, chopped

¼ cup dried currants

Juice of ½ lemon (1 tablespoon plus 2 teaspoons)

3 tablespoons pine nuts, toasted

1½ ounces Parmesan, shaved with vegetable peeler (about ½ cup)

1 **BRING** a large pot of water to a boil on high heat. Add the linguine and cook to al dente according to package directions. Carefully scoop about ½ cup of the pasta cooking water out of the pot just before draining the linguine and set aside. Drain the linguine.

2 **HEAT** the oil in a large skillet on medium-low heat. Add the garlic and cook, stirring, about 1 minute. Add the kale and reserved pasta cooking water and bring to a simmer. Cook, stirring frequently, until the kale is tender and the liquid has nearly evaporated, 8 to 10 minutes. Stir in the olives, currants, and lemon juice and remove from the heat.

3 **RETURN** the drained linguine to the pot it was cooked in (off the heat). Add the kale mixture and pine nuts and toss to combine. Season to taste with salt and freshly ground black pepper. Divide among 4 bowls and top evenly with the Parmesan.

NUTRITION *(per serving: 1¾ cups)* 435 calories, 16 g protein, 68 g carbs, 13 g fat, 3 g saturated fat, 676 mg sodium

Vc 233% (140 mg) daily vitamin C   Ca 27% (270 mg) daily calcium   Cr 2 servings carotenoid-rich food (kale)

Fi 44% (11 g) daily fiber

Spaghetti with Sardines, Caramelized Fennel, and Buttery Garlic Bread Crumbs

If there is any recipe that will turn you into a sardine fan, it's this one. The combination of the fish, the sweet silky fennel, and the garlic bread crumbs will win over your taste buds—and the fact that sardines require virtually no preparation will make this dish a weeknight favorite.

PREP TIME: 10 MINUTES / **TOTAL TIME:** 50 MINUTES / **SERVINGS:** 4

1 tablespoon plus 1 teaspoon olive oil

3 fennel bulbs, trimmed, cored, and thinly sliced

2 teaspoons unsalted butter

3 cloves garlic, chopped

⅓ cup whole wheat panko

8 ounces whole wheat spaghetti

3 cans (3.75 ounces each) water-packed sardines, drained

Juice of 1 lemon (about 3 tablespoons)

2 tablespoons chopped fresh flat-leaf parsley

1 **HEAT** 1 tablespoon of the oil in a large skillet on medium-low heat. Add the fennel and cook, stirring occasionally, until tender and lightly browned, 20 to 25 minutes. If the fennel sticks to the skillet during cooking, add 3 to 4 tablespoons water to deglaze. Season to taste with salt and freshly ground black pepper.

2 **HEAT** the butter and the remaining 1 teaspoon olive oil in a small skillet on medium-low heat. When the butter is just melted, add the garlic and cook 30 seconds. Add the panko and cook, stirring frequently, until coated with butter and lightly toasted, 2 to 3 minutes. Season to taste with salt and freshly ground black pepper.

3 **BRING** a large pot of water to a boil over high heat. Cook the spaghetti to al dente according to package directions. Carefully scoop out about ½ cup of the pasta cooking water from the pot just before draining the spaghetti and set aside. Drain the spaghetti and return to the pot off the heat. Add the sardines, lemon juice, fennel, and panko. Toss well to combine. Add the reserved pasta water, about 2 tablespoons at a time, to moisten as desired (you will not use all the pasta water). Divide among 4 bowls and sprinkle with the parsley.

NUTRITION *(per serving: 2 cups)* 482 calories, 29 g protein, 42 g carbs, 13 g fiber, 16 g fat, 3 g saturated fat, 454 mg sodium

O3	104% (1,040 mg) daily omega-3s	Vc	50% (30 mg) daily vitamin C	Fe	33% (6 mg) daily iron
B12	100% (6 mcg) daily vitamin B12	Ca	38% (380 mg) daily calcium	K	33% (1,157 mg) daily potassium
Fi	52% (13 g) daily fiber	VD	34% (135 IU) daily vitamin D		

Stuffed Eggplant with Couscous, Roasted Red Peppers, and Goat Cheese

Whole wheat couscous cooks just as quickly as the white flour variety (it is a pasta, not a whole grain) and is easy to find in most supermarkets. After you've made this recipe as written, consider trying it with different veggies (sautéed mushrooms, onions, or zucchini), cheeses (feta or fresh mozzarella), and nuts.

PREP TIME: 15 MINUTES / **TOTAL TIME:** 1 HOUR 15 MINUTES / **SERVINGS:** 4

2 medium eggplant (about 1¼ pounds each), halved lengthwise

¾ cup whole wheat couscous

1 jar (16 ounces) roasted red bell peppers, drained and chopped (about 1¾ cups)

½ cup walnuts, toasted and chopped

1 teaspoon ground cumin

Juice of 1 lemon (about 3 tablespoons)

⅓ cup plus 2 tablespoons chopped fresh mint, parsley, or basil

2 ounces goat cheese, crumbled (about ½ cup)

1 **HEAT** the oven to 425°F. Coat a baking sheet with cooking spray. Place the eggplant on the baking sheet flesh side down. Roast until the flesh is browned and yields when pressed and the skin starts to wrinkle (do not roast until the skin collapses), 35 to 40 minutes. Reduce the oven temperature to 350°F.

2 **SCOOP** the flesh into a large bowl when the eggplant is cool enough to handle, leaving some flesh attached to the skin to maintain its shape. Place the shells back on the same baking sheet skin side down.

3 **BRING** 1 cup water to a boil in a small saucepan. Stir in the couscous and ¼ teaspoon salt. When the water returns to a boil, cover and remove from the heat. Let stand 10 minutes. Add to the bowl with the eggplant flesh. Add the bell pepper, walnuts, cumin, lemon juice, and ⅓ cup of the mint. Stir to combine. Season to taste with salt and freshly ground black pepper.

4 **SPOON** the couscous mixture evenly into the eggplant skin and top with the goat cheese. Roast until the cheese is lightly browned and the couscous mixture is heated through, 17 to 20 minutes. Sprinkle with the remaining herbs and serve.

NUTRITION (per serving: 1 stuffed eggplant half) 290 calories, 10 g protein, 39 g carbs, 13 g fat, 3 g saturated fat, 113 mg sodium

Vc 110% (66 mg) daily vitamin C

Fi 56% (14 g) daily fiber

An 2 servings anthocyanin-rich food (eggplant)

O3 ALA omega-3s

Pizza with Butternut Squash, Spinach, and Fontina

Using mashed butternut squash as the "sauce" is a tasty departure that packs this pizza with nutrients. Along with the squash, pine nuts and fontina make this vegetarian meal highly satisfying.

PREP TIME: 15 MINUTES / **TOTAL TIME:** 1 HOUR 15 MINUTES / **SERVINGS:** 4

1 small butternut squash (about 2 pounds), halved lengthwise

1 tablespoon olive oil

1 large red onion, halved lengthwise and thinly sliced

5 cups baby spinach leaves (about 5 ounces)

1 pound fresh whole wheat pizza dough, at room temperature

4 ounces fontina cheese, grated (about 1 cup)

2 tablespoons pine nuts, toasted

1 **HEAT** the oven to 400°F. Coat a baking sheet with cooking spray. Scoop out the squash seeds and spray the flesh with cooking spray. Place on the prepared baking sheet flesh side down. Roast until golden brown, 30 to 35 minutes. Turn flesh side up and roast until tender when pierced with a fork, 20 to 25 minutes longer. When cool, scrape the flesh into a medium bowl and mash. Season to taste with salt and freshly ground black pepper.

2 **PLACE** a pizza stone on a rack in the center of the oven and raise the temperature to 550°F. Heat the oil in a large skillet on medium-low heat. Add the onion and cook, stirring occasionally, until tender and lightly browned, 20 to 25 minutes. Season to taste with salt and freshly ground black pepper. Transfer to a bowl. Raise the heat to medium and coat the skillet with cooking spray. Cook the spinach, stirring frequently, until wilted, 2 to 3 minutes.

3 **LIGHTLY** flour the dough and roll into a 12" circle, ⅛" to ¼" thick, on parchment paper. Spread about 1½ cups squash over the dough. Top with the onion and spinach. Transfer the pizza to the oven using a pizza peel or large cutting board, sliding the parchment directly onto the pizza stone (the peel or board does not go into the oven). Bake until the edges are lightly browned, 7 to 9 minutes. Carefully pull out the rack with the pizza stone and top the pizza with the cheese and pine nuts. Bake until the cheese is melted, about 1 minute. Rest 5 minutes, cut into 8 pieces, and serve.

NUTRITION (per serving: 2 slices) 471 calories, 18 g protein, 63 g carbs, 20 g fat, 6 g saturated fat, 759 mg sodium

Fi 52% (13 g) daily fiber

Vc 35% (21 mg) daily vitamin C

Fe 28% (5 mg) daily iron

Ca 26% (257 mg) daily calcium

Cr 2 servings carotenoid-rich foods (butternut squash, spinach)

Picadillo-Stuffed Red Bell Peppers

Picadillo is a mix of ground beef, tomatoes, and an array of seasonings, depending on the country and the cook. You'll find variations all over Latin and South America; this one relies on raisins and green olives for a punch of flavor.

PREP TIME: 15 MINUTES / **TOTAL TIME:** 50 MINUTES / **SERVINGS:** 4

4 red bell peppers

¾ pound lean ground beef or 90% lean ground beef

2 teaspoons canola oil

½ medium onion, chopped (about ½ cup)

¼ teaspoon dried oregano

¼ teaspoon red-pepper flakes

2 cloves garlic, chopped

2 tablespoons tomato paste

1 can (14 ounces) no-salt-added diced tomatoes

2 tablespoons red wine vinegar

⅓ cup raisins

12 large green olives, chopped

1 **HEAT** the oven to 350°F. Bring a large pot of water to a boil on high heat. Cut off and discard the tops of the peppers, and cut out the stems, ribs, and seeds with a paring knife. Add the peppers to the pot, cover, and boil until crisp-tender when pierced with a fork, 5 to 7 minutes. Drain.

2 **HEAT** a large skillet on medium-high heat and coat with cooking spray. Add the beef and cook, crumbling the meat with a large spoon, until no longer pink, 5 to 6 minutes. Season to taste with salt and freshly ground black pepper. Transfer to a paper towel–lined plate with a slotted spoon to drain. Wipe out the skillet.

3 **HEAT** the oil in the same skillet you used to cook the beef on medium heat. Add the onion, oregano, and pepper flakes and cook, stirring frequently, until the onion is tender and lightly browned, 6 to 7 minutes. Add the garlic and cook, stirring 1 minute. Add the tomato paste and stir well to combine. Add the diced tomatoes and bring to a simmer. Cook until the liquid evaporates but the mixture is still moist, 4 to 6 minutes. Add the vinegar, raisins, and olives and stir to combine. Simmer until the raisins are plump, 1 to 2 minutes. Stir in the beef and cook 1 to 2 minutes.

4 **FILL** the bell peppers evenly with the beef mixture (about 1 cup per pepper) and stand in an 8" × 8" baking dish. Add ¼ cup water to the baking dish. Bake until the tops of the peppers are lightly browned, 11 to 13 minutes. Serve hot.

NUTRITION *(per serving: 1 stuffed pepper)* 314 calories, 21 g protein, 31 g carbs, 12 g fat, 2.5 g saturated fat, 409 mg sodium

Vc 382% (229 mg) daily vitamin C

Cr 3 servings carotenoid-rich foods (bell peppers, tomato paste, diced tomatoes)

Wild Rice–Stuffed Acorn Squash

Many supermarkets and natural foods stores carry a wild rice and brown rice "medley," which works especially well in this dish. If you can't find one, use half wild rice and half brown rice.

PREP TIME: 15 MINUTES / **TOTAL TIME:** 55 MINUTES / **SERVINGS:** 4

4 small acorn squash (¾ to 1 pound each)

1 tablespoon plus 2 teaspoons olive oil

⅔ cup wild rice–brown rice mixture

1 medium carrot, peeled and diced (about ½ cup)

1 medium zucchini, chopped (about 2 cups)

½ medium onion, finely chopped (about ½ cup)

1 cup canned chickpeas, rinsed and drained

½ cup dried currants

1 teaspoon ground cumin

½ teaspoon chili powder

½ teaspoon cinnamon

1 **HEAT** the oven to 400°F and coat a baking sheet with cooking spray. Cut the squash in half lengthwise (stem end to blossom end) and scoop out the seeds. Cut a thin slice from the skin side of each half, creating a flat surface so the squash sits flesh side up like a bowl. Place on the prepared baking sheet. Brush the flesh with 2 teaspoons of the olive oil and sprinkle with ⅛ teaspoon salt and freshly ground black pepper. Roast until the flesh is very tender when pierced with a fork, 35 to 40 minutes.

2 **BRING** 1⅓ cups water to a boil in a small saucepan over high heat. Stir in the rice and ⅛ teaspoon salt. Reduce the heat to low, cover, and simmer until the rice is tender and the liquid is absorbed, 50 minutes. Remove from the heat and rest, covered, 10 minutes.

3 **HEAT** the remaining 1 tablespoon oil in a large skillet on medium-high heat. Add the carrot and zucchini and cook, stirring occasionally, until lightly browned, 10 minutes. Add the onion and cook until soft and translucent, about 5 minutes. Stir in the chickpeas, currants, cumin, chili powder, and cinnamon and cook until heated through, about 2 minutes. Remove from the heat and stir in the rice. Season to taste with salt and freshly ground black pepper. Fill each squash half with about ½ cup of the rice mixture and serve.

NUTRITION *(per serving: 2 filled squash halves)* 462 calories, 10 g protein, 94 g carbs, 8 g fat, 1 g saturated fat, 225 mg sodium

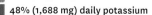 90% (54 mg) daily vitamin C
Fi 52% (13 g) daily fiber
K 48% (1,688 mg) daily potassium

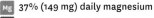 37% (149 mg) daily magnesium
Fo 31% (122 mcg) daily folate
Fe 28% (5 mg) daily iron

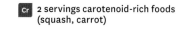 2 servings carotenoid-rich foods (squash, carrot)

Roasted Chicken Breasts with Sautéed Cabbage and Apples

The term "split chicken breast" refers to one side of a chicken's breastbone, or what we would think of as a whole chicken breast. Cooking the chicken with the skin on keeps it moist, but remove it before eating to keep calories and fat low.

PREP TIME: 25 MINUTES **/ TOTAL TIME:** 1 HOUR 15 MINUTES **/ SERVINGS:** 4

2 tablespoons chopped fresh sage plus 16 sage leaves

1¼ teaspoons dried thyme

4 split bone-in chicken breasts (about 12 ounces each)

1 tablespoon olive oil

½ medium onion, chopped (about ½ cup)

½ large red cabbage, cored and sliced (about 5 cups)

1 tablespoon balsamic vinegar

1 tablespoon honey

1 large Granny Smith apple, cored and thinly sliced

2 teaspoons unsalted butter

1 **HEAT** the oven to 400°F. Coat a baking sheet with cooking spray. Combine the chopped sage, 1 teaspoon of the thyme, ½ teaspoon salt, and freshly ground black pepper in a small bowl. Rub one-third of the herb mixture evenly on the bottom sides (not the skin side) of the chicken breasts. Turn skin side up. Gently lift the skin and slide the remaining seasoning between the skin and the flesh with your fingers. Place on the prepared baking sheet and roast until cooked through, 35 to 40 minutes.

2 **HEAT** the oil in a large skillet on medium heat. Add the onion and the remaining ¼ teaspoon thyme and cook, stirring occasionally, until onion is lightly browned, 4 to 5 minutes. Raise the heat to medium high. Cook the cabbage, tossing constantly with tongs or a spatula, until just wilted, about 2 minutes. Add the vinegar and honey and cook, stirring frequently, until the liquid is nearly evaporated and the cabbage is crisp-tender, 4 to 5 minutes. Add the apple and cook until just softened, about 2 minutes. Season to taste with salt and freshly ground black pepper.

3 **MELT** the butter in a small saucepan on medium-low heat. Cook the sage leaves until crisp and golden brown, 1 to 2 minutes. Transfer to a paper towel–lined plate with a slotted spoon. Divide the chicken and the cabbage mixture among 4 plates and garnish with sage leaves.

NUTRITION (per serving: 1 chicken breast without skin and about 1 cup cabbage) 445 calories, 60 g protein, 23 g carbs, 12 g fat, 3 g saturated fat, 587 mg sodium

Vc 112% (67 mg) daily vitamin C   K 39% (1,367 mg) daily potassium   An 2½ servings anthocyanin-rich food (red cabbage)

Braised Chicken with Dates, Ginger, and Almonds

Dried dates are intensely sweet when eaten on their own, but here they subtly balance the savory flavors of the stew. We call for Medjool dates, which are larger, softer, and sweeter than the other variety, Deglet Noor. Either one, however, will work in this recipe.

PREP TIME: 25 MINUTES / **TOTAL TIME:** 1 HOUR 10 MINUTES / **SERVINGS:** 4

1 tablespoon olive oil

2½ pounds split bone-in chicken breasts, skin removed

1 medium white onion, chopped (about 1 cup)

1" piece fresh ginger, peeled and finely chopped (about 1 tablespoon)

2 cloves garlic, chopped

1 teaspoon ground coriander

Dash of cayenne

4 cups low-sodium chicken broth

½ pound red potatoes, chopped (about 1¾ cups)

2 medium carrots, sliced (about 1 cup)

⅔ cup pitted Medjool dates, chopped

Juice of ½ lemon (1 tablespoon plus 2 teaspoons)

2 tablespoons sliced almonds, toasted

2 tablespoons chopped fresh flat-leaf parsley

1 **HEAT** the oil in a large pot or Dutch oven on medium-high heat. Season the chicken with ¼ teaspoon salt and freshly ground black pepper. Place in the pot and sear, turning once about halfway through, until deep golden brown, 8 to 10 minutes. Transfer to a plate.

2 **REDUCE** the heat to medium, add the onion, and cook, stirring occasionally, until tender and lightly browned, 6 to 7 minutes. Add the ginger, garlic, coriander, and cayenne and cook, stirring frequently, about 1 minute. Add the broth, raise the heat to high, and bring to a boil. Add the chicken, reduce the heat to medium low, and simmer, uncovered, 15 minutes. Turn the chicken breasts. Add the potatoes, carrots, and about three-quarters of the dates and simmer until the vegetables are tender and the chicken is cooked through, 10 to 15 minutes. Stir in the lemon juice and remove from the heat. Season to taste with salt and freshly ground black pepper.

3 **TRANSFER** the chicken to a cutting board. Discard the bones and skin and cut the chicken into smaller serving pieces. Divide the broth, vegetable mixture, and chicken evenly among 4 bowls. Sprinkle with the almonds, parsley, and the remaining dates.

NUTRITION (per serving: 1½ cups broth mixture and ¾ cup chicken) 477 calories, 53 g protein, 41 g carbs, 11 g fat, 2 g saturated fat, 481 mg sodium

K 42% (1,482 mg) daily potassium   **Vc** 42% (25 mg) daily vitamin C   **Mg** 26% (105 mg) daily magnesium

Baked Chicken Parmesan with Homemade Tomato Sauce

Baking the chicken breasts rather than pan-frying results in a crisp, golden crust without any added fat. To save time, look for thin sliced or filleted chicken breasts at your supermarket, which are the perfect thickness for this recipe. You can make the tomato sauce up to 2 days ahead, but jarred marinara (look for brands with less sodium) works just as well.

PREP TIME: 15 MINUTES **/ TOTAL TIME:** 1 HOUR 15 MINUTES **/ SERVINGS:** 4

SAUCE

2 teaspoons olive oil

½ large onion, chopped (about ¾ cup)

1 small carrot, peeled and chopped (about ½ cup)

1 small rib celery, chopped (about ½ cup)

¼ teaspoon dried thyme

¼ teaspoon dried oregano

3 cloves garlic, chopped

¼ teaspoon red-pepper flakes

2 cans (14 ounces each) no-salt-added diced tomatoes

1 dried bay leaf

2 tablespoons balsamic vinegar

2 tablespoons chopped fresh basil

1 **PREPARE THE SAUCE:** Heat the oil in a large saucepan on medium heat. Add the onion, carrot, celery, thyme, and oregano and cook, stirring occasionally, until tender and lightly browned, 8 to 10 minutes. Add the garlic and pepper flakes and cook, stirring, 1 minute. Add the tomatoes and bay leaf and bring to a simmer. Reduce the heat to medium low and simmer, stirring occasionally, until the vegetables are very soft and the sauce is slightly thickened, about 25 minutes. Add the vinegar and basil and simmer until the flavors blend, about 5 minutes. Remove from the heat, discard the bay leaf. Working in batches, transfer the sauce to a blender (or use an immersion blender) and puree until smooth (be careful when blending hot liquids). Season to taste with salt and freshly ground black pepper. Cover and set aside.

2 **PREPARE THE CHICKEN:** Heat the oven to 400°F. Coat a baking sheet with cooking spray. Place 3 shallow bowls in front of you. Add the flour to the first bowl. Crack the eggs into the second bowl, beat, and season with ¼ teaspoon salt and freshly ground black pepper. Combine the bread crumbs, oregano, and three-

(continued)

CHICKEN

½ cup all-purpose flour

2 large eggs

½ cup whole wheat bread crumbs

1½ teaspoons dried oregano

2 ounces Parmesan cheese, grated (about ½ cup)

4 boneless, skinless chicken breast halves (about 6 ounces each), pounded ¼" to ½" thick

½ cup grated part-skim mozzarella cheese (about 2 ounces)

quarters of the Parmesan in the third bowl. Dip the chicken breasts in the flour, shaking off the excess. Dip in the egg, then press into the bread crumbs so the mixture adheres to the chicken. Place on the prepared baking sheet. Bake, turning once about halfway through, until golden brown and cooked through, 15 to 20 minutes. Switch the oven to broil.

3 **REHEAT** the sauce over low heat if necessary. Spread 1½ cups of the sauce inside a 2½- to 3-quart baking dish. Add the chicken in a single layer, overlapping slightly if necessary. Spread about ¼ cup of the sauce over each chicken breast (you may have some leftover). Top evenly with the mozzarella and the remaining Parmesan. Transfer to the center rack of the oven and broil until the cheese is melted, 2 to 4 minutes. Serve with an arugula salad, if desired.

NUTRITION (*per serving*) 500 calories, 51 g protein, 36 g carbs, 16 g fat, 6 g saturated fat, 695 mg sodium

Vc 62% (37 mg) daily vitamin C   Ca 37% (367 mg) daily calcium   Cr 2 servings carotenoid-rich foods (tomatoes, carrot)

Roast Chicken with Brussels Sprouts, Roasted Grapes, and Hazelnuts

Roasting the grapes until they just start to burst makes them soft and juicy and intensifies their sweetness. They also look beautiful on a serving platter scattered around this simple roast chicken, so consider bringing it to the table before carving.

PREP TIME: 25 MINUTES **/ TOTAL TIME:** 1 HOUR 25 MINUTES **/ SERVINGS:** 4

2 tablespoons plus 1 teaspoon chopped fresh rosemary

1 teaspoon dried thyme

1 roasting chicken (about 4 pounds)

½ lemon

1½ pounds Brussels sprouts, trimmed and halved

1 tablespoon plus 1 teaspoon olive oil

1 pound red seedless grapes, still attached to stems

1½ ounces toasted hazelnuts, chopped (about ⅓ cup)

1 **ARRANGE** one rack in the lower third of the oven and one in the middle of the oven. Heat the oven to 400°F. Combine 1 tablespoon plus 2 teaspoons of the rosemary, ¾ teaspoon of the thyme, ¾ teaspoon salt, and freshly ground black pepper in a small bowl. Place the chicken in a roasting pan and pull up the skin covering the breast so you can slide your fingers underneath it. Rub about one-third of the rosemary mixture under the skin. Turn the chicken and repeat on the bottom side of the breast. Sprinkle the remaining rosemary mixture inside the cavity. Squeeze the lemon juice into the cavity and stuff the lemon inside. Roast in the middle of the oven breast side up until an instant-read thermometer reaches 165°F when inserted into the thickest part of the meat (without touching bone) and the juices run clear, about 1 hour for a 4-pound chicken, or 15 minutes per pound. Rest 10 minutes.

Giving Fruit and Veggies a New Meaning

Pairing savory roasted Brussels sprouts with jammy red grapes may sound strange at first, but one bite will reveal the method behind the madness. Sweet foods make savory ones even more addictive (evidence: chocolate-covered pretzels, peanut butter and jelly). And for the vegetable-averse, sweetness can suddenly make an acquired taste like Brussels sprouts more palatable. If the idea has your mouth watering, try these other fruit and veggie combos: roasted beets with orange sections, spinach salad with sliced strawberries, sautéed cabbage with apples (see page 153), and tomato salsa with diced mango.

2 **COAT** a large baking sheet with cooking spray. Add the Brussels sprouts, 1 tablespoon of the oil, ¼ teaspoon salt, and freshly ground black pepper. Toss well to combine. Roast in the lower third of the oven (below the chicken), until the bottom sides are browned, 9 to 12 minutes, depending on the size of the sprouts. Remove from the oven and turn the sprouts so the browned sides are face up.

3 **PREPARE** the grapes while the sprouts roast. Cut the grape clusters into 6 to 8 smaller clusters, if large. Add the grapes, the remaining olive oil, the remaining rosemary, the remaining thyme, ⅛ teaspoon salt, and freshly ground black pepper to a medium bowl and toss well to combine. Add to the baking sheet with the sprouts and return to the oven. Roast, turning grape clusters halfway through, until the sprouts are tender when pierced with a fork and the grapes are beginning to burst, 8 to 10 minutes. Transfer the chicken to a serving platter. Arrange the sprouts and grapes around the chicken, sprinkle with the hazelnuts, and serve.

NUTRITION (per serving: ¾ cup light meat and ¼ cup dark meat without skin, ¾ cup sprouts, and ½ cup grapes) 443 calories, 36 g protein, 36 g carbs, 20 g fat, 3 g saturated fat, 666 mg sodium

Vc 242% (145 mg) daily vitamin C	**Fo** 28% (113 mcg) daily folate
K 33% (1,161 mg) daily potassium	**Fe** 28% (5 mg) daily iron
Fi 32% (8 g) daily fiber	**Cr** 2 servings carotenoid-rich food (Brussels sprouts)

O3 ALA omega-3s

Pumpkin Seed– Coated Chicken Breasts with Bulgur Pilaf

You're probably most familiar with bulgur as the grain in tabbouleh, the Middle Eastern salad of diced tomatoes, cucumbers, and herbs. This type of crushed wheat is already cooked and dried, so rehydrating it is easy work.

PREP TIME: 15 MINUTES / **TOTAL TIME:** 50 MINUTES / **SERVINGS:** 4

¾ cup bulgur

¾ cup pumpkin seeds

½ teaspoon chili powder

½ cup all-purpose flour

2 large eggs

4 boneless, skinless chicken breasts (about 5 ounces each)

1 tablespoon olive oil

3 medium carrots, sliced into rounds (1½ cups)

1 medium onion, chopped (about 1 cup)

1½ teaspoons cumin seeds

Juice of 2 limes (about ¼ cup)

⅓ cup dried cranberries

4 scallions, white and some green, thinly sliced (about ⅓ cup)

¼ cup chopped flat-leaf parsley, plus leaves for garnish

1 **HEAT** the oven to 400°F. Bring 1⅛ cups water to a boil in a medium saucepan. Stir in the bulgur and ⅛ teaspoon salt. Return to a boil, cover, and remove from the heat. Let stand 30 minutes.

2 **COAT** a baking sheet with cooking spray. Pulse the pumpkin seeds in a food processor until coarsely ground. Add the chili powder and ⅛ teaspoon salt and pulse once or twice to combine.

3 **PLACE** 3 shallow bowls in front of you. Add the flour to the first bowl. Beat the eggs in the second bowl and season with ¼ teaspoon salt and freshly ground black pepper. Add the pumpkin seeds to the third bowl. Dip the chicken breasts in the flour, shaking off the excess. Dip in the egg, then press into the pumpkin seeds so the mixture adheres. Place on the prepared baking sheet. Bake, turning once about halfway through, until golden brown and cooked through, 15 to 20 minutes.

4 **HEAT** the oil in a large skillet on medium heat. Add the carrots and cook, stirring occasionally, until partially softened, 7 to 8 minutes. Add the onion and cumin seeds and cook until tender and lightly browned, 7 to 8 minutes. Add the bulgur and stir to combine. Stir in the lime juice, cranberries, scallions, and chopped parsley. Divide the chicken and bulgur among 4 plates and garnish with parsley leaves.

NUTRITION *(per serving: 1 chicken breast and about 1 cup bulgur)* 561 calories, 45 g protein, 52 g carbs, 21 g fat, 4 g saturated fat, 471 mg sodium

Mg 55% (220 mg) daily magnesium   **K** 31% (1,067 mg) daily potassium   **Fe** 28% (5 mg) daily iron

Fi 36% (9 g) daily fiber

Black Bean–Turkey Chili with Butternut Squash

If your supermarket sells peeled and chopped butternut squash in the produce section, take advantage of this great time-saver— just be sure to cut any large chunks into bite-size pieces. If you do buy a whole squash, a vegetable peeler is the best tool for removing the skin.

PREP TIME: 15 MINUTES **/ TOTAL TIME:** 50 MINUTES **/ SERVINGS:** 6

1 tablespoon canola oil

1 large onion, chopped (about 1½ cups)

¼ cup tomato paste

3 cloves garlic, chopped

2 teaspoons ground cumin

2 teaspoons dried oregano

¾ teaspoon allspice

¼ teaspoon ground cloves

1 can (28 ounces) crushed tomatoes

1 can (14 ounces) no-salt-added fire-roasted tomatoes

½ medium butternut squash, peeled, seeded, and chopped (about 3½ cups)

1 large poblano chile, seeded and sliced (about 1¼ cups)

1 pound ground turkey breast

2 cans (14½ ounces each) black beans, rinsed and drained

2 to 4 canned chipotle peppers in adobo sauce, finely chopped, plus 1 to 2 tablespoons adobo sauce (optional)

6 tablespoons reduced-fat (light) sour cream

6 scallions, white and some green, sliced (about ⅓ cup)

¼ cup chopped cilantro

Lime wedges

1 **HEAT** the oil in a large pot or Dutch oven on medium heat. Add the onion and cook, stirring occasionally, until tender and lightly browned, 7 to 8 minutes. Add the tomato paste, garlic, cumin, oregano, allspice, and cloves and cook, stirring until the spices are fragrant, 1 to 2 minutes. Add 1¾ cups water, crushed tomatoes, and fire-roasted tomatoes. Cover, raise the heat to high, and bring to a simmer. Add the squash, reduce the heat to medium, and simmer, uncovered, stirring occasionally, until the squash is partially cooked, 10 minutes. Add the poblano and simmer until the squash is tender, 5 to 10 minutes.

Good to Glow

This stew not only tastes terrific, but eating it can also make you look terrific. People who loaded up on carotenoid-rich fruits and vegetables had more red and yellow tones in their skin—the pigments in the produce are distributed to the skin's surface—according to a study from the University of St. Andrews in Scotland. As a result, they were perceived to be healthier and more attractive. The researchers found that upping your daily fruit and veggie intake by about three servings is enough to improve your complexion in just 6 weeks.

2 **COAT** a large skillet with cooking spray and heat on medium-high heat. Add the turkey and cook, stirring frequently and crumbling the meat with a large spoon, until no longer pink, 6 to 8 minutes. Season to taste with salt and freshly ground black pepper.

3 **ADD** the turkey and black beans to the tomato-squash mixture and stir to combine. Simmer until heated through and the flavors blend, about 5 minutes. Stir in the chipotle peppers and adobo sauce, if using, starting with the smaller amount and adding more according to taste. Remove the chili from the heat, season to taste with salt and freshly ground black pepper, and serve with sour cream, scallions, cilantro, and lime wedges.

NUTRITION *(per serving: about 1½ cups)* 399 calories, 26 g protein, 53 g carbs, 11 g fat, 3 g saturated fat, 548 mg sodium

Vc 138% (83 mg) daily vitamin C	**Fe** 39% (7 mg) daily iron	**Cr** 3½ servings carotenoid-rich foods (butternut squash, poblano, tomatoes)
Fi 60% (15 g) daily fiber	**K** 32% (1,115 mg) daily potassium	

Grilled Steak with Peperonata Sauce

Once you make this classic Italian sauce, you'll want to use it in a variety of ways: on sandwiches, as a topping for ricotta crostini, or on pizza with fresh mozzarella. Steamed broccolini with a squeeze of fresh lemon juice makes a great side dish, rich in carotenoids, vitamin C, and folate.

PREP TIME: 20 MINUTES **/ TOTAL TIME:** 55 MINUTES + MARINATING TIME **/ SERVINGS:** 4

4 cloves garlic

2 whole sprigs fresh basil, roughly chopped, plus 2 tablespoons chopped leaves

½ cup red wine

1 teaspoon dried rosemary

4 tablespoons olive oil

1½ pounds flank steak

1 large onion, sliced (about 1½ cups)

2 large red bell peppers, sliced

2 large yellow bell peppers, sliced

½ teaspoon dried oregano

1 tablespoon plus 2 teaspoons capers, rinsed

1 tablespoon balsamic vinegar

1 **SMASH** 2 of the garlic cloves with the flat side of a knife. Add to a large zip-top bag along with the basil sprigs, wine, rosemary, and 2 tablespoons the oil. Add the steak and refrigerate 6 hours. Bring to room temperature before grilling.

2 **HEAT** 1 tablespoon of the oil in a large pot with a lid or Dutch oven on medium heat. Cook the onion, stirring occasionally, until tender and lightly browned, about 10 minutes. Add the remaining 1 tablespoon oil, heat 30 seconds, and add the bell peppers and oregano. Cover and cook, stirring occasionally, until the texture is soft and silky (avoid browning), about 5 minutes. Finely chop the remaining garlic cloves. Add to the pot and cook, stirring, 1 to 2 minutes. Stir in the capers and vinegar and cook 2 to 3 minutes. Season to taste with salt and freshly ground black pepper.

3 **BRUSH** a grill rack with vegetable oil and heat the grill to medium-high. Discard the marinade and season the steak with ¼ teaspoon salt and freshly ground black pepper. Grill about 6 minutes per side for medium rare. Rest 3 minutes and thinly slice against the grain. Top with the peperonata, sprinkle with the chopped basil leaves, and serve.

NUTRITION *(per serving)* 381 calories, 39 g protein, 15 g carbs, 18 g fat, 5 g saturated fat, 325 mg sodium

Vc 465% (279 mg) daily vitamin C   B12 33% (2 mcg) daily vitamin B12   K 29% (1,021 mg) daily potassium

Beef Stew with Root Vegetables

Taking the time to brown the flour-coated beef in batches creates a caramelized exterior that builds flavor. Be sure not to crowd the meat—otherwise, it will steam rather than brown properly.

PREP TIME: 30 MINUTES **/ TOTAL TIME:** 2 HOURS 10 MINUTES **/ SERVINGS:** 4

1¼ pounds grass-fed beef chuck, cut into 1½" cubes

⅓ cup all-purpose flour

2 tablespoons olive oil

½ large onion, chopped (about ¾ cup)

¼ teaspoon dried thyme

¼ teaspoon dried rosemary

2 tablespoons tomato paste

2 cloves garlic, finely chopped

¾ cup red wine

3 to 4 cups low-sodium chicken broth

2 large parsnips, cut into 1" pieces (about 1½ cups)

3 medium carrots, cut into 1" pieces (about 1½ cups)

1 medium rutabaga peeled and cut into 1" cubes (about 2 cups)

2 cups frozen lima beans

2 tablespoons red wine vinegar

2 tablespoons chopped fresh flat-leaf parsley

1 **SEASON** the beef with ½ teaspoon salt and freshly ground black pepper. Place the flour in a wide, shallow bowl. Add about a quarter of the beef to the flour and toss to coat completely. Shake off the excess and transfer to a plate. Repeat with the remaining beef in three batches.

2 **HEAT** 1 tablespoon of the oil in a large pot or Dutch oven on medium-high heat. Add half the beef, spacing pieces at least ½" apart to avoid crowding (if the pot isn't large enough to hold half the beef without crowding, cook it in three batches). Cook without moving the beef until the bottom sides are browned, about 3 minutes. Turn and cook until the opposite sides are browned, about 2 minutes. Transfer to a bowl and repeat with the remaining 1 tablespoon oil and beef.

3 **REDUCE** the heat to medium and add the onion, thyme, and rosemary. Cook, stirring occasionally, until the onion is tender and lightly browned, about 7 minutes. Add the tomato paste and garlic and cook, stirring, about 1 minute. Add the wine and simmer until the liquid is reduced by half, 3 to 4 minutes.

A Hearty Vegetarian Stew

With so much flavor and a slew of nutrients from the root vegetables and lima beans, this dish can easily become a satisfying meat-free supper. Here's how: Cut out the beef and flour and skip step 1. Reduce the oil to 2 teaspoons and proceed with step 2, swapping the chicken broth for vegetable. Jump to step 3 and add 1½ cups chopped sweet potatoes when you add the rutabaga. This variation not only accommodates everyone at the table, it also shaves about 45 minutes off the total time!

4 **ADD** 3 cups of the broth, cover, and bring to a boil on high heat. Add the beef and any juice that has accumulated in the bowl. Reduce the heat to medium low and simmer, uncovered, stirring occasionally, 30 minutes.

5 **ADD** the parsnips and carrots. Add the remaining broth, if necessary, to just cover the vegetables. Cover, and simmer, stirring occasionally, 20 minutes. Add the rutabaga, cover, and simmer, stirring occasionally, until all the vegetables are tender and the beef is very tender, 20 minutes. Add the lima beans and simmer, stirring frequently, until heated through, about 5 minutes. Stir in the vinegar. Season to taste with salt and freshly ground black pepper. Divide among 4 bowls and sprinkle with the parsley.

NUTRITION *(per serving: 2 cups)* 549 calories, 42 g protein, 50 g carbs, 11 g fiber, 17 g fat, 5 g saturated fat, 544 mg sodium

B₁₂ 100% (6 mcg) daily vitamin B₁₂	Fi 44% (11 g) daily fiber
Vc 85% (51 mg) daily vitamin C	Fe 33% (6 mg) daily iron
K 53% (1,868 mg) daily potassium	Fo 31% (122 mcg) daily folate

Mg 29% (115 mg) daily magnesium

Cr 1 serving carotenoid-rich foods (carrots, tomatoes)

Beef and Broccoli with Brown Rice

Try using tamari soy sauce in this dish. Compared to regular soy sauce, it's made with less or no wheat and tends to be smoother, more complex, and less salty. You'll find it in the Asian section of large supermarkets.

PREP TIME: 20 MINUTES **/ TOTAL TIME:** 1 HOUR 20 MINUTES **/ SERVINGS:** 4

1 cup brown rice

⅓ cup reduced-sodium soy sauce

1 tablespoon rice vinegar

1 tablespoon honey

2 teaspoons sesame oil

2 teaspoons cornstarch

8 ounces white mushrooms, sliced (about 1½ cups)

2 teaspoons canola oil

1¼ pounds sirloin tip steak, top sirloin, or top round, thinly sliced

1 large head broccoli (about 2¼ pounds), trimmed, florets cut into bite-size pieces

1 large orange bell pepper, sliced (about 1¼ cups)

1 tablespoon peeled, chopped fresh ginger (1" piece)

3 cloves garlic, chopped

2 teaspoons sesame seeds, toasted

1 **BRING** 2 cups water to a boil in a medium saucepan on high heat. Stir in the rice, cover, reduce heat to low, and simmer until the rice is tender and the liquid is evaporated, about 50 minutes. Remove from the heat and let stand 10 minutes.

2 **WHISK** the soy sauce, vinegar, honey, sesame oil, cornstarch, and 3 tablespoons water together in a small bowl. Set aside.

3 **COAT** a large skillet with cooking spray and heat on medium heat. Add the mushrooms and cook, stirring occasionally, until tender and lightly browned, 8 to 10 minutes. Transfer to a bowl. Add the canola oil to the skillet and raise the heat to medium high. Add the beef and cook, stirring occasionally, until browned and just cooked through, 3 to 5 minutes. Add to the mushrooms.

4 **ADD** the broccoli and bell pepper to the skillet and cook, stirring, until lightly browned, about 2 minutes. Add ⅔ cup water and simmer until evaporated, about 2 minutes. (If the skillet is too small to fit all the vegetables at once, cook in two batches, using ⅓ cup water per batch. Return all vegetables to the skillet before proceeding.) Add the ginger and garlic and cook 1 minute, stirring constantly. Add the soy sauce mixture and simmer until slightly thickened, about 3 minutes. Stir in the beef and mushrooms and cook until heated through, 1 to 2 minutes. Spoon over the rice, sprinkle with sesame seeds, and serve.

NUTRITION *(per serving: ¾ cup rice and 1¾ cups beef mixture)* 554 calories, 40 g protein, 56 g carbs, 19 g fat, 5 g saturated fat, 629 mg sodium

Vc 258% (155 mg) daily vitamin C	Fo 35% (138 mcg) daily folate	Fe 28% (5 mg) daily iron
K 37% (1,299 mg) daily potassium	B₁₂ 33% (2 mcg) daily vitamin B₁₂	Cr 4 servings carotenoid-rich foods (broccoli, bell pepper)
Mg 36% (143 mg) daily magnesium	Fi 28% (7 g) daily fiber	O₃ ALA omega-3s

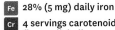

Grilled Steak au Poivre with Sautéed Broccoli Rabe

Traditionally, these peppercorn-coated fillets are sautéed in a skillet, and the rendered fat is then used to make a sauce enriched with brandy, cream, and butter. Grilling the steaks ensures that the rendered fat doesn't end up on your plate, and skipping the cream and butter cuts even more saturated fat.

PREP TIME: 10 MINUTES **/ TOTAL TIME:** 50 MINUTES **/ SERVINGS:** 4

1 pound broccoli rabe, ends trimmed and cut into 3" lengths

2 tablespoons olive oil

2 cloves garlic, chopped

¼ teaspoon red-pepper flakes

1 can (15 ounces) chickpeas, drained and rinsed

Juice of ½ lemon (1 tablespoon)

1 tablespoon whole peppercorns (black, white, pink, or any combination)

7 whole dried allspice berries or ½ teaspoon ground allspice

4 grass-fed beef tenderloin steaks (about 5 ounces each; filet mignon)

4 medium shallots, thinly sliced (about ½ cup)

½ cup brandy

½ cup chicken stock

2 teaspoons Dijon mustard

2 tablespoons chopped fresh parsley

1 **BRING** a large pot of water to a boil on high heat. Add the broccoli rabe and boil until crisp-tender, 3 to 4 minutes. Drain. Heat 1 tablespoon of the olive oil in a large skillet on medium-low heat. Add the garlic and pepper flakes and cook, stirring, 1 minute. Add the broccoli rabe and stir well to combine. Stir in the chickpeas and lemon juice. Cook, stirring occasionally, until heated through, 2 to 3 minutes. Season to taste with salt and freshly ground black pepper. Cover and keep warm.

2 **BRUSH** a grill rack with vegetable oil and heat the grill to medium-high heat. Crush the peppercorns and allspice berries as coarse or fine as you prefer with a mortar and pestle or in a spice grinder. Transfer to a small bowl (if using ground allspice, add to the bowl and stir to combine). Brush the steaks with 1 teaspoon of the olive oil and season with ½ teaspoon salt. Sprinkle both sides of the steaks with the peppercorn mixture, pressing lightly to adhere (if you like less spice, do not use all of the mixture).

All about Broccoli Rabe

This vitamin C, potassium, and iron-packed vegetable is often cause for confusion. For starters, it sometimes goes by the name rapini, and though it's in the same plant family, it isn't broccoli at all. It has a strong, somewhat bitter flavor that pairs well with bold ingredients such as garlic, chiles, or balsamic vinegar. To complicate things further, it's frequently mixed up with broccolini, another vegetable that has become common in supermarket produce sections only recently. In this recipe, mustard greens (remove the thick stems) or the mild-tasting broccolini may be substituted.

3 **PLACE** the steaks on the grill, cover, and cook over direct heat to the desired degree of doneness, 6 to 7 minutes per side for medium rare and 8 to 9 minutes per side for medium. Transfer to a plate and rest 5 minutes.

4 **HEAT** the remaining 2 teaspoons olive oil in a medium skillet on medium-low heat. Add the shallots and cook, stirring frequently, until soft and lightly browned, about 4 minutes. Add the brandy and chicken stock, bring to a simmer, and cook until reduced to about ⅓ cup and slightly thickened, 4 to 5 minutes. Reduce the heat to low, add the mustard, and stir to combine. Remove from the heat. Divide the broccoli rabe and steaks among 4 plates. Top steaks evenly with the shallot mixture, sprinkle with parsley, and serve.

NUTRITION *(per serving)* 512 calories, 40 g protein, 30 g carbs, 19 g fat, 5 g saturated fat, 565 mg sodium

Vc	47% (28 mg) daily vitamin C
Fo	40% (161 mcg) daily folate
Fe	33% (6 mg) daily iron
B_{12}	28% (1.7 mcg) daily vitamin B_{12}
Fi	28% (7 g) daily fiber
K	27% (936 mg) daily potassium
Cr	1 serving carotenoid-rich food (broccoli rabe)

Roast Pork Tenderloin with Edamame Succotash

Variations abound, but succotash is a Southern sauté that usually consists of corn and lima beans. Here, we've replaced the beans with magnesium-rich edamame, brought in basil for summery flavor, and used a small amount of butter, which is traditionally added at the end for extra richness.

PREP TIME: 15 MINUTES **/ TOTAL TIME:** 50 MINUTES **/ SERVINGS:** 4

1 teaspoon ground cumin

¾ teaspoon chili powder

½ teaspoon oregano

1¼ pounds pork tenderloin

1 tablespoon olive oil

1 large sweet onion, chopped (about 1½ cups)

1 large red bell pepper, chopped (about 1¼ cups)

3 cloves garlic, chopped

3 cups frozen shelled edamame

1 cup frozen corn

1 tablespoon plus 1 teaspoon apple cider vinegar

1 tablespoon unsalted butter

3 tablespoons chopped fresh basil, plus leaves for garnish

1 **HEAT** the oven to 450°F. Coat a baking sheet with cooking spray. Combine the cumin, chili powder, oregano, ½ teaspoon salt, and freshly ground black pepper. Rub the pork all over with the spice mixture and place on the prepared baking sheet. Roast until an instant-read thermometer inserted in the thickest part registers 145°F. Let stand 5 minutes.

2 **HEAT** the oil in a large skillet on medium heat. Add the onion and bell pepper and cook, stirring frequently, until the pepper is crisp-tender and the onion is lightly browned, 6 to 7 minutes. Add the garlic and cook, stirring, for 1 minute. Add the edamame, corn, and vinegar and cook, stirring occasionally, until the liquid evaporates and the vegetables are heated through, 2 to 3 minutes. Stir in the butter until melted and remove from the heat. Add the chopped basil. Thinly slice the pork. Divide the pork and succotash among 4 plates, garnish with the basil leaves, and serve.

NUTRITION (per serving: 5 ounces pork and 1¼ cups succotash) 361 calories, 41 g protein, 24 g carbs, 11 g fat, 3 g saturated fat, 331 mg sodium

Vc 123% (74 mg) daily vitamin C

Fo 78% (311 mg) daily folate

K 36% (1,272 mg) daily potassium

Fi 28% (7 g) daily fiber

Mg 27% (108 mg) daily magnesium

Pork Braised in Kiwi-Coconut Sauce with White Beans

Look for curry paste in the Asian section of your supermarket (the Thai Kitchen brand is widely available). It's a combination of spices and ingredients like lemongrass and curry leaves; try adding it to chicken broth as the base for an Asian-inspired soup.

PREP TIME: 25 MINUTES / **TOTAL TIME:** 1 HOUR / **SERVINGS:** 6

1 tablespoon canola oil

6 (1¼" thick) boneless center cut pork loin chops (about 5 ounces each)

½ large red onion, chopped (about ¾ cup)

1 can (14 ounces) light coconut milk

1 tablespoon green curry paste

11 kiwi, peeled and chopped (about 4 cups)

1 can (15 ounces) cannellini beans, drained and rinsed

1 can (8 ounces) pineapple chunks, drained and chopped

6 tablespoons roasted unsalted sunflower seeds

3 tablespoons thinly sliced shallots

3 tablespoons chopped cilantro

1 **HEAT** the oil in a large pot or Dutch oven on medium-high heat. Season the pork with ¼ teaspoon salt and freshly ground black pepper. Brown the pork in batches without moving until the bottoms are deep golden brown, 2 to 3 minutes. Turn and repeat on the opposite sides. Transfer to a plate as browned.

2 **REDUCE** the heat to medium low, add the onion, and cook, stirring occasionally, until softened, about 6 minutes. Add the coconut milk, curry paste, and 1⅓ cups of the kiwi. Bring to a simmer, reduce the heat to low, cover, and cook until the kiwi is soft, about 5 minutes. Remove from the heat. Working in batches, transfer to a blender and puree (be careful when blending hot liquids).

3 **RETURN** the coconut mixture to the pot and bring to a simmer on medium-high heat. Add the pork and any juices accumulated on the plate. Reduce the heat to low, cover, and simmer, turning halfway through, until the pork feels firm and the center is just barely pink, 12 to 14 minutes. Let stand off the heat, uncovered, 5 minutes. Season to taste with salt and freshly ground black pepper.

4 **COMBINE** the beans, pineapple, sunflower seeds, shallots, 2 tablespoons of the cilantro, and the remaining kiwi in a large bowl. Divide among 6 plates. Divide the sauce evenly among the plates and top with a pork chop. Garnish with the remaining cilantro, and serve.

NUTRITION (per serving: 1 chop, ¼ cup sauce, ¾ cup beans) 501 calories, 37 g protein, 45 g carbs, 20 g fat, 7 g saturated fat, 307 mg sodium

VC 268% (161 mg) daily vitamin C   K 30% (1,033 mg) daily potassium   VE 27% (8 IU) daily vitamin E

Fi 36% (9 g) daily fiber

Roasted Cedar-Plank Salmon with Mustard-Maple Glaze

A cedar plank infuses the salmon with the flavor of slow-smoked fish. No smoker or grill is needed—your oven does all the work. Be sure to use mustard with the seeds still intact to add texture to the savory-sweet topping.

PREP TIME: 5 MINUTES **/ TOTAL TIME:** 40 MINUTES + SOAKING TIME **/ SERVES:** 4

1½ pounds center-cut wild salmon fillet with skin

⅓ cup pure maple syrup

2½ tablespoons whole grain mustard

2 cloves garlic, chopped

Juice of ½ lemon (1 tablespoon plus 2 teaspoons)

Dash of cayenne

1 **SOAK** a large cedar plank in water 1 hour. Pat dry. Heat the oven to 400°F and line a baking sheet with foil. Heat the cedar plank in the oven 10 minutes. Place on the prepared baking sheet and put the salmon on top. Season with ⅛ teaspoon salt. Roast until nearly opaque in the thickest part, 10 to 12 minutes. Remove from the oven and switch the oven to broil.

2 **BRING** the maple syrup, mustard, and garlic to a simmer in a small saucepan on medium-high heat while the salmon cooks. Reduce the heat to low and simmer until thickened and reduced to about ⅓ cup, 8 minutes. Stir in the lemon juice and cayenne and remove from the heat.

3 **TRANSFER** about 2 tablespoons of the mustard-maple glaze to a small bowl and reserve. Spoon the remaining glaze over the salmon and broil 6" from the heat until the top is lightly browned and the flesh is opaque in the thickest part, 3 to 5 minutes. Immediately spoon the reserved glaze over the salmon, slice into 4 equal pieces, and serve with steamed green beans flavored with lemon zest, if desired.

NUTRITION (per serving) 399 calories, 39 g protein, 23 g carbs, 16 g fat, 3 g saturated fat, 230 mg sodium

VD 330% (1,319 IU) daily vitamin D   O3 180% (1,800 mg) daily omega-3s   B12 133% (8 mcg) daily vitamin B12

Pan-Roasted Salmon with Lentil Pilaf

Green lentils are slighter firmer and hold their shape better than the more common brown variety, making them ideal for a pilaf. Also called "French lentils" or "lentilles du puy," they can be found in large supermarkets and health food stores, but brown lentils will work in a pinch.

PREP TIME: 15 MINUTES **/ TOTAL TIME:** 55 MINUTES **/ SERVINGS:** 4

1¼ cups green lentils

1 dried bay leaf

1 tablespoon plus 2 teaspoons olive oil

1 large carrot, diced (about ¾ cup)

½ large onion, chopped (about ¾ cup)

1 rib celery, diced (about ½ cup)

2 sprigs fresh thyme

½ teaspoon fennel seeds

¼ teaspoon dried rosemary

½ cup dry red wine

4 salmon fillets with skin (about 5 ounces each)

¼ teaspoon dried thyme

Juice of ½ lemon (1 tablespoon plus 2 teaspoons)

1 teaspoon fresh thyme leaves

1 **HEAT** the oven to 350°F. Bring 5 cups water to a boil in a medium saucepan on high heat. Add the lentils and bay leaf, reduce the heat to medium low, and simmer, partially covered, until the lentils are cooked through yet still firm to the bite, 20 to 22 minutes. Drain and discard the bay leaf.

2 **HEAT** 1 tablespoon of the oil in a large skillet on medium heat. Add the carrot, onion, celery, thyme sprigs, fennel seeds, and rosemary. Cook, stirring occasionally, until the carrot is just tender, about 10 minutes. Add the wine and simmer until nearly evaporated, 3 to 4 minutes. Remove the thyme sprigs and bay leaf. Stir in the lentils and cook until heated through, about 1 minute. Season to taste with salt and freshly ground black pepper.

3 **HEAT** the remaining 2 teaspoons of olive oil in a large ovenproof skillet on medium-high heat. Season the salmon with ¼ teaspoon salt and freshly ground black pepper. Rub the dried thyme between your fingers to crumble and rub over the salmon. Add to the skillet, flesh side down, and cook until golden brown, 2 to 3 minutes. Turn and sear skin, 1 minute. Transfer to the oven and roast until the flesh is opaque in the thickest part, 4 to 8 minutes, depending on thickness. Drizzle with the lemon juice and serve over the lentils. Garnish with the fresh thyme leaves.

NUTRITION *(per serving: 1½ cups lentils and 1 salmon fillet)* 522 calories, 43 g protein, 41 g carbs, 19 g fat, 3 g saturated fat, 221 mg sodium

VD 258% (1,032 IU) daily vitamin D	B12 117% (7 mcg) daily vitamin B12	K 34% (1,199 mg) daily potassium
O3 180% (1,800 mg) daily omega-3s	Fi 40% (10 g) daily fiber	Fe 28% (5 mg) daily iron

Individual Tuna Casseroles with Peas and Tarragon

Personal-size casseroles are a fun change of pace and provide built-in portion control. Or make one casserole—use a 9" × 13" baking dish, cover, and bake 25 minutes, then uncover and bake 5 minutes longer.

PREP TIME: 20 MINUTES **/ TOTAL TIME:** 55 MINUTES **/ SERVINGS:** 8

1 pound whole wheat shell pasta

1 tablespoon unsalted butter

2 cloves garlic, finely chopped

½ cup whole wheat panko

2 tablespoons olive oil

⅓ cup all-purpose flour

5 cups fat-free milk

4 ounces reduced-fat Monterey Jack cheese, grated (about 1 heaping cup)

2 cups frozen peas

2 cans (5 ounces) tuna packed in water, drained

2 cans (5 ounces) tuna packed in olive oil, drained

¼ cup plus 2 tablespoons chopped fresh tarragon

1½ ounces Parmesan, grated (about ⅓ cup)

1 **HEAT** the oven to 350°F and spray 8 individual 10-ounce casserole dishes or ramekins with cooking spray. Bring a large pot of water to a boil on high heat and cook the pasta to just barely al dente. Drain. Wipe the inside of the pasta pot dry and reserve.

2 **MELT** the butter in a small skillet on medium-low heat. Add the garlic and cook, stirring, about 30 seconds. Add the panko and stir frequently until lightly toasted, 2 to 3 minutes. Season to taste with salt and freshly ground black pepper. Set aside.

3 **HEAT** the oil in the reserved pasta pot on medium heat. Whisk in the flour and cook, whisking constantly, until the flour is lightly toasted, about 2 minutes. Add 4 cups of the milk, pouring in a slow, steady stream while whisking constantly; bring to a simmer. Simmer, whisking constantly, until slightly thickened, about 2 minutes.

4 **WHISK** in the Monterey Jack cheese off the heat until melted. Add the peas, tuna, ¼ cup of the tarragon, pasta, and remaining 1 cup milk and stir to combine. Divide among the casserole dishes and top with the panko mixture and Parmesan. Cover with foil and place on 2 baking sheets. Bake in the upper and lower thirds of the oven 10 minutes. Switch positions and bake 5 minutes longer. Remove the foil and bake until the sauce is bubbling and the cheese is melted, about 5 minutes. Let stand 5 minutes, sprinkle with the remaining tarragon, and serve.

NUTRITION (per serving) 498 calories, 39 g protein, 59 g carbs, 5 g fiber, 14 g fat, 5 g saturated fat, 530 mg sodium

B₁₂ 43% (2.6 mcg) daily vitamin B₁₂   VD 34% (137 IU) daily vitamin D   O3 28% (280 mg) daily omega-3s
Ca 38% (382 mg) daily calcium

Steamed Clams and Chickpeas in Tomato-Leek Broth

When purchasing live shellfish like clams and oysters, it's best to buy and cook them on the same day. If the fishmonger puts your clams in a plastic bag, be sure to leave it partially open so they can breathe. When steaming, lightly tap clams that are slow to open and discard any that stay closed after all the other clams are cooked.

PREP TIME: 15 MINUTES **/ TOTAL TIME:** 40 MINUTES **/ SERVINGS:** 4

1 medium leek, white and light green parts

1 tablespoon unsalted butter

2 cloves garlic, finely chopped

¾ cup dry white wine, such as sauvignon blanc

1 can (14 ounces) no-salt-added diced tomatoes

1 can (15 ounces) chickpeas, drained and rinsed

24 littleneck clams, scrubbed and rinsed

3 tablespoons chopped fresh flat-leaf parsley

Lemon wedges

1 **TRIM** the leek, halve lengthwise, and thinly slice. Wash well in a bowl of cold water. Let stand. Lift the leek out of the water with a slotted spoon and transfer to a colander to drain.

2 **MELT** the butter in a large pot on medium heat. Add the leek and cook, stirring frequently, until soft and lightly browned, about 5 minutes. Season with salt and freshly ground black pepper to taste. Add the garlic and cook, stirring, 1 minute. Add the wine, bring to a simmer, and cook until reduced by half. Add the tomatoes and chickpeas and return to a simmer.

3 **ADD** the clams and reduce the heat to medium low. Cover and simmer until the clams open, checking frequently and transferring the clams to a bowl as they open, 10 to 13 minutes. Divide the chickpea mixture among 4 bowls and top with 6 clams each. Sprinkle with the parsley and serve with the lemon wedges.

NUTRITION (per serving: ¾ cup chickpeas and 6 clams) 248 calories, 17 g protein, 32 g carbs, 2 g fat, 0 g saturated fat, 175 mg sodium

B_{12} **717% (43 mcg) daily vitamin B_{12}**   Fe **83% (15 mg) daily iron**   Vc **67% (40 mg) daily vitamin C**

Seafood Paella

Spanish chorizo is generously seasoned with paprika and other spices, so a small amount adds unique flavor to dishes like this. Look for it in specialty markets and butcher shops.

PREP TIME: 20 MINUTES / **TOTAL TIME:** 1 HOUR 30 MINUTES / **SERVINGS:** 4

3 ounces dried Spanish chorizo, diced

1 pound medium shrimp, peeled, deveined, and patted dry

½ teaspoon smoked paprika

1 large red bell pepper, chopped (about 1¼ cups)

1 medium onion, chopped (about 1 cup)

3 cloves garlic, chopped

¼ teaspoon dried oregano

1 cup short- or medium-grain white rice

½ cup plus 2 tablespoons chopped fresh flat-leaf parsley

1 can (14.5 ounces) no-salt-added diced tomatoes

1 cup frozen peas

¼ teaspoon saffron

16 littleneck clams, scrubbed and rinsed

Lemon wedges

1 **HEAT** a large heavy skillet or paella pan on medium heat. Add the chorizo and cook, stirring frequently, until lightly browned, about 5 minutes. Transfer to a paper towel–lined plate with a slotted spatula and press lightly with another paper towel to drain.

2 **DISCARD** all but 1 tablespoon of the rendered fat from the chorizo and raise the heat to medium high. Season the shrimp with the paprika, ¼ teaspoon salt, and freshly ground black pepper. Add to the skillet and cook, turning halfway through, until lightly browned and opaque in the thickest part, about 4 minutes. Transfer to a bowl and set aside.

3 **ADD** the bell pepper and onion to the skillet and cook, stirring occasionally, until tender and lightly browned, about 7 minutes. Add the garlic, oregano, rice, and ½ cup of the parsley and cook, stirring almost constantly, until the rice turns opaque, about 2 minutes. Add the tomatoes, peas, saffron, and 1 cup water. Bring to a simmer and reduce the heat to low. Simmer, stirring occasionally during the first 20 minutes of cooking, until the rice is cooked through, the bottom layer of rice has turned light brown and crisp in spots, and the liquid is absorbed, 24 to 28 minutes. (If the water evaporates before the rice is cooked through, add more as needed.) Stir in the chorizo and shrimp and remove from the heat.

4 **FILL** a large pot with about ½" water, insert a steamer basket, cover, and bring to a boil over high heat. Reduce the heat to medium low, add the clams, and steam, covered, until the shells open, 5 to 10 minutes. Transfer the clams to a bowl as they open and discard any that do not open. Divide the paella among 4 bowls and top with the clams. Serve with the lemon wedges.

NUTRITION *(per serving: 1¾ cups rice mixture and 4 clams)* 525 calories, 42 g protein, 60 g carbs, 11 g fat, 4 g saturated fat, 680 mg sodium

| B12 | 500% (30 mcg) daily vitamin B12 | Fe | 83% (15 mg) daily iron | Fo | 43% (172 mcg) daily folate |
| Vc | 173% (104 mg) daily vitamin C | O3 | 75% (750 mg) daily omega-3s | | |

Shrimp and Asparagus Stir-Fry with Rice Noodles

You only need a few flavorful ingredients to create the savory-sweet orange sauce for this quick stir-fry. Light-colored miso, which can be found in natural food stores and Asian markets, tends to be sweeter and less salty than dark miso, so it works well in the delicate sauce. For the best texture, be sure to stop cooking the rice noodles when they're still a bit chewy.

PREP TIME: 20 MINUTES / **TOTAL TIME:** 40 MINUTES / **SERVINGS:** 4

Zest of 1 orange (about 1 tablespoon)

Juice of 1 orange (about ⅓ cup)

2 tablespoons honey

1 tablespoon white or yellow miso paste

2 teaspoons reduced-sodium soy sauce

10 ounces rice noodles (pad Thai noodles)

2 teaspoons canola oil

1¼ pounds medium shrimp, shelled and deveined

3 pounds asparagus, tough ends trimmed, cut into 3" lengths

8 scallions, white and some green, sliced (about ½ cup)

1 tablespoon peeled, chopped fresh ginger (1" piece)

½ teaspoon red-pepper flakes

1 **WHISK** together the orange zest, orange juice, honey, miso, and soy sauce in a small bowl. Set aside. Bring a large pot of water to a boil on high heat and add the rice noodles. Reduce the heat to medium low and simmer until al dente, 5 to 7 minutes. Drain.

2 **HEAT** the oil in a large skillet on medium-high heat. Add the shrimp and cook until the outsides are golden brown and the centers are opaque, 3 to 4 minutes, stirring once or twice. Transfer to a bowl.

3 **ADD** the asparagus to the skillet and cook, stirring frequently, 1 to 2 minutes. Add ⅔ cup water and simmer until evaporated, stirring frequently, 3 to 4 minutes. Add the scallions and ginger and cook, stirring frequently, until the asparagus is crisp-tender, about 1 minute.

4 **ADD** the reserved orange juice mixture and simmer until slightly thickened, 2 to 3 minutes. Add the shrimp and rice noodles and cook, stirring constantly, until heated through and coated with the sauce, 1 to 2 minutes. Divide among 4 serving bowls and sprinkle with the pepper flakes to taste.

NUTRITION *(per serving: 2¼ cups)* 370 calories, 7 g protein, 81 g carbs, 3 g fat, 0 g saturated fat, 307 mg sodium

| Vc | 38% (23 mg) daily vitamin C | Fo | 28% (111 mcg) daily folate | Cr | 2½ servings carotenoid-rich food (asparagus) |
| Fe | 33% (6 mg) daily iron | | | | |

SIDES 7

Asparagus : **FOLATE**
Eggplant : **ANTHOCYANINS**
Quinoa : **FIBER**
Kale : **CALCIUM**

Broiled Asparagus with Sun-Dried Tomato Vinaigrette

Look for jars of sun-dried tomatoes packed in olive oil, often found in the supermarket produce section. You'll use the tomatoes, as well as their flavorful oil, to make the vinaigrette in this side dish.

PREP TIME: 10 MINUTES **/ TOTAL TIME:** 20 MINUTES **/ SERVINGS:** 4

2¾ pounds asparagus, tough ends trimmed

1 tablespoon olive oil

1 tablespoon balsamic vinegar

¼ teaspoon sugar

2 tablespoons chopped sun-dried tomatoes packed in olive oil, plus 2 tablespoons of the oil

1 tablespoon chopped shallot

1 **HEAT** the broiler to high. Arrange the asparagus on a baking sheet in a single layer and drizzle with the olive oil. Broil 6" to 8" from the heat source, turning occasionally, until the asparagus is lightly browned and tender, 5 to 7 minutes. Transfer to a serving platter and season with salt and freshly ground black pepper to taste.

2 **WHISK** the vinegar, sugar, and the oil from the sun-dried tomato jar until emulsified in a small bowl. Whisk in the sun-dried tomatoes and shallot and season with salt and freshly ground black pepper to taste. Drizzle over the hot asparagus and serve.

NUTRITION *(per serving)* 113 calories, 5 g protein, 10 g carbs, 8 g fat, 1 g saturated fat, 81 mg sodium

Fo **26% (104 mcg) daily folate**

 Cr **3 servings carotenoid-rich food (asparagus)**

Sweet and Tangy Baked Beans and Tomatoes

Just 45 minutes in the oven makes these beans taste like they've been slow cooking all day. Be sure *not* to stir them, so the top layer and edges can develop a crisp, caramelized "crust" that adds texture to the dish.

PREP TIME: 10 MINUTES / **TOTAL TIME:** 1 HOUR 30 MINUTES / **SERVINGS:** 6

2 teaspoons canola oil

½ large onion, chopped (about ¾ cup)

½ teaspoon dried rosemary

2 cloves garlic, chopped

½ cup tomato paste

1 can (14 ounces) fire-roasted diced tomatoes

3 cans (15 ounces) great Northern or navy beans, drained and rinsed

3 tablespoons pure maple syrup

2 tablespoons apple cider vinegar

1 **HEAT** the oven to 350°F. Heat the oil in a large ovenproof pot or Dutch oven on medium heat. Add the onion and rosemary and cook, stirring occasionally, until the onion is tender and lightly browned, 7 to 8 minutes. Add the garlic and cook, stirring, 1 minute. Stir in the tomato paste and cook until some of the moisture evaporates, 2 minutes. Add the diced tomatoes and bring to a boil.

2 **ADD** the beans, maple syrup, and vinegar and stir to combine. Season to taste with salt and freshly ground black pepper. Bring to a simmer and transfer to the oven. Bake, uncovered, without stirring, until the edges are browned, 45 minutes. Cool 15 minutes and serve.

NUTRITION *(per serving: ¾ cup)* 241 calories, 13 g protein, 44 g carbs, 2 g fat, <1 g saturated fat, 325 mg sodium

Fi 44% (11 g) daily fiber

Fo 36% (142 mcg) daily folate

Cr 1 serving carotenoid-rich food (tomatoes)

O3 ALA omega-3s

Roasted Beet and Beet Green Sauté

Don't toss those leaves! Beet greens have a mild flavor and are tender enough for a quick sauté. This dish makes a beautiful nutrient-packed side, but it would be equally good mixed with whole wheat pasta or quinoa as a vegetarian entrée.

PREP TIME: 20 MINUTES / **TOTAL TIME:** 1 HOUR 25 MINUTES / **SERVINGS:** 4

4 medium beets

1 tablespoon olive oil

2 cloves garlic, finely chopped

1 pound beet greens (about 2 bunches), stems trimmed, chopped

Juice of ½ lemon (1 tablespoon plus 2 teaspoons)

1 **HEAT** the oven to 425°F. Trim the beet stems and roots, leaving about 1" attached to the beets. Wrap the beets together tightly in foil, place on a baking sheet, and roast until a paring knife inserted into the beets goes in and out with minimal resistance, 55 to 65 minutes. When the beets are cool enough to handle, unwrap them from the foil. Trim the root and stem ends, slip the skin off the beets with your fingers, and chop. (May be done up to 1 day ahead, then cover and refrigerate.)

2 **HEAT** the oil in a large skillet on medium-low heat. Add the garlic and cook, stirring, 1 minute. Raise the heat to medium, add the beet greens, toss well to coat with the garlic and oil, and cook until wilted, about 3 minutes. Add enough water to create a thin layer in the skillet (about ¼ cup) and bring to a simmer. Cook, stirring frequently, until the greens are tender and the liquid is evaporated, 3 to 4 minutes. Stir in the beets and lemon juice and cook until heated through, about 1 minute. Remove from the heat. Season to taste with salt and freshly ground black pepper and serve.

NUTRITION (*per serving: ¾ cup*) 97 calories, 4 g protein, 15 g carbs, 4 g fat, 1 g saturated fat, 272 mg sodium

Vc	57% (34 mg) daily vitamin C
Fo	31% (125 mcg) daily folate
Fi	28% (7 g) daily fiber

| K | 28% (995 mg) daily potassium |
| Cr | 3 servings carotenoid-rich food (beet greens) |

 2 servings anthocyanin-rich food (beets)

Braised Kale
with Black-Eyed Peas

Miso paste, soy sauce, and tomato paste add complexity to this
vegan dish. Miso can be found in health food stores or Asian grocery
stores, or increase the soy sauce to 2 tablespoons if miso is
unavailable.

PREP TIME: 10 MINUTES / **TOTAL TIME:** 45 MINUTES / **SERVINGS:** 4

1 tablespoon olive oil

1 medium onion, chopped (about
   1 cup)

1 large carrot, chopped (about
   ¾ cup)

¼ cup tomato paste

2 cloves garlic, chopped

¼ teaspoon red-pepper flakes

1 tablespoon yellow or white miso
   paste

1 tablespoon reduced-sodium
   soy sauce

2 pounds kale (about 3 bunches),
   thick stems trimmed, chopped

1½ cups frozen black-eyed peas

Zest of ½ lemon (about 1 teaspoon)

Juice of ½ lemon (1 tablespoon
   plus 2 teaspoons)

1 **HEAT** the oil in a large pot or Dutch oven on medium heat. Add the
onion and carrot and cook, stirring occasionally, until soft and
lightly browned, about 10 minutes. Add the tomato paste, garlic,
and pepper flakes and cook, stirring, about 1 minute. Add the
miso, soy sauce, and 1½ cups water and bring to a simmer. Add the
kale, reduce the heat to medium low, cover, stirring once or twice,
and simmer until the kale is just tender, about 10 minutes.

2 **ADD** the peas and simmer, uncovered, until the kale is very tender
and the peas are heated through, 8 to 10 minutes. Stir in the
lemon zest and juice. Season to taste with freshly ground black
pepper and serve.

NUTRITION *(per serving: 1¼ cups)* 251 calories, 13 g protein, 43 g carbs, 5 g fat, 1 g saturated fat, 445 mg sodium

 355% (213 mg) daily vitamin C

Fi 36% (9 g) daily fiber

Fe 28% (5 mg) daily iron

Ca 26% (260 mg) daily calcium

K 25% (879 mg) daily potassium

 3 servings carotenoid-rich foods
(kale and carrots)

O₃ ALA omega-3s

Carrot Gratin with Creamy Goat Cheese Sauce

Not all gratins require copious amounts of heavy cream. We get that rich texture with milk and tangy goat cheese instead, trimming both calories and saturated fat.

PREP TIME: 15 MINUTES / **TOTAL TIME:** 45 MINUTES / **SERVES:** 6

2 pounds carrots, sliced on the diagonal ¼" thick

2 tablespoons olive oil

½ large onion, chopped (about ¾ cup)

⅛ teaspoon dried thyme

1 tablespoon plus 2 teaspoons all-purpose flour

1½ cups 2% milk

½ teaspoon allspice

4 ounces goat cheese, crumbled (about 1 cup)

1 teaspoon fresh thyme leaves

3 tablespoons whole wheat panko

1 **HEAT** the oven to 375°F. Bring a large pot of water to a boil on high heat. Add the carrots and boil until tender, 6 to 8 minutes. Drain.

2 **WIPE** the pot dry, add the oil, and heat on medium heat. Add the onion and dried thyme and cook, stirring occasionally, until soft and translucent, about 6 minutes. Add the flour and cook, stirring constantly, until golden, about 2 minutes. Raise the heat to high and, whisking constantly, add the milk in a slow, steady stream. Add the allspice and continue whisking frequently until the milk comes to a simmer. Simmer, whisking constantly, until thickened, 1 to 2 minutes. Remove from the heat.

3 **STIR** in about two-thirds of the goat cheese, ¾ teaspoon of the thyme leaves, and the carrots. Season to taste with salt and freshly ground black pepper. Transfer to a 2-quart oven-safe baking dish. Sprinkle the panko and the remaining goat cheese over the carrot mixture. Bake until the liquid is bubbling, 12 to 15 minutes. Switch the oven to broil and broil 10" from the heat until the cheese is lightly browned, 2 to 6 minutes. Let stand 10 minutes. Sprinkle with the remaining thyme leaves and serve.

NUTRITION (per serving: ¾ cup) 200 calories, 8 g protein, 21 g carbs, 10 g fat, 4 g saturated fat, 193 mg sodium

Cr **2 servings carotenoid-rich food (carrots)**

Red Potatoes with Edamame Pesto

Edamame usually pops up in Asian dishes, but we've put an Italian twist on these healthy legumes by making them the basis for a chunky pesto. To save time, look in your supermarket's freezer section for shelled edamame, rather than the ones still in their pods.

PREP TIME: 20 MINUTES **/ TOTAL TIME:** 35 MINUTES **/ SERVINGS:** 6

4 cloves garlic

2 pounds red potatoes, chopped (about 6 cups)

½ cup chopped fresh, flat-leaf parsley

½ cup chopped fresh basil

⅔ cup pine nuts, toasted

Zest of ½ lemon (about 1 teaspoon), plus extra for garnish

Juice of ½ lemon (1 tablespoon plus 2 teaspoons)

3 cups frozen shelled edamame, thawed

1 ounce Parmesan cheese, grated (about ¼ cup), and 1 ounce Parmesan cheese, shaved with a vegetable peeler

2 tablespoons olive oil

¾ cup low-sodium chicken or vegetable broth

1 **FILL** a large pot with about 1" of water. Smash 3 of the garlic cloves with the flat side of a knife and add to the water. Place a steamer basket in the pot and bring to a boil on high heat. Add the potatoes, cover, and reduce the heat to medium low. Steam until tender when pierced with a fork, 8 to 12 minutes.

2 **FINELY** chop the remaining garlic clove. Combine it with the parsley, basil, pine nuts, lemon zest, lemon juice, 1½ cups of the edamame, and the grated Parmesan in the bowl of a food processor. Process until roughly chopped, scraping down the sides of the bowl as needed. With the processor running, pour the oil through the feed tube to form a slightly chunky puree. Pour ½ cup of the broth through the feed tube to thin. Add the remaining broth if a thinner consistency is desired.

3 **COMBINE** the potatoes (discard the garlic) and the remaining edamame in a large bowl. Add the pesto and stir to combine. Season to taste with salt and freshly ground black pepper. Garnish with the shaved Parmesan and lemon zest.

NUTRITION *(per serving: 1⅔ cups)* 327 calories, 14 g protein, 33 g carbs, 17 g fat, 3 g saturated fat, 224 mg sodium

| Fo | 56% (224 mcg) daily folate | K | 32% (1,121 mg) daily potassium | Mg | 26% (102 mg) daily magnesium |
| Vc | 48% (29 mg) daily vitamin C | Fi | 28% (7 g) daily fiber | | |

Braised Spinach and Potatoes with Indian Spices

Black mustard seeds, which can be found at Indian grocery stores, add a pleasantly bitter flavor to this dish. They don't taste like regular mustard, so don't substitute regular mustard seeds. Garam masala is a spice mixture that usually includes cumin, coriander, and cardamom and can be found in the spice section of most supermarkets.

PREP TIME: 20 MINUTES **/ TOTAL TIME:** 50 MINUTES **/ SERVINGS:** 4

¾ pound red potatoes, cut into 1" chunks (about 3 cups)

1 tablespoon canola oil

¾ teaspoon cumin seeds

¾ teaspoon black mustard seeds (optional)

½ large onion, chopped (about ¾ cup)

1 fresh jalapeño, seeded and chopped (about 3 tablespoons)

2 cloves garlic, finely chopped

1 teaspoon turmeric

¾ teaspoon garam masala

8 cups spinach leaves (about 8 ounces), chopped

1 **BRING** a large pot of water to a boil on high heat. Add the potatoes and boil until tender, but not soft, 7 to 10 minutes. Drain.

2 **HEAT** the oil in a large pot or Dutch oven on medium heat. Add the cumin seeds and black mustard seeds, if using. Cook, stirring often, until fragrant, about 1 minute. Add the onion and jalapeño and cook until tender and lightly browned, 7 to 8 minutes. Add the garlic and cook, about 1 minute. Add the potatoes, turmeric, and garam masala. Cook, stirring, until well combined, 1 minute.

3 **ADD** ¾ cup water and one-third of the spinach. Stir until the spinach is just wilted and add another third of the spinach. Stir until just wilted and add the remaining spinach. Cook, stirring often, until most of the liquid evaporates and the spinach is tender, 6 to 8 minutes. Season with salt and freshly ground black pepper to taste.

NUTRITION *(per serving: ¾ cup)* 123 calories, 4 g protein, 20 g carbs, 4 g fat, <1 g saturated fat, 53 mg sodium

 47% (28 mg) daily vitamin C

 33% (133 mg) daily folate

Cr 2 servings carotenoid-rich food (spinach)

Honey-Lime Glazed Carrots

The term "glaze" suggests a thick, sugary coating that takes a long time to make. Not so here. Honey is the only thickener required, and its sweetness is cut with the bright acidity of lime juice.

PREP TIME: 10 MINUTES / TOTAL TIME: 20 MINUTES / SERVINGS: 4

1 pound carrots, sliced on the diagonal ¼" thick (about 4½ cups)

Juice of 3 limes (about 6 tablespoons)

3 tablespoons honey

3 tablespoons chopped fresh cilantro or flat-leaf parsley

1 **BRING** a large pot of water to a boil on high heat. Add the carrots and boil until crisp-tender, 3 to 4 minutes. Drain.

2 **WHISK** together the lime juice and honey in a small bowl. Heat a large skillet on medium-low heat. Add the carrots and lime juice mixture and bring to a simmer. Cook, stirring occasionally, until the liquid thickens to a glaze, 5 to 7 minutes. Season to taste with salt and freshly ground black pepper. Stir in the cilantro or parsley.

NUTRITION *(per serving: 1 cup)* 100 calories, 1 g protein, 26 g carbs, <1g fat, 0 g saturated fat, 80 mg sodium

Cr 2 servings carotenoid-rich food (carrots)

Shredded Carrot and Chickpea Salad

Grate the carrots in a food processor fitted with a shredding disk or on the large holes of a box grater to create this fresh-tasting salad.

PREP TIME: 10 MINUTES / TOTAL TIME: 15 MINUTES / SERVINGS: 4

1 pound carrots (about 7 medium), shredded

1 can (15 ounces) chickpeas, drained and rinsed

½ cup raisins

¼ cup red wine vinegar

1 tablespoon olive oil

1 tablespoon cumin seeds, toasted

Juice of ½ lemon (about 1 tablespoon plus 2 teaspoons)

½ cup chopped fresh flat-leaf parsley

COMBINE THE carrots, chickpeas, raisins, vinegar, oil, cumin, lemon juice, and parsley in a large bowl. Toss well to combine. Season to taste with salt and freshly ground black pepper.

NUTRITION *(per serving: 1⅓ cups)* 258 calories, 7 g protein, 49 g carbs, 5 g fat, <1 g saturated fat, 197 mg sodium

Vc 40% (24 mg) daily vitamin C

Fi 32% (8 g) daily fiber

Cr 2 servings carotenoid-rich food (carrots)

Grilled Japanese Eggplant with Miso Glaze

Japanese eggplant is slender and smaller than the more common Italian variety. While both types taste similar, the Japanese one cooks quickly, making it ideal for grilling. If you can't find it, baby eggplant (smaller version of the Italian variety) is a good alternative and will cook in the same amount of time.

PREP TIME: 15 MINUTES / **TOTAL TIME:** 25 MINUTES / **SERVINGS:** 4

1 tablespoon plus 2 teaspoons light miso

Juice of ½ lemon (1 tablespoon plus 2 teaspoons)

2 teaspoons honey

1 teaspoon soy sauce

½ teaspoon ground ginger

¼ teaspoon garlic powder

2½ pounds Japanese or baby eggplant (about 6), halved lengthwise

1 tablespoon canola oil

2 tablespoons chopped fresh cilantro

Lemon wedges

1 **BRUSH** a grill rack with vegetable oil and heat the grill to medium-high. Whisk together the miso, lemon juice, honey, soy sauce, ginger, and garlic powder in a small bowl. Set aside.

2 **BRUSH** the flesh side of the eggplant with the canola oil and season with freshly ground black pepper. Grill over direct heat, flesh side down, until golden brown grill marks appear, 5 to 7 minutes. Turn and grill until light grill marks appear on the bottom side and the flesh offers some resistance when pierced with a fork, 4 to 5 minutes. Brush the miso glaze over the flesh and continue grilling until very tender and the flesh offers no resistance when pierced, 1 to 2 minutes. Transfer to a serving plate and sprinkle with cilantro. Serve with lemon wedges.

NUTRITION (per serving) 124 calories, 4 g protein, 21 g carbs, 4 g fat, <1 g saturated fat, 362 mg sodium

Fi **40% (10 g) daily fiber**

 An **4½ servings anthocyanin-rich food (eggplant)**

Quinoa with Black Beans, Tomatoes, Corn, and Feta

Quinoa comes in a variety of colors—red, black, and gold. Feel free to use any shade you like in this dish.

PREP TIME: 15 MINUTES / **TOTAL TIME:** 50 MINUTES / **SERVINGS:** 6

¾ cup quinoa, rinsed

2 teaspoons canola oil

½ large onion, chopped (about ¾ cup)

¾ cup frozen corn

1 can (15 ounces) black beans, drained and rinsed

1 pint cherry tomatoes, quartered (about 1½ cups)

1 teaspoon ground cumin

½ teaspoon chili powder

Juice of 2 to 3 limes (about 4 to 6 tablespoons)

3 ounces feta cheese, crumbled (about ¾ cup)

⅓ cup fresh cilantro leaves

1 **BRING** 1¼ cups water to a boil in a medium saucepan on high heat. Stir in the quinoa and ¼ teaspoon salt. Reduce the heat to low, cover, and simmer until the quinoa is cooked through but still firm to the bite and the water is evaporated, 15 to 18 minutes. Remove from the heat and rest, covered, 10 minutes.

2 **HEAT** the oil in a large skillet on medium heat. Add the onion and cook, stirring occasionally, until soft and lightly browned, about 6 minutes. Add the corn and cook 2 minutes, then add the beans and cook until heated through, about 2 minutes. Transfer to a large bowl. Add the quinoa, tomatoes, cumin, chili powder, and lime juice to taste and stir gently to combine. Stir in the feta and cilantro and season to taste with salt and freshly ground black pepper.

NUTRITION (per serving: 1 heaping cup) 222 calories, 11 g protein, 33 g carbs, 6 g fat, 2 g saturated fat, 501 mg sodium

Fi 28% (7 g) daily fiber

Red Cabbage Slaw with Tangy Poppy Seed Dressing

This crunchy slaw pairs well with grilled foods like barbecued pork, steak, and burgers. It's also a perfect match for our Fish Tacos with Black Bean–Papaya Salsa (page 88).

PREP TIME: 20 MINUTES **/ TOTAL TIME:** 20 MINUTES **/ SERVINGS:** 6

5 tablespoons cider vinegar

3 tablespoons canola oil

3 tablespoons honey

1 tablespoon Dijon mustard

1 tablespoon plus 2 teaspoons poppy seeds

½ red cabbage, cored and thinly sliced (about 5 cups)

2 yellow bell peppers, thinly sliced (about 2 cups)

1½ cups shredded carrots

½ cup coarsely chopped fresh flat-leaf parsley

WHISK the vinegar, oil, honey, and mustard together in a large bowl. Whisk in the poppy seeds. Add the cabbage, bell peppers, carrots, and parsley and toss well to combine. Season to taste with salt and freshly ground black pepper and serve.

NUTRITION *(per serving: 1¼ cups)* 158 calories, 2 g protein, 21 g carbs, 9 g fat, 1 g saturated fat, 99 mg sodium

Vc 190% (114 mg) daily vitamin C

 An 1½ servings anthocyanin-rich food (red cabbage)

Cr 1 serving carotenoid-rich foods (yellow bell pepper and carrots)

Curried Roasted Cauliflower with Flaxseeds

A trick for getting great browning and caramelization when roasting cruciferous vegetables like cauliflower, broccoli, and Brussels sprouts is to start with veggies that are completely dry. Wash and air dry in advance or toss them around in a kitchen towel to soak up as much water as possible if you're pressed for time.

PREP TIME: 15 MINUTES / **TOTAL TIME:** 40 MINUTES / **SERVINGS:** 4

1 large head cauliflower (about 2 pounds), trimmed, florets cut into bite-size pieces
1 tablespoon canola oil
2 tablespoons curry powder
3 tablespoons ground flaxseeds
Juice of 1½ limes (about 3 tablespoons)
2 tablespoons fresh cilantro leaves

1 **HEAT** the oven to 400°F and coat a baking sheet with cooking spray. Pat the cauliflower dry if damp and spread it on the baking sheet. Whisk together the oil and curry powder and toss with cauliflower to coat. Season with ½ teaspoon salt and freshly ground black pepper. Roast in the lower third of the oven until deep golden brown on the bottom sides, about 15 minutes.

2 **ADD** the flaxseeds and toss. Roast until the cauliflower is tender, 7 to 10 minutes. Transfer to a serving bowl. Add the lime juice and cilantro and toss.

NUTRITION *(per serving: 1 cup)* 115 calories, 5 g protein, 12 g carbs, 7 g fat, 1 g saturated fat, 273 mg sodium

| Vc | **192% (115 mg) daily vitamin C** | Fi | **28% (7 g) daily fiber** | O3 | **ALA omega-3s** |

Fingerling Potato Salad with Creamy Mustard-Anchovy Dressing

The anchovies don't make this creamy dressing taste fishy, but they do add a complex savory flavor that makes this salad addictive. If you've had a traditional, freshly made Caesar dressing, which also contains anchovies, this is the same idea at play.

PREP TIME: 15 MINUTES / **TOTAL TIME:** 30 MINUTES / **SERVES:** 4

1½ pounds fingerling potatoes

½ cup low-fat plain Greek yogurt

6 canned anchovy fillets, finely chopped

Juice of 1 lemon (about 3 tablespoons)

2 tablespoons grainy mustard

1 tablespoon olive oil

2 teaspoons honey

5 cups arugula (about 5 ounces)

1½ cups cherry tomatoes, halved

1 **CUT** the potatoes in half (or in thirds, if large) crosswise on the diagonal. Fill a large pot with about ½" of water, insert a steamer basket, cover, and bring to a boil on high heat. Reduce the heat to medium, add the potatoes, cover, and steam until fork-tender, 10 to 12 minutes.

2 **WHISK** together the yogurt, anchovies, lemon juice, mustard, oil, and honey in a large serving bowl. Add the arugula, tomatoes, and potatoes and toss to combine. Season with freshly ground black pepper to taste. Serve immediately.

NUTRITION *(per serving: 1⅔ cups)* 225 calories, 9 g protein, 40 g carbs, 4 g fat, 1 g saturated fat, 348 mg sodium

 97% (58 mg) daily vitamin C | K 25% (863 mg) daily potassium | Cr 2 serving carotenoid-rich foods (arugula and tomatoes)

Tuscan Kale Salad with Almonds and Parmesan

Tuscan kale is also known as Lacinato or dinosaur kale because of its pebbled texture (like one might imagine dinosaur skin). It is more tender than regular kale, which makes it the best choice for salads like this. Working the oil and coarse salt into the leaves with your fingers for a full 5 minutes softens them enough that this traditional cooking green may be eaten raw.

PREP TIME: 20 MINUTES **/ TOTAL TIME:** 20 MINUTES **/ SERVINGS:** 4

1½ pounds Tuscan kale (2 small bunches)

Juice of 1 lemon (about 3 tablespoons)

2 tablespoons olive oil

½ teaspoon coarse sea salt or kosher salt

¼ cup whole almonds, toasted

2 ounces Parmesan, shaved

1 **TRIM** the ends and cut each kale leaf in half lengthwise, completely removing ribs. Thinly slice the kale about ⅛" thick. Dry the kale in a salad spinner and transfer to a large bowl.

2 **ADD** the lemon juice, oil, and salt to the kale. Rub the ingredients into the kale, working them between your hands and fingers, until the leaves are soft and tenderized, about 5 minutes. Add almonds and freshly ground black pepper and toss to combine. Divide among 4 salad bowls and top evenly with the Parmesan.

NUTRITION (per serving: 1½ cups) 196 calories, 9 g protein, 10 g carbs, 16 g fat, 3 g saturated fat, 463 mg sodium

Vc 137% (82 mg) daily vitamin C

Ca 26% (260 mg) daily calcium

Cr 1 serving carotenoid-rich food (kale)

Crab Fried Rice with Tofu

Most restaurant versions of this dish contain precious little crab, and it's likely to be of the imitation variety. This one gives you plenty of satisfying protein from the shellfish, as well as tofu, and the brown rice adds filling fiber.

PREP TIME: 20 MINUTES / **TOTAL TIME:** 1 HOUR 35 MINUTES / **SERVINGS:** 4

¾ cup brown rice

2 large eggs

2 tablespoons reduced-sodium soy sauce

1 teaspoon dark sesame oil

¼ to ½ teaspoon red-pepper flakes

1 tablespoon canola oil

1 medium red bell pepper, chopped (about 1 cup)

½ package (7 ounces) extra-firm tofu, drained, patted dry, and cut into ½" cubes

8 ounces canned crabmeat, drained and picked over for shells

¾ cup frozen peas

4 scallions, white and light green parts, sliced (about ¼ cup)

1 can (8 ounces) pineapple chunks, drained and chopped

Lemon wedges

1 **BRING** 1½ cups water to a boil in a small saucepan on high heat. Add the rice and ¼ teaspoon salt, reduce the heat to low, cover, and simmer until the rice is tender and the liquid is evaporated, 50 minutes. Remove from the heat and let stand, covered, 10 minutes.

2 **WHISK** together the eggs, soy sauce, sesame oil, and pepper flakes (use a smaller amount if you like less heat) in a small bowl and reserve.

3 **HEAT** the canola oil in a large skillet on medium heat. Add the bell pepper and tofu and cook, stirring occasionally, until the pepper is tender and the tofu is lightly browned, 7 to 9 minutes. Season to taste with salt and freshly ground black pepper. Add the rice, crabmeat, and peas and stir to combine. Add the soy mixture to the rice mixture and cook, stirring frequently, until the eggs are set and the rice mixture is moist but not wet, 3 to 4 minutes. Add the scallions and pineapple and stir gently until the scallions are softened, 1 to 2 minutes. Divide among 4 bowls and serve with lemon wedges.

NUTRITION *(per serving: 1 cup)* 253 calories, 16 g protein, 29 g carbs, 8 g fat, 2 g saturated fat, 409 mg sodium

B_{12} 50% (3 mcg) daily vitamin B_{12} Vc 50% (30 mg) daily vitamin C   O3 44% (440 mg) daily omega-3s

SNACKS AND DESSERTS

8

Strawberries : **VITAMIN C**
Walnuts : **OMEGA-3s**
Yogurt : **CALCIUM**

Blueberry Fool

The origin of its name is uncertain, but one thing we do know is that this simple combination of fruit and cream is incredibly easy to make. Adding as many berries as possible, both cooked and fresh, ups the nutrient content and makes the small amount of heavy cream practically virtuous.

PREP TIME: 5 MINUTES **/ TOTAL TIME:** 35 MINUTES **/ SERVINGS:** 4

3 tablespoons granulated sugar

Juice of 1 lemon (about 3 tablespoons)

4 cups fresh blueberries

½ cup cold heavy cream

1½ tablespoons confectioners' sugar

1 **BRING** the granulated sugar, lemon juice, and 2½ cups of the blueberries to a simmer in a medium saucepan on medium heat. Simmer, stirring occasionally, until the berries break down and the liquid thickens, 10 to 12 minutes. Remove from the heat and stir in all but 12 of the remaining blueberries; set those aside.

2 **PLACE** the saucepan in a larger bowl or baking dish (not glass) filled with ice water. Let stand, stirring occasionally, until chilled, 10 to 15 minutes. Alternatively, cool at room temperature, cover, and refrigerate 2 hours or up to 24 hours.

3 **BEAT** the cream with an electric mixer on medium-high speed in a large bowl until the volume doubles and soft peaks form, 2 to 3 minutes. Add the confectioners' sugar and beat until combined, about 30 seconds.

4 **PLACE** about 1½ tablespoons of the blueberry mixture in each of 4 dessert glasses or small bowls. Fold all but 2 tablespoons of the remaining blueberry mixture into the whipped cream. Divide the cream among the dessert glasses and top evenly with the remaining blueberry mixture. Garnish with the reserved blueberries and serve.

NUTRITION (per serving) 224 calories, 2 g protein, 33 g carbs, 12 g fat, 7 g saturated fat, 13 mg sodium

 33% (20 mg) daily vitamin C

An 2 servings anthocyanin-rich food (blueberries)

Dark Chocolate Pudding with Whipped Ricotta

Once you try homemade pudding, you'll never go back to the store-bought kind in the little plastic cups. Aerating the ricotta with an electric mixer makes a fluffy calcium-rich topping.

PREP TIME: 10 MINUTES **/ TOTAL TIME:** 25 MINUTES + CHILLING TIME **/ SERVINGS:** 4

⅓ cup plus 1 tablespoon sugar

⅓ cup unsweetened natural cocoa powder (not Dutch process)

2½ tablespoons cornstarch

2½ cups fat-free milk

2 large egg yolks

1¼ teaspoons vanilla extract

1½ ounces dark chocolate (60% to 70% cocoa), chopped or chips (about ¼ cup)

⅓ cup part-skim ricotta cheese

8 to 12 raspberries (optional)

Mint leaves (optional)

1 **WHISK** together ⅓ cup sugar, cocoa, cornstarch, and ¼ teaspoon salt in a medium saucepan. Add the milk, pouring in a slow, steady stream, whisking constantly.

2 **HEAT** the mixture on high, whisking constantly, and bring to a simmer. Reduce the heat to medium and simmer until thickened, about 1 minute. Remove from the heat.

3 **WHISK** together the egg yolks and 1 teaspoon of the vanilla in a medium bowl. Add about ½ cup of the milk mixture in a slow, steady stream, whisking constantly as you pour to prevent the yolks from curdling. Immediately pour the egg mixture into the saucepan, whisking constantly. Bring to a simmer on medium-high heat, whisking constantly. Reduce the heat to medium low and, whisking constantly, simmer, 1 minute. Remove from the heat and immediately add the chocolate and whisk until smooth. Divide among 4 dessert cups or ramekins. Place plastic wrap over pudding, directly touching the surface to prevent a skin from forming. Refrigerate 2 hours.

4 **ADD** the ricotta and the remaining 1 tablespoon sugar and vanilla to a medium bowl. Beat with an electric mixer on medium-high speed until smooth, about 1 minute. Top pudding evenly with the ricotta and garnish with raspberries and mint, if using.

NUTRITION *(per serving)* 287 calories, 11 g protein, 43 g carbs, 9 g fat, 5 g saturated fat, 215 mg sodium

Ca 26% (255 mg) daily calcium

Strawberry-Ricotta Crepes

Although they contain less vitamin C, raspberries can be substituted for strawberries in this recipe. Raspberries have the most fiber of all the berries—8 grams per cup.

PREP TIME: 15 MINUTES / **TOTAL TIME:** 1 HOUR / **SERVINGS:** 10

Juice of 1 lemon (about
    3 tablespoons)

2 tablespoons granulated sugar

2 pounds strawberries, cored and
    finely chopped (about 4 cups)

1 cup part-skim ricotta cheese

3 ounces reduced-fat cream cheese
    (Neufchâtel), about ⅓ cup

5 tablespoons confectioners' sugar
    plus extra (optional) for serving

¾ cup all-purpose flour

¾ cup white whole wheat flour

2 large eggs

2 cups fat-free milk

1 teaspoon vanilla extract

Zest of 2 lemons (about
    4 teaspoons)

1 **ADD** the lemon juice, granulated sugar, and 2 cups of the strawberries to a medium saucepan and bring to a simmer on medium-high heat. Simmer, stirring frequently, until the berries are very soft and broken down and the liquid is thickened, 15 to 20 minutes. Remove from the heat, cover, and set aside.

2 **COMBINE** the ricotta, cream cheese, 4 tablespoons of the confectioners' sugar, and the remaining berries in a medium bowl. Cover and refrigerate until ready to use.

3 **WHISK** together both flours, the remaining 1 tablespoon confectioners' sugar, and ¼ teaspoon salt in a large bowl. Whisk the eggs in a medium bowl, add the milk and vanilla extract, and whisk to combine. Pour into the flour mixture and whisk until no lumps remain.

4 **HEAT** an 8" skillet on medium heat. Spray with cooking spray and pour about ¼ cup of the batter into the skillet. Immediately tilt the skillet and swirl the batter around to coat the entire cooking surface. Cook until the bottom side is golden brown, 1 to 1½ minutes. Loosen with a spatula and flip, using the spatula and your fingers to help turn the crepe. Cook until the opposite side is golden brown, reducing the heat to medium low if the crepe browns too quickly, about 45 seconds. Transfer to a plate and cover with a kitchen towel.

(continued)

Crepes 101

Crepes are fun and easy to make once you get the hang of it. Tilt the skillet immediately after pouring the batter so it thinly coats the entire cooking surface; make sure the pan is hot enough so that the crepe cooks quickly and doesn't stick (it should sizzle a little on contact); and take the crepe out of the pan as soon as both sides are light golden brown so it's tender, not crispy.

5 **REPEAT** with the remaining batter, spraying the skillet with cooking spray each time. Stack the finished crepes, placing wax paper or parchment paper between them to prevent sticking, and keep covered with the towel.

6 **SPREAD** about ¼ cup of the ricotta mixture over each crepe. Loosely fold in half and fold again to form triangles. Reheat the reserved strawberry sauce on low heat, if necessary. Top each crepe with about 2 tablespoons of the sauce and garnish with the lemon zest. Sift confectioners' sugar over the top, if using.

NUTRITION *(per serving: 1 crepe)* 209 calories, 9 g protein, 31 g carbs, 5 g fat, 3 g saturated fat, 151 mg sodium

Vc **87% (52 mg) daily vitamin C**

Baked Apples with Walnuts, Cinnamon, and Raisins

This dessert is like apple crisp without loads of extra sugar and butter. Since you don't need to peel and chop the apples, you can have it in the oven in just 15 minutes.

PREP TIME: 15 MINUTES / **TOTAL TIME:** 1 HOUR 10 MINUTES / **SERVINGS:** 4

4 medium apples
Juice of 1 lemon (about 3 tablespoons)
1 tablespoon unsalted butter
½ cup chopped walnuts
¼ cup brown sugar
2 tablespoons raisins
1 teaspoon cinnamon

1 **HEAT** the oven to 375°F. Cut a thin slice off the stem ends of the apples, removing the stems. Core the apples three-quarters of the way to the bottom (do not cut through the bottoms), cutting a 1"-wide cavity with a paring knife, removing the seeds. Place in an 8" × 8" baking dish. Drizzle the lemon juice evenly into the apple cavities to prevent discoloring.

2 **PLACE** the butter in a small microwaveable bowl. Microwave until melted, 45 seconds to 1 minute. Add the walnuts, sugar, raisins, cinnamon, and ⅛ teaspoon salt and stir to combine. Pack the mixture evenly into the apple cavities.

3 **POUR** ½ cup boiling water into the baking dish. Bake until the apples are soft and offer almost no resistance when pierced with a paring knife, 40 to 45 minutes. Cool 10 minutes and serve.

NUTRITION *(per serving)* 291 calories, 3 g protein, 48 g carbs, 12 g fat, 3 g saturated fat, 67 mg sodium
03 ALA omega-3s

Dark Chocolate Walnut Brownies

Brownies made with cocoa powder like these tend to stay perfectly chewy, not heavy or greasy. Since about three-quarters of the cocoa butter has been removed from the powder, it is lower in fat than solid chocolate. As for what type to buy, we think Dutch cocoa, which is treated to remove its acidic component, makes for a deeper chocolate flavor in brownies.

PREP TIME: 15 MINUTES **/ TOTAL TIME:** 1 HOUR **/ SERVINGS:** 16

6 tablespoons unsalted butter

½ cup granulated sugar

½ cup light brown sugar

½ cup Dutch process cocoa powder

1 teaspoon vanilla extract

2 large eggs

½ cup all-purpose flour

⅓ cup chopped walnuts, toasted

16 large walnut pieces

1 **HEAT** the oven to 350°F. Line an 8" × 8" baking dish with nonstick foil or parchment paper, leaving a few inches hanging over two opposite sides, forming a "sling" to lift the brownies out.

2 **MELT** the butter in a medium saucepan on medium heat. Stir in the sugars and reduce the heat to low. Heat the mixture (avoid simmering), stirring often, until the sugar is partially dissolved, 2 to 3 minutes. Transfer to a medium bowl and stir in the cocoa, vanilla and ½ teaspoon salt. Beat the eggs lightly in a small bowl. Add to the cocoa mixture, stirring until just combined. Add the flour and stir until just combined. Stir in the chopped walnuts.

3 **TRANSFER** the batter to the prepared baking dish and place the walnut pieces on top, spacing evenly in 4 rows of 4. Bake until a wooden pick inserted in the center comes out with a few moist crumbs, 24 to 26 minutes. Cool in the baking dish 10 minutes. Lift out of the dish, transfer to a rack, and cool completely. Cut into 16 squares.

NUTRITION (per serving) 147 calories, 3 g protein, 18 g carbs, 8 g fat, 3 g saturated fat, 69 mg sodium

O3 ALA omega-3s

Strawberry Cocoa Shortcakes with Amaretto Whipped Cream

Amaretto is an almond-flavored liqueur that adds subtle flavor to the whipped cream. Hazelnut or orange liqueur may be substituted or skip the alcohol and use ¼ teaspoon almond extract.

PREP TIME: 35 MINUTES **/ TOTAL TIME:** 1 HOUR + CHILLING TIME **/ SERVINGS:** 10

2½ pounds strawberries, cored and sliced (about 5 cups)

3 tablespoons granulated sugar

Juice of ½ lemon (1 tablespoon plus 2 teaspoons)

2 cups all-purpose flour

2 tablespoons unsweetened cocoa powder

⅓ cup light brown sugar

2 teaspoons baking powder

¼ cup canola oil

½ cup low-fat plain yogurt

¼ cup low-fat milk

1 egg, lightly beaten, plus 1 egg white, lightly beaten

¼ cup bittersweet chocolate chips

1 teaspoon vanilla extract

2 tablespoons sliced almonds

½ cup plus 2 tablespoons cold whipping cream

1 tablespoon confectioners' sugar

1 tablespoon amaretto

1 **ADD** the strawberries, granulated sugar, and lemon juice to a large bowl. Stir and refrigerate 1 hour or up to 8 hours. Bring to room temperature before serving.

2 **HEAT** the oven to 425°F and line a baking sheet with parchment paper. Whisk together the flour, cocoa, brown sugar, baking powder, and ½ teaspoon salt in a large bowl. Whisk together the oil, yogurt, milk, whole egg, chips, and vanilla extract in a medium bowl. Add to the flour mixture and stir until moistened (dough will not come together completely).

3 **TRANSFER** the dough to a floured surface and knead into a ball with floured hands. Pat into a thick disk and lightly sprinkle with flour. Roll into a ¾"-thick circle. Cut out as many circles as you can with a 2½" biscuit cutter and transfer to the prepared baking sheet. Keep rolling and cutting the dough until you have 10 biscuits. Lightly brush the tops with the egg white. Sprinkle evenly with almonds, pressing lightly to adhere. Bake until the bottom sides are lightly browned and a wooden pick comes out clean, 10 to 11 minutes. Transfer to a rack and cool 10 minutes.

4 **COMBINE** the whipping cream, confectioners' sugar, and amaretto in a large bowl. Beat on high speed until soft peaks form, 2 to 3 minutes. Split the biscuits horizontally. Top each bottom half with about ½ cup strawberries and about 2 tablespoons whipped cream. Cover with the top halves and serve immediately.

NUTRITION (per serving: 1 biscuit) 323 calories, 6 g protein, 43 g carbs, 15 g fat, 5 g saturated fat, 136 mg sodium

Vc 82% (49 mg) daily vitamin C

Strawberry-Mango Smoothie

Frozen fruit also works well in this recipe. Reduce the amount of ice slightly, to ¾ cup.

PREP TIME: 15 MINUTES **/ TOTAL TIME:** 15 MINUTES **/ SERVINGS:** 1

1 cup cored, sliced strawberries
½ mango, chopped (about ¾ cup)
¼ cup fat-free plain Greek yogurt
½" piece fresh ginger, finely grated
　　(about ½ teaspoon)

ADD all of the ingredients plus 1 cup ice cubes to a blender. Blend on high speed until smooth. Pour into a glass and serve.

NUTRITION *(per serving)* 160 calories, 7 g protein, 35 g carbs, <1 g fat, 0 g saturated fat, 25 mg sodium
Vc　**207% (124 mg) daily vitamin C**

Kiwi-Banana Smoothie with Sunflower Seeds

Ripe kiwis and the banana give this smoothie plenty of sweetness. If you're craving a little more, adding 1 to 2 teaspoons of honey would do the trick.

PREP TIME: 15 MINUTES **/ TOTAL TIME:** 15 MINUTES **/ SERVINGS:** 1

3 kiwis, peeled and chopped
½ medium banana, sliced
1 tablespoon unsalted sunflower
　　seeds

ADD all of the ingredients plus 1 cup ice cubes to a blender. Blend on high speed until smooth. Pour into a glass and serve.

NUTRITION *(per serving)* 255 calories, 5 g protein, 53 g carbs, 5 g fat, 1 g saturated fat, 14 mg sodium
Vc　**328% (197 mg) daily vitamin C**　　K　**32% (1,129 mg) daily potassium**　　Mg　**26% (103 mg) daily magnesium**
Fi　**44% (11 g) daily fiber**　　Ve　**27% (8 IU) daily vitamin E**

Cardamom Yogurt Cheesecake with Caramelized Plums

We cut out the soggy, butter-laden crust that goes with most cheesecakes to make room for more of the good stuff: rich, creamy filling with a hint of tanginess. Draining the yogurt overnight through cheesecloth creates a texture similar to soft goat cheese and results in a dessert with more calcium and less saturated fat than the typical all-cream cheese version.

PREP TIME: 10 MINUTES **/ TOTAL TIME:** 1 HOUR 15 MINUTES + STANDING AND COOLING TIME **/ SERVINGS:** 8

1 quart low-fat plain yogurt

8 ounces reduced-fat cream cheese (Neufchâtel)

1¼ cups sugar

2 tablespoons cornstarch

1 tablespoon vanilla extract

½ teaspoon cardamom

4 large eggs

4 ripe but firm medium plums (about 1¼ pounds), halved, pitted, and sliced ⅓" thick

3 tablespoons sliced almonds, toasted

1 **LINE** 2 large fine mesh strainers with 2 layers each of cheesecloth. Place each strainer over a bowl deep enough to leave at least 4" between the bottom of the strainer and the bottom of the bowl. Divide the yogurt between the strainers and cover with plastic wrap. Refrigerate until about ¾ cup liquid has collected in each bowl and the yogurt feels firm, at least 8 hours or up to 24 hours. Discard drained liquid.

2 **HEAT** the oven to 325°F. Cut out a 9½"-diameter circle of parchment paper. Butter the base and sides of a 9" springform pan and line the base with the circle of parchment. Place the pan on a baking sheet.

3 **ADD** the cream cheese, 1 cup sugar, cornstarch, vanilla extract, cardamom, and the yogurt to the bowl of a food processor and puree until very smooth, scraping down the sides of the bowl as needed. Add 2 eggs and process just until combined, about 30 seconds. Add the remaining 2 eggs and process until thoroughly combined, about 1 minute. Pour into the prepared springform pan. Transfer the pan to a baking sheet and bake until the center is just set and a thin knife comes out coated with thick, creamy (not wet) batter, 50 to 55 minutes. Cool 10 minutes, then run a thin knife along the sides of the cheesecake to loosen it, allowing

(continued)

it to contract as it cools and prevent cracking. Cool at room temperature, 2 to 3 hours. Remove the sides from the springform pan and refrigerate the cake until thoroughly chilled, at least 2 hours, or overnight.

4 **HEAT** a large nonstick skillet on medium heat just before you are ready to serve. Combine the remaining ¼ cup sugar and ½ cup water in the skillet and heat until the sugar starts to dissolve, about 1 minute. Add the plums, bring to a simmer, and cook, stirring occasionally, until the liquid reduces to a thick syrup and the plums are tender, 6 to 9 minutes. (If the liquid evaporates before the plums finish cooking, add additional water by the tablespoon.) Cut the cheesecake into 8 slices. Top evenly with the plums and almonds and serve.

NUTRITION *(per serving)* 345 calories, 12 g protein, 53 g carbs, 11 g fat, 5 g saturated fat, 205 mg sodium

Ca 25% (253 mg) daily calcium

Date Squares with Easy Banana "Ice Cream"

These squares get most of their sweetness from dates, not added sugar, and tons of orange flavor from the zest. But the really fun part is the one-ingredient banana "ice cream." Blitzing frozen banana chunks in a food processor creates a consistency that's remarkably similar to your favorite frozen treat without the fat.

PREP TIME: 10 MINUTES **/ TOTAL TIME:** 35 MINUTES + FREEZING TIME **/ SERVINGS:** 9

9 ripe large bananas, peeled

2 cups Medjool dates, pitted and chopped

1 cup fat-free evaporated milk

Zest of ½ large orange (about 2 teaspoons)

1 teaspoon vanilla extract

1 cup all-purpose flour

¾ cup oat bran

5 tablespoons canola oil

3 tablespoons honey

¼ cup chopped pecans

1 **SLICE** the bananas about 1½" thick. Divide between 2 large zip-top bags and freeze at least 4 hours or overnight.

2 **HEAT** the oven to 400°F and line an 8" × 8" baking dish with parchment paper. Combine the dates, evaporated milk, zest, and vanilla extract in a medium saucepan. Bring to a simmer, stirring almost constantly, until thickened, 4 to 5 minutes.

3 **WHISK** together the flour, oat bran, and ½ teaspoon salt in a large bowl. Whisk together the canola oil and honey in a small bowl. Add to the flour mixture and stir until moistened. Transfer to the prepared baking dish and firmly press into an even layer with a spatula or the back of a large spoon. Spread the date mixture evenly over the top and sprinkle with the pecans.

4 **BAKE** until the edges are lightly browned, 18 to 20 minutes. Cool completely and cut into 9 squares.

5 **ADD** 1 bag of frozen bananas to the bowl of a food processor. Process until smooth and the consistency of slightly soft ice cream, breaking up any large chunks as needed if the processor gets stuck. Transfer to a large bowl and place in the freezer while you process the second batch. Repeat with the remaining bananas. Serve immediately with the date squares.

NUTRITION (per serving: 1 square and ½ cup banana "ice cream") 369 calories, 8 g protein, 74 g carbs, 9 g fat, 4 g saturated fat, 142 mg sodium

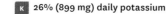

Fi 32% (8 g) daily fiber   K 26% (899 mg) daily potassium

Cocoa-Roasted Peanuts with Cayenne

Egg whites are the base for the peanuts' crispy coating, and a small amount of confectioners' sugar balances the natural bitterness of unsweetened cocoa powder. If heat is not your thing, just skip the cayenne—or swap it for ½ teaspoon of cinnamon.

PREP TIME: 10 MINUTES / **TOTAL TIME:** 25 MINUTES / **SERVINGS:** 4

3 tablespoons confectioners' sugar

⅛ teaspoon cayenne

2 large egg whites

4 tablespoons unsweetened natural cocoa powder (not Dutch process)

1¾ cups roasted unsalted peanuts

1 **HEAT** the oven to 350°F. Coat a baking sheet with cooking spray. Whisk together the sugar, cayenne, egg whites, 2 tablespoons of the cocoa, and ¾ teaspoon salt in a large bowl until smooth. Add the peanuts and toss to combine. Spread onto the prepared baking sheet in a single layer, keeping the nuts from touching as much as possible.

2 **BAKE** until the egg white mixture appears dry, 7 to 8 minutes. Cool on the baking sheet 3 minutes. Immediately transfer the warm nuts to a large bowl and sprinkle with the remaining 2 tablespoons cocoa. Toss well to combine, breaking up any nuts that may be stuck together. Serve immediately or cool completely and store in an airtight container up to 2 days.

NUTRITION *(per serving: ⅓ cup)* 378 calories, 18 g protein, 18 g carbs, 30 g fat, 5 g saturated fat, 397 mg sodium

| Fo | 36% (145 mcg) daily folate | Fi | 28% (7 g) daily fiber | VE | 27% (8 IU) daily vitamin E |

| Mg | 32% (128 mg) daily magnesium |

Spiced Walnuts with Orange Zest and Rosemary

You often see cumin and coriander in spicy Indian dishes, but this recipe highlights the subtle orange flavor of the coriander by pairing it with orange zest.

PREP TIME: 15 MINUTES **/ TOTAL TIME:** 30 MINUTES **/ SERVINGS:** 8

2 cups walnut halves and pieces

1 tablespoon chopped fresh rosemary

Zest of 1 orange (about 1 tablespoon)

¾ teaspoon coarse kosher or sea salt

½ teaspoon ancho chili powder (or other mild to medium chili powder)

½ teaspoon ground cumin

½ teaspoon ground coriander

2 tablespoons unsalted butter, melted and still hot

1 **HEAT** the oven to 350°F. Spread the walnuts out on a baking sheet and bake until lightly browned, tossing once halfway through, about 10 minutes.

2 **COMBINE** the rosemary, zest, salt, chili powder, cumin, and coriander in a large bowl. Add the hot nuts and stir to combine. Add the butter and stir well until combined. Serve warm or at room temperature. These are best served the day they are made.

NUTRITION *(per serving: ¼ cup)* 190 calories, 4 g protein, 4 g carbs, 19 g fat, 4 g saturated fat, 181 mg sodium

O3 **ALA omega 3s**

Make Every Day Super Healthy

We've combined recipes in this book with select healthy snacks and side dishes to create a week's worth of nutrient-packed menus. You'll see how easy it is to mix and match our recipes in order to get the Essential 13 from food, not pills.

DAY 1

BREAKFAST

Creamy Steel-Cut Oats with Dried Cranberries and Pistachios (p 63)

LUNCH

Mediterranean Edamame Patties in Whole Wheat Pita with Tahini Sauce (p 86)

SNACK

Cocoa-Roasted Peanuts with Cayenne (p 230)

STARTER

Brussels Sprout Poppers with Orange-Poppy Seed Dipping Sauce (p 118)

DINNER

Baked Chicken Parmesan with Homemade Tomato Sauce (p 155)

1 cup arugula with 1 teaspoon olive oil and balsamic vinegar

DAILY NUTRITION 1,812 calories, 80 g fat, 15 g saturated fat

An 0 servings anthocyanin-rich foods, Ca 102% calcium, Cr 6 servings carotenoids-rich foods, Fi 124% fiber, Fo 150% folate, Fe 92% iron, Mg 99% magnesium, O3 ALA omega-3s, K 106% potassium, B12 34% vitamin B12, Vc 765% vitamin C, VD 34% vitamin D, VE 46% vitamin E

DAY 2

BREAKFAST

Eggs Florentine on English Muffins (p 69)

LUNCH

Chopped Vegetable Salad with Sardines and Toasted Pita Croutons (p 77)

STARTER

Pumpkin Seed Dip with 1 cup sugar snap peas (p 122)

DINNER

Fettuccine with Lentil Bolognese (p 142)

DESSERT

Blueberry Fool (p 214)

DAILY NUTRITION 1,520 calories, 60 g fat, 17 g saturated fat

An 2 servings anthocyanin-rich foods, Ca 95% calcium, Cr 6 servings carotenoids-rich foods, Fi 176% fiber, Fo 135% folate, Fe 91% iron, Mg 90% magnesium, O3 114% omega-3s plus ALA, K 77% potassium, B12 126% vitamin B12, Vc 274% vitamin C, VD 50% vitamin D, VE 35% vitamin E

DAY 3

BREAKFAST

Tropical Ambrosia Salad (p 71)

LUNCH

Grilled Eggplant, Tomato, and Fresh Mozzarella Sandwiches (p 96)

SNACK

1 cup low-fat plain yogurt and 12 roasted almonds

DINNER

Beef Stew with Root Vegetables (p 166)

DESSERT

Dark Chocolate Walnut Brownies and 1 cup low-fat milk (p 222)

DAILY NUTRITION 1,681 calories, 54g fat, 18 g saturated fat

An 2 servings anthocyanin-rich foods, **Ca** 131% calcium, **Cr** 6 servings carotenoids-rich foods, **Fi** 138% fiber, **Fo** 81% folate, **Fe** 68% iron, **Mg** 84% magnesium, **O₃** ALA omega-3s, **K** 127% potassium, **B₁₂** 116% vitamin B₁₂, **Vc** 583% vitamin C, **Vᴅ** 31% vitamin D, **Vᴇ** 55% vitamin E

DAY 4

BREAKFAST

Blueberry-Oatmeal Casserole with Baked Yogurt Topping (p 59)

LUNCH

Roasted Sweet Potato and Pumpkin Seed Salad (p 74)

SNACK

Kiwi Banana Smoothie with Sunflower Seeds (p 225)

SOUP

Creamy Broccoli–Pea Soup with Bacon and Cheddar (p 110)

DINNER

Roasted Cedar-Plank Salmon with Mustard-Maple Glaze and 1 cup steamed green beans (p 176)

DAILY NUTRITION 1,619 calories, 46 g fat, 12 g saturated fat

An 2 servings anthocyanin-rich foods, **Ca** 76% calcium, **Cr** 11½ servings carotenoids-rich foods, **Fi** 144% fiber, **Fo** 91% folate, **Fe** 65% iron, **Mg** 109% magnesium, **O₃** 180% omega-3s, **K** 108% potassium, **B₁₂** 133% vitamin B₁₂, **Vc** 680% vitamin C, **Vᴅ** 329% vitamin D, **Vᴇ** 47% vitamin E

DAY 5

BREAKFAST

Almond-Apricot Scones (p 56)

LUNCH

Date Ricotta Crostini and Arugula Salad
(p 85)

STARTER

Crab Cocktail with Mango (p 121)

DINNER

Linguini with Kale, Olives, and Currants
(p 145)

DAILY NUTRITION 1,400 calories, 58 g fat, 14 g saturated fat

An 0 servings anthocyanin-rich foods, **Ca** 95% calcium,
Cr 4 servings carotenoids-rich foods, **Fi** 120% fiber,
Fo 65% folate, **Fe** 125% iron, **Mg** 44% magnesium,
O3 35% omega-3s, **K** 70% potassium, **B12** 67% vitamin B_{12},
Vc 288% vitamin C, **VD** 3% vitamin D, **VE** 70% vitamin E

DAY 6

BREAKFAST

Poached Eggs with Steamed Asparagus and
Asiago Cheese (p 65)

LUNCH

Tuna and Chickpea Salad in Tomato Cups
(p 105)

DINNER

Pumpkin Seed–Coated Chicken Breasts with
Bulgur Pilaf (p 160)

SIDE

Curried Roasted Cauliflower with Flaxseeds
(p 207)

DESSERT

Dark Chocolate Pudding with Whipped
Ricotta (p 217)

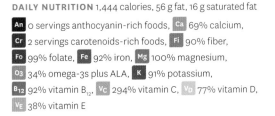

DAILY NUTRITION 1,444 calories, 56 g fat, 16 g saturated fat

An 0 servings anthocyanin-rich foods, **Ca** 69% calcium,
Cr 2 servings carotenoids-rich foods, **Fi** 90% fiber,
Fo 99% folate, **Fe** 92% iron, **Mg** 100% magnesium,
O3 34% omega-3s plus ALA, **K** 91% potassium,
B12 92% vitamin B_{12}, **Vc** 294% vitamin C, **VD** 77% vitamin D,
VE 38% vitamin E

DAY 7

BREAKFAST

Blueberry-Cornmeal Waffles with Blueberry
Sauce (p 60)

LUNCH

Roasted Tomato Soup with White Cheddar
Grilled Cheese Sandwiches (p 94)

DINNER

Wild Rice–Stuffed Acorn Squash (p 151)

SIDE

Tuscan Kale Salad with Almonds and
Parmesan (p 210)

DESSERT

Baked Apples with Walnuts, Cinnamon, and
Raisins (p 221)

DAILY NUTRITION 1,809 calories, 62 g fat, 14 g saturated fat

An 2 servings anthocyanin-rich foods, **Ca** 95% calcium,
Cr 4½ servings carotenoids-rich foods, **Fi** 152% fiber,
Fo 67% folate, **Fe** 92% iron, **Mg** 129% magnesium,
O3 ALA omega-3s, **K** 111% potassium, **B12** 0% vitamin B_{12},
Vc 465% vitamin C, **VD** 2% vitamin D, **VE** 22% vitamin E

ACKNOWLEDGMENTS

It didn't take quite 101 people to produce *101 Recipes You Can't Live Without,* but it was a group effort.

Diane Salvatore, editor-in-chief of *Prevention,* championed the idea. A strong believer in the healing power of food, she was convinced that people were ready for a different kind of healthy cookbook.

Recipe developer and writer Julie O'Hara's creativity under deadline pressure was truly amazing. It also didn't hurt that she always had an upbeat and can-do attitude.

Editor Trisha Calvo pulled everything together. Nancy Bailey, Debbie McHugh, and Chris Krogermeier provided clear guidance and sage advice. JoAnn Brader and her team tested the recipes. The dishes look as good as they taste thanks to designer Kara Plikaitis, design director George Karabotsos, photographer Mitch Mandel, food stylist Mariana Velasquez, and prop stylist Amy Wilson.

A thousand thank-yous.

INDEX

Underscored page references indicate boxed text. **Boldfaced** page references indicate photographs.

D

E

F